PRAISE FOR
The Power of Surprise
How Your Brain Secretly Changes Your Beliefs

"*The Power of Surprise* provides an incredibly accurate and practical description of how our brain turns raw information into creative ideas to help us survive and thrive. We learn, we build beliefs, we turn them into memories, and then we go through life on automatic pilot. Those beliefs turn into biases that hinder our ability to be creative, productive, and happy. How do you get over these neurological roadblocks? Seek out surprises, because in those surprising moments both you and your brain have a golden opportunity to turn limiting beliefs and biases into a life filled with discovery and joy. Through delightful storytelling, the author brilliantly gives the reader new tools for using surprise strategically to create new life-enhancing experiences, avoiding destructive influences. A rare and enjoyably readable book on the neuroscience of personal transformation. Highly, highly recommended for anyone!" —**Mark Robert Waldman**, executive MBA faculty, Loyola Marymount University (2009–2019); coauthor of *Born to Believe* and the bestseller *How God Changes Your Brain*

"In *The Power of Surprise*, Michael Rousell shares his insights into the ways in which little surprises about ourselves transform our lives. Rousell, a PhD psychologist, with 40 years of experience as a teacher and counselor, demystifies the power of surprise and its complexity and shows us how to use surprise strategically to improve lives. Surprise, we learn, is more subtle that being startled and more lasting that being shocked. Rousell shows how surprise works behind the curtain of our consciousness to change beliefs and behavior by changing the ways we see ourselves and the world. Well written and clear, *The Power of Surprise* helps us understand our emotions and cognitive biases and offers several artful tips to harness surprise at just the right moment." —**Edwin Battistella**, author of *Dangerous Crooked Scoundrels*

"As a scientist and mindfulness teacher, I firmly believe that *The Power of Surprise*, either positive or negative, is one of the best teaching moments in our life. Because we can get lost in unawareness and trapped in wrong beliefs, we often miss its potentially transformative power. In his book, Michael Rousell brilliantly outlines several principles about surprise that each person—who has a certain hunger to learn—must reflect on; he also creatively explains how to 'play with' surprises along the bumpy road of our life in order to promote a successful growth mindset. I truly enjoyed reading this inspiring book and I recommend it to everyone." —**Silvia Papalini**, PhD, Laboratory of Biological Psychology, KULeuven, Belgium.

"*The Power of Surprise* is full of powerful ideas about how we come to be who we are and how to engineer small revolutions in our own identities. This book will help you better understand the people around you and, if you let it, will help you become a better version of yourself." —**Tania Luna**, coauthor of *Surprise: Embrace the Unpredictable and Engineer the Unexpected*

"If you want to break with stress for good, learn how to fuel your brain with *The Power of Surprise*, living a life that is both amazing and amusing even in the most challenging times.—**Heidi Hanna**, *New York Times* best-selling author of *The Sharp Solution, Stressaholic and Recharge*.

"It may be a surprise that surprise is our least understood of emotions. Yet in a moment of surprise, we often form a new belief that becomes part of our identity. And our identity, our sense of self—of who we are—guides our actions every day. Most surprises are processed unconsciously by our brain, but the power of surprise is to be in a ready state and on the look out for the smallest surprises that come along, process them consciously, interpret them, and use them strategically to enhance our self-esteem.

"Rousell writes about the power of surprise in a lucid, scientific, and accessible way. He brings the science to life with a plethora of examples that entertain, inform, and educate the reader.

"Surprise has the power to create a neurological storm—the brain loves novelty—that arouses our self-bias. Our sense of self is at the heart of our conscious awakening and a repository of the life story we tell ourselves. Our ability to process surprise helps us organise our emotional lives.

Surprise can of course be a negative experience, like losing your job, and training the mind to process experiences less destructively can improve mental health and well-being especially during the current pandemic.

"As an educator and coach, the power of surprise can be used tactically to build people's confidence, for example, when giving feedback. Praise makes people grow. Kindness and compassion connect us all as fellow human beings. This book is full of wonderful stories of how surprise can uplift the human spirit and provide hope out of the depths of despair.

"Channeling positive thought and energy out of deeply emotional surprises and wiring them into our consciousness can ultimately result in a more positive, more resilient self-image. This book is a timely gift in a fast-changing world where people are feeling increasingly uncertain and anxious." —**Nick Marson**, author *Leading by Coaching*

The Power of Surprise

How Your Brain Secretly Changes Your Beliefs

Michael Rousell

ROWMAN & LITTLEFIELD
Lanham • Boulder • New York • London

Published by Rowman & Littlefield
An imprint of The Rowman & Littlefield Publishing Group, Inc.
4501 Forbes Boulevard, Suite 200, Lanham, Maryland 20706
www.rowman.com

6 Tinworth Street, London SE11 5AL, United Kingdom

British Library Cataloguing in Publication Information Available

Library of Congress Cataloging-in-Publication Data

ISBN: 978-1-5381-5241-6 (cloth)
ISBN: 978-1-5381-5242-3 (electronic)

To those who inspire me every day:
Paige, Lauren, Kaitlin, Nathalie

~

Contents

~

Acknowledgments

This book contains brilliant ideas, discoveries, and theories by those mentioned in my references. To all of them, I offer my utmost regards for their hard work, creativity, and influence. I synthesized their efforts within my conceptual framework to produce the book you are about to read.

Special thanks to those who told me their stories of influence about how surprise played a role in their formative moments. These stories breathe life into science.

This book took an inordinately long time to move from conception to print. Literary consultant Elizabeth Lyon stayed with me through countless rewrites. Her skills in editing played an instrumental role in this work. She frequently referred to me as a poster boy for perseverance. Thanks also to my editor Suzanne Staszak-Silva at Rowman & Littlefield who encouraged and nurtured me through the publishing process.

On a personal note, my wife and children indulged me and allowed me to spend thousands of hours on research and writing. I tried not to cheat them out of the important things in life. That said, I could have cleaned, painted, mended, and cooked more often. I love you and appreciate your patience and support.

I dedicate this work to my grandchildren: Paige, Lauren, Kaitlin, and Nathalie. They inspire me to be better every day. I have not met that mark, but they love me nonetheless.

To Laura, to whom I owe everything, and to my daughters Leanne and Kary, who know courage.

~

Introduction

Why leave many of our most formative moments to chance when we can create them?

Imagine sitting in a traffic jam when the car in front of you suddenly hovers, scoots over the gridlock, lands smoothly, and drives away. Until then, you believed that cars couldn't fly. Surprise! Physiologically, your eyes flew wide open, your jaw dropped. Neurologically, you experienced a brief burst of dopamine telling you that something important just happened. Learn quickly: *Is this an invasion, am I safe?* Cognitively, your senses piqued, and you stopped what you were thinking. Then, you instantly formed a new belief: Cars *can* hover. A belief change happens so fast we often miss it, as if in secret. The change happens *to* you, not *by* you. You don't will it, nor can you stop it, ignore it, or undo it. Beliefs materialize instantly, without any agency on our part, during moments of surprise.

We are hardwired to make sense of our environment so that it can become a safe and predictable place. Learning instantly when surprised kept us alive. Surprise happens to all of us, with widespread effects, but we rarely notice because the instant learning is, well, instant.

A surprise is a neurological error signal. It means that your expectations, how you understand the world and feel secure in it, suddenly

1

don't work. In our evolutionary past, a surprise often meant immense opportunity or imminent danger. *Alert! Am I safe? Is this an opportunity?* Those who stopped to think didn't make it to the gene pool. Accordingly, evolution hardwired us to learn instantly during a moment of surprise.

What if you see your trusted friend steal someone's smartphone at a coffee shop? Shocked, you'll spontaneously form a new belief about your friend. Before your eyes, Honest Owen morphs into Crooked Cal. Again, this belief developed automatically, and you couldn't have stopped it. When a surprise happens, it creates an alarm that screams, "Oh my gosh! Your belief doesn't work. Hurry, and make a new one!"

Surprises, insignificant or monumental, and the beliefs they alter, can be about external matters or about ourselves. In the external world of our senses, we can often objectively test and verify our new beliefs. We can follow the driver of the car and watch it lift off, hover, and land. We can question our friend about the theft incident.

You wake up to see a monkey on your lawn. Surprise! Is it a prank, an illusion, a prop for a movie set, or are you still dreaming? The monkey moves away before you can confirm your sighting. You run outside to see if it lingers in the neighborhood. Did it leave tracks? Are your friends laughing in the bushes? Is there a movie set? Nothing. The sighting remains on your mind all day. You find yourself glancing at news reports to see if others shared your sighting or if a monkey escaped from a traveling circus. During the evening news, you smile as you watch the reporter describe a police raid on an illegal exotic animal home. The incursion accidentally released a monkey, a python, and a jackal. *Whew. I'm not crazy after all.* You verified your surprise by looking for and finding evidence. But that's not at all what happens when you have a surprise to your self-concept, your understanding of who you are and how you understand yourself.

Beliefs we hold about the external world, monkey sightings, are objectively verifiable. What about beliefs we hold about ourselves, our self-concept? Those beliefs that define us, how we experience and understand ourselves?

Your supervisor comments on "your uncanny ability to capture the essence of complex issues." Surprise! You didn't think you had this "uncanny ability." You now find that you pride yourself on this aptitude and see it as a signature feature of your personality. You don't instinctively question this new belief. Not only that, a new belief about yourself also drives a cognitive disposition to find or even create evidence to support it. You now see your "uncanny ability" everywhere you look.

These are the types of surprises I examine in this book. Alert. This book isn't about the impressive and colorful cases of surprise. They engage us and make great conversation, but they don't change us. Formative moments differ. For example, Jane thought she wasn't creative until her boss surprised her by saying, "You keep coming up with clever solutions." While this example is less stunning, it's potentially transformative. If it was a simple comment, Jane could dismiss it as empty flattery, or accept it as a thoughtful comment from a supportive supervisor. But, if it surprised her, a host of neurological and cognitive processes take place that generate an instant new belief: "I'm clever." That's what surprises do.

The process occurs as if in secret, beyond our awareness, and verification isn't as straightforward as for an external event. That's what you'll find in these pages. No flash-bang here. Only Jane was surprised. To any witness or even the supervisor, it was just a mundane event in the day. Yes, it's tried-and-true advice to give positive comments, but when you do it with a surprise, it's a game changer. Learning to use surprise strategically relies upon the wonders of science mixed with the art of timing and delivery.

Are you clever? Beliefs often form incrementally, but they may also erupt suddenly. Do you believe you're clever? How did that belief develop? Was it incremental, parents and teachers lauding your efforts and commenting on your brilliant creative efforts? Did this belief erupt suddenly through a surprise, like Jane's? Regardless of how beliefs form, they affirm themselves through confirmation bias. This means that you can test for monkeys in your neighborhood by looking for empirical evidence. Jane will instinctively test for cleverness by looking at her behavior, which she now views through the lens of "I'm clever." She sees examples of her cleverness everywhere.

The nuances and complexities inherent in the element of surprise defy a quick explanation. Can I explain these critical elements in a minute or two? No. That's akin to asking Tiger Woods to describe the critical elements of golf during an elevator ride. "You hit a small ball with a stick to a hole four-hundred yards away. Repeat this seventeen times, but with the target at various distances. Whoever does it with the least number of hits is the winner. The sticks, called clubs, come in different lengths and handedness. They come with curved bottoms that slope at a variety of angles. While the sticks vary, the balls and holes are always the same sizes. Dress in bright-colored clothing that you wouldn't wear anywhere else." Time's up.

Most of what readers will learn about the element of surprise and its strategic use is new. New means building a foundation from the ground up. For the reader, taking on this task requires patience and careful reading. But the payoff is tremendous. Once you know how formative moments emerge, you can create them as a parent, teacher, supervisor, coach, therapist, or friend to intentionally produce a decisive change in someone's life.

We use surprise when we give an unexpected gift, turn up unexpectedly, or delight in sharing exciting news. Accordingly, we all think we know it well. But our everyday understandings are like the proverbial tip of the iceberg. They miss the nuances and complexities that make it a powerful tool, ripe for strategic use to create formative moments, to trigger inspirational mindsets. This examination of surprise illustrates the hidden yet critical nuances inherent in surprise. I demystify the complexities. You'll see how minor features create profound differences.

Think about this brief list of surprises. A barking cat puzzles us. A shark sighting while swimming terrifies us. Seeing a magician make an elephant disappear mystifies us. Not receiving the promised promotion disheartens us. Watching our favorite team mount a historic comeback, then win, elates us. Do surprises puzzle, terrify, mystify, dishearten, or elate us? Yes, and no. While vivid and dazzling, these examples illustrate a small spectrum of surprise. What about less intense examples: A friend shows up unexpectedly at work, a mouse runs across your desk, the network cancels your favorite show without warning. Are the same neurological and cognitive processes still at play? Yes, and no.

Although we use the term "surprise" frequently, it encompasses very specific scientific properties that differentiate it from other emotions. The concept of surprise is actually pretty complex and pervasive. It comes in a variety of forms, a variety of intensities, and is a fundamental but often overlooked phenomenon of the human condition. What

I discovered and share in this book is how to use it strategically to significantly improve lives.

Whenever I tell someone that I study surprise, they usually reply with, "Like getting surprised at a party?" "An unexpected visit from an old friend?" or "A surprise event, like a news story?" I tell them, "Not those kinds of surprises. While surprising, those events didn't change you at a personal level. The ones that I study are the personal ones that change your life and the beliefs you hold about yourself." Then I get, "Like when my parents divorced? I didn't see that coming," or "Like the time my mother got her cancer diagnosis." Once again, I have to say no. "While those surprise events changed your day-to-day life circumstances, they didn't change you, your beliefs about yourself." These are surprising events that change our behavior because we have to adapt.

When I ask people to tell me a story of a surprise in their lives, I rarely get a story about a surprise that changed a personal belief about themselves. We don't tend to see surprise as a trigger for personal transformation. So, I ask them to tell me about an event that changed how they think about themselves, a formative moment. When I ask it this way, I often get a story that illustrates surprise as the initial stimulus. *Formative moments, if remembered it at all, are remembered as life-altering moments, not surprise events.*

Think of the Carly Simon story. As a teen, Academy Award-winning singer and songwriter Carly Simon dreaded that her stammer would become an item of ridicule among her peers. While hanging out with her boyfriend Nick, he surprised her by laughing compassionately at her anguish and referring to her stammer as "charming." She credits this surprise episode as a turning point in her life. She now had a new belief about her stammer—charming. That surprise changed how she felt about herself. After this story, they usually get it.[1]

One of the essential elements of a belief change triggered by surprise is that it isn't always dazzling. Rather, it's often subtle if noticed at all. The change of belief frequently takes place suddenly with little fanfare. That's part of how it works, behind the scenes of consciousness. And that's also part of what makes it so powerful. It changes beliefs and behavior outside of any conscious resistance. One day you believe this and act this way, a surprise event happens, then suddenly you believe something else and act a different way. When we believe something, we see or manufacture evidence for it everywhere. It becomes our filter for interpreting the world, our rose-colored spectacles. Often, a new belief is like a small seed that grows into a mighty oak. Even though we often miss it, it can be extremely powerful. We can harness that power strategically.

Occasionally, we get vivid and dazzling portrayals, but that's not the norm. It's important to avoid the idea that surprise always makes immense, visible, and immediate effects. Surprise-triggered belief change happens to all of us, all the time, and often so fast that we frequently miss it. If surprise-triggered belief change was obvious, vivid, and immediate, we would all already know this.

I watched my first hypnosis act in my late teens. Wow! The act captivated me. How could the hypnotist get participants to perform hilarious and remarkable antics? Several years later, I decided to give hypnosis a try. I took a few classes and read whatever books I could find on the subject. I started experimenting with this newly acquired skill by hypnotizing friends at parties. While hypnosis proved to be a fun party trick, I experienced a deep yearning to learn more. What inherent human propensity did this so-called hypnosis tap into? How did hypnosis work, and what was the essential mechanism? Friends often asked perplexing questions that I couldn't answer: "Can you hypnotize people without them knowing?" and "What would happen if you hypnotized someone and they didn't come out of it?"

My hypnosis instructor suggested I consider a career in chiropractic medicine. He told me he knew several chiropractic practitioners who use hypnosis in their treatments. Intrigued, I attended an intensive weekend workshop on an introduction to chiropractic medicine. Dr. Rudolf,[2] a visiting chiropractor with an impressive reputation for spontaneous cures, offered it. I started the workshop bubbling with eager anticipation, excited to take part in this prominent audience of forty health-care workers. I sat amazed by his electrifying delivery, enthusiastic laughter, and heartwarming tales. He captivated the participants' imagination with compelling stories from his extraordinary practice. A bearded gentleman with over thirty years of experience, his imposing yet paternal presence provided a feeling of approachable intimacy. When I started the workshop, I hadn't expected that the end would be a monumental turning point for me, instilling a sudden realization that would send me on a journey lasting nearly four decades.

He opened the workshop with a promise to give all the participants a chiropractic neck adjustment at the conclusion of the workshop. After three enthralling days, the time for the adjustments arrived. Twenty-five of us sat in the conference room. The host invited us one at a time to seat ourselves on a chair at the front of the room. As Dr. Rudolf slowly manipulated the participant's head from side to side, he told stories and laughed enthusiastically. Then suddenly he would stop, sometimes midsentence, as if he'd discovered some critical feature in the participant's body. Electrified, we all awaited his diagnostic pronouncement. Instead, he would make a declaration about that person's character and what positive lot he or she would inevitably find in life: "I can tell by the alignment in C5 that this person finds it easy to work well with difficult patients, and in fact thrives on these challenges—Haha!" He always delivered these declarations just as he gave the person's head a sudden twist, an action that always produced eerie snapping and popping sounds. *Whack!* He'd clap his hands loudly. The wide-eyed participant would then blink a few times, arise, and thank Dr. Rudolf.

I was one of the last to be called. When the attendant called my name, I felt the adrenaline surge through my body. The cracking sounds from previous attendants made me apprehensive to say the very least. I pushed my anxiety aside and joined Dr. Rudolf in the front of the room. As I sat there, listening intently, he continued in the same fashion he'd done with the others. Slowly, my resistance diminished. I began to relax and allow him to move my head freely, loosening the muscles for the inevitable cracking to come. Shortly after letting myself relax, he stopped and concentrated on a small muscle on the side of my neck. He said, "Now this is interesting. This man will always achieve more than simple appearances indicate. Haha!" A sudden twist of my neck—*snap!*—*whack!*—a loud clap, and they escorted me back to my seat. That was nearly forty years ago, and I still recall his words.

His pronouncement surprised me. "What just happened?" I experienced a sudden insight that catapulted me into a lifelong inquiry. It was at that moment that I realized that hypnosis is a "belief-formation episode." The hypnotist gives the subject a suggestion, "You're in the

Arctic and you forgot your coat." The subject temporarily accepts this suggestion, wraps his arms snugly around his body, and acts as if this suggestion (a new belief) is real. This all takes place after a rather time-consuming and tedious induction period to get the recipient into a suggestible state.

My world turned upside down. I had just witnessed an expert create a moment of profound suggestibility, instantly, and deliver a suggestion (new belief) purposefully and permanently. And all this with no volition from me, the recipient. I now had the answers to my friends' perplexing questions. Yes, you can powerfully influence someone without them knowing, and yes, you can create a permanent belief while in this state. But if it's not hypnosis, then what is *this state*?

Some readers may wonder about the statement Dr. Rudolf delivered to me. Did it genuinely create a permanent belief? Herein lies the artistry of a well-crafted suggestion and how beliefs work. Do I achieve much more than my appearances indicate? I don't know if I do or don't, but I believe I do. That's how a belief works. Regarding Dr. Rudolf's comment, I've already surpassed my grandest plans in almost every aspect of my life. Even if I hadn't, my belief that I have makes all the difference. Note also the intentional vagueness of his shrewd comment. Was Dr. Rudolf referring to my intellectual, academic, financial, physical, or creative accomplishments, or all of them? He created a perception in me that became self-perpetuating. We all perpetuate our beliefs through confirmation bias, interpreting events in a way that fits our worldview.

Armed with this new worldview, new perspectives bubbled up in my psyche. As a teacher, I saw my public-school students differently. Was the class clown a child who acted out a suggestion that someone inadvertently gave him: "You always find the lighter side"? Did the student with math anxiety actually find math difficult, or was she merely acting out a self-affirming belief? If so, where did she get this belief? I already knew that people perceived their world and acted according to their beliefs. Could changing someone's belief about math change how he or she acted, and would this new belief create a new self-affirming cycle? Questions like this led me to graduate school at the University of Oregon. I earned my doctorate in 1990 and I titled my dissertation, "Hypnotic Conditions: Are They Present in the Elementary Classroom?" My dissertation showed that the very conditions created by clinical hypnotists were regularly present in the elementary classroom. The next two decades of continued research led me to my first book in 2007, *Sudden Influence: Spontaneous Events That Shape Our Lives*. This book currently sits in more than 1,200 libraries in sixty countries.

In the decade since, I pored over the research in a variety of disciplines related to the brain sciences: cognition, motivation, neuroscience, psychology, artificial intelligence, persuasion, evolution, and learning. I also studied practices and expert opinion in magic, advertising, cinematic arts, and influence in general. A common pattern for instant learning and sudden belief formation emerged. *I discovered that the emotional mechanism of surprise is the most common catalyst for transforming our beliefs.*

At the same time, I accumulated thousands of anecdotes of formative moments triggered by surprise. Many of these belief transformations sparked life-changing moments. I now teach graduate students in education, nursing, psychology, and business how to harness this magnificent mechanism for the benefit of those in their care. Like any tool, it constructs or destructs. This book is about the construction process. The primary purpose is to illuminate the power of surprise and the wisdom of using it deliberately.

The Power of Surprise: How Your Brain Secretly Changes Your Beliefs is the next logical progression from my first book. It shows how the element of surprise, like no other emotion, can secretly change your personal beliefs, your fundamental identity, instantly. It then shows you how to harness this magnificent power.

What makes *The Power of Surprise* unique is that we rarely look at these moments as developmental opportunities. But the mechanism of surprise can be a purposeful tool used intentionally to create beliefs, changing how and what we think. Unfortunately, most of these moments arise from an accident or luck. Beliefs about our abilities, confidence, and self-esteem often arise from unpredictable events when we're surprised. But why should we leave many of our most formative moments to chance when we can create them?

The Power of Surprise shows you how to craft moments of surprise strategically, to be the creator of richer lives for your children, students, athletes, employees, and patients. For example, eleven-year-old Cindy used to believe her slow test-taking indicated a lack of intelligence, but that changed instantly. While Cindy anxiously finished a test, the librarian surprised her by naming her slowness as "attentive deliberation that shows grit." She now writes her tests slowly, with confidence. After all, she's got grit. The comment surprised Cindy, giving her a burst of the motivator neurotransmitter dopamine and creating a window for belief formation. Now when Cindy writes tests, her instincts prompt her to go slowly, with attentive deliberation, and feel proud because it confirms her grit.

As it turns out, the neurological event of surprise is the most important spark for instantly constructing or transforming a belief. Parents, teachers, personnel in mental health, coaches, employers, and those who work to influence others will find this work captivating. You'll discover the evolutionary purpose of beliefs, how they form, maintain themselves, and why they constantly change how we define ourselves. Using current research from a wide variety of disciplines in the brain and behavioral sciences, I identify and map the consequences of *surprise* as a trigger for instant belief formation.

Surprise not only differs from other emotions by tone, but *surprise is the only emotion that requires an interpretation.* This distinctive feature makes the meaning of surprise hackable, the fundamental premise of this book. Imagine that you are working on a shared project when your friend unexpectedly roars, "Wow! That's just great!" Surprised, you don't instantly know whether the comment is sarcasm or genuine delight. The nuanced meaning of the tone and words is not immediately clear. How you perceive (interpret) this event makes an enormous difference: shame, "I'm an idiot," or elation, "I'm brilliant." Other emotions, such as happiness and fear, come with neurological signals to approach or avoid. During the cognitive alarm sparked by a surprise, we instinctively grasp at the first thought or comment that arises, positive or negative. Confirmation bias, our inherent impulse to find affirming evidence, further entrenches this new belief.

While surprises in the external world of concrete objects are usually verifiable through our senses, this drive to find a meaning for surprises to our self-concept makes us vulnerable. Because we typically accept the first thoughts or comments we hear during moments of surprise, not all new beliefs are positive, productive, rational, or accurate. Many can be limiting (math phobia) or destructive ("I'm no good"). The meaning we make from a surprise is intensely personal. These intensely personal, defining moments happen regularly, to all of us, anywhere and anytime.

You'll learn how to see negative experiences as magnificent opportunities and how you can be the instrument of a defining moment. You may ask, "If this is such a powerful tool, why isn't it more prominent?" It is, but it's often used intuitively or under different guises. You'll hear how Marine Corps General Charles Krulak intentionally instituted a training rule that instills the use of strategic surprise: "You can only compliment people on things that are unexpected." He trains his drill sergeants to tell the wimpy kids that they did a good job running, and compliment shy people who take a leadership role.

In chapter 6, *Surprise Is All Around Us*, you'll see how some professional groups use it knowingly, many individuals use it intuitively, and still others use it unwittingly. Common intentional uses include the following:

- Comedians use surprise to set up the punch line. Are people born with photographic memories, or does it take time to develop?
- Magicians depend on it. They intentionally set up expectations in order to violate them. You don't expect to see a pigeon emerge from a puff of smoke.
- Moviemakers use it to dramatically change the viewers' beliefs. Darth Vader tells Luke Skywalker, "No, I am your father."
- News anchors give surprise teasers to keep you watching after commercial breaks. "You might think dogs are a man's best friend until you meet this cat. Stay tuned after the break."
- Our favorite commercials often use surprise to engage us. Two entranced boys watch as a glamourous supermodel pulls a Pepsi out of a vending machine. One boy says, "Is that a great new Pepsi can or what?"
- It's even the basis of some forms of psychotherapy. In exposure therapy, therapists carefully expose patients to conditions with which they have an abnormal fear (e.g., introducing a therapy dog to someone with a dog phobia). The surprise of surviving the event creates a new and more functional belief.

- The police, military, and criminals use surprise to distract their foes.

These intentional uses teach us a great deal. In *The Power of Surprise*, I distill them into the essential components that we can all use to make lives better.

You'll learn how to be an effective and deliberate agent of positive influence, how to strategically elicit surprise moments. But that's just the window of influence opening. I also illustrate how to create effective linguistic structures to instill positive and functional mindsets.

I took everything I know about beliefs, surprise, and productive linguistic structures into the lab. My lab for applying and examining surprise is practicing teachers. I focus on teachers because they have an immense opportunity to trigger surprise and deliver methodical linguistic structures. They work with the same people from day to day, are interested in building personal assets in their population, are trained observers of behavior, and show a willingness to discuss their results. I teach graduate students in education how to use surprise strategically to prompt productive beliefs in their students.

Armed with the knowledge of how surprise events arise, these teachers watch for opportunities to create formative moments for their students. For instance, high-school student Jeremy regularly requests a library pass because he thinks he's not smart enough to participate in class. Karla, his teacher, knows he has impressive technical savvy because he helps his father repair computers. During one of his regular requests, she decides to surprise him by saying, "Are you kidding me? You're one of the smartest kids I know. Anyone who can do what you do with computers is brilliant." After that, his attendance improved, and he didn't request library passes anymore.

Karla surprised Jeremy by *doing the opposite of what is expected* and *linking an attribute to a new context*. Recall the Carly Simon surprise episode. Her boyfriend used a different strategy: *reframing an apparent weakness* (her stammer) *as an asset* (charming). You'll discover how to create prudent moments to underscore a skill or aptitude and maybe even spawn a new belief.

The strategies noted in their examples also work outside the class-room, improving the quality of work, interpersonal relationships, health, and also the overall quality of life.

- Employer: Adam believed he lacked leadership skills until his boss surprised him with a powerful comment. He now leads confidently.
- Parent: Jenna credits her successful musical career to a surprise comment from her grieving mother.
- Coach: Samantha used to believe her shyness was a weakness, but she how feels quietly powerful after a surprise comment from her coach.
- Instructor: Ryan credits his signature grittiness to a surprise comment by his karate instructor.
- Librarian: Cindy believed her slow reading hampered her academic success until a surprise comment from a librarian instilled a belief that she learns thoroughly.
- Ranch hand: After a frightening event while riding, Janet credits her sudden love of spirited horses to a surprise comment from a ranch hand.

Learning how beliefs work, why they perpetuate themselves, and how to change them, raises the question: What beliefs are most productive? Belief systems vary as much as our fingerprints. Some are functional and some dysfunctional. We rarely know which is which. Is a belief in an afterlife functional or accurate? These *believe-in* beliefs are personal and outside the scope of this book. I examine the literature on human potential. Is grit, passion with perseverance, functional for all of us, or just a select few? What leadership qualities are most effective, and do we all need them? In the end, the informed reader will decide what beliefs are most functional and for whom.

To illuminate the power of surprise and the wisdom of using it deliberately, this book focuses on five goals, in five sections.

Section I, chapters 1 through 3, explores why we have beliefs. To understand how surprise works to make formative moments you must understand *beliefs*; why we have them and how they work. Are they environmentally driven or genetic? What role does emotion play in producing urges to act, and how do beliefs initiate behavior?

Section II, chapter 4, illustrates how inherent biases work to keep our beliefs robust. Beliefs, once formed, are notoriously difficult to change. What mechanisms work to ensure rigid beliefs and what purpose does a persistent belief system serve? During our day-to-day existence, confirmation bias works to sustain our beliefs, keeping them robust so that every minor incident doesn't make our life unstable and uncomfortable. This same confirmation bias that keeps belief threats at bay, suddenly switches sides during a surprise, now supporting the new belief. That's what a surprise does; it signals that a belief is deficient, activates a new belief, then brings confirmation bias along with it. They travel together. Bias plays a critical, complex, and often contradictory role.

Section III, chapters 5 and 6, explores the neurological and cognitive components of surprise. It puts the spotlight on how surprise activates a sudden belief formation.

Section IV, chapters 7 through 10, turns to the practical application of surprise. Using anecdotes and specific instructions, this section shows the reader several methods to artfully elicit surprise and what to say during these formative moments. What are the most effective communication structures, and how do they produce results?

Section V, chapter 11, discusses several critical components of positive beliefs and how to embed them. I devote the first section to the "Growth Mindset," an empirically proven approach that shows how we can develop our intelligence and abilities through dedication and hard work. This well-documented field delivers the foundation for productive outlooks to success. Other components include grit and self-efficacy.

Learning instantly when surprised is a fixed element of the human condition. But here's the key: What we learn is malleable.

This book is for the psychologically curious, those who are willing to patiently discover the subtle nuances that can make the element of surprise a powerful tool. Readers will learn how to use surprise as an instrument to strategically create moments of inspiration and productive self-affirming mindsets for others. Whether you're a parent, a teacher, supervisor, coach, therapist, or friend, you'll find immense value here.

That's it. Read the book, practice the strategies, and make others' lives better. But don't always smile while you're doing it. You'll learn in chapter 8 that one strategy to trigger a surprise is to *not laugh* or *not be impressed* when those responses are expected.

Note to the reader: Some authors use the terms "belief" and "mindset" interchangeably. I do not. In this book, a belief is a mental representation of the pattern our brain makes to understand the world. A mindset is an inclination to think, feel, respond, act, and interpret the world in a way that reflects that underlying belief.

SECTION I

~

BELIEFS

CHAPTER ONE

～

We Are Our Beliefs

What determines the meaning of an event? Will this event form a belief or contribute as a component to a broader belief? How will it be remembered if recalled at all? Does the person who experiences the event play any conscious role in how it's perceived? Can you refuse to allow an event to affect you? Once an event occurs, can you, or some agent, manipulate its meaning? This chapter provides insight into these questions and more.

How are you at math? Where did your beliefs about your math ability come from? Let's examine a typical classroom scenario for a young child. Events like this take place regularly, leaving their influence behind, often outside any awareness or intent. Ms. Givens gives a short math lesson that includes successful strategies to tackle similar math questions. After the lesson, she gives the students a few problems to solve and then walks around the room to monitor their work. Compare the following two comments to an anxious first-grade student who is struggling with a math problem. Comment A: "Goodness, Samuel. You sure struggle with math." Comment B: "Goodness, Samuel. Your willingness to stick with tough problems makes you a strong student." The first comment suggests that Samuel is "weak at math." The second suggests he is a "strong learner." Statements such as these might easily shape Samuel's belief regarding his math ability.

If Samuel accepts "You sure struggle with math," he may give up on math when it becomes difficult. After all, he's just not good at math. Avoid it. We know how that cycle ends up. Now imagine if Samuel accepts the second remark, "Your willingness to stick with tough problems makes you a strong student." This would play out differently. When problems get harder, he tries harder and sticks with it. We also know how this positive cycle develops. He gets a little motivational boost from the neurotransmitter dopamine whenever he sticks with it, because after all, that's the sign of a good learner, and he's a good learner.

Our brains are always accessing the environment, sensing opportunity or threat, and then immediately releasing neurotransmitters to optimize the response to a situation. Emotions, operating below our conscious radar, allocate brain resources based on these assessments. If important, allocate more resources, if unimportant, allocate fewer. These emotions activate either "avoid" or "engage" behavior.

If Samuel believes he's not good at math, a cognitive assessment of "don't waste effort here" allocates fewer resources. An underlying negative emotion neurologically activates "avoid" plans of action: Stay away from math and don't waste your time. Samuel now has fewer cognitive resources and an emotionally activated avoid mindset.

If Samuel believes he is a strong learner, that assessment drives greater cognitive resources and an emotionally activated engage mindset. Then he eagerly attempts to solve new problems. It's easy to see how either of these beliefs trigger a self-perpetuating cycle. This all stems from a seemingly simple comment.

Serendipitous events such as these happen to us regularly, outside our control, and shape us outside our awareness. Statements about our ability and identity form our beliefs about who we are and how the world operates. This process happens naturally as we interact with the world. We don't choose beliefs as much as we merely discover we have them. While we may reflect on them, it's rare to know exactly when they first formed. We are not in full control of whether or how our brains take in new information and what we do with it or how we think.

We Don't Choose Our Beliefs

When an event like the one Samuel experienced takes place, it's unlikely that he would remember it. It's even less likely that Samuel would perceive it as the origin of a belief about his math ability. We rarely get to choose which events transform us and how they transform us, nor are we always conscious of the influence when it takes place. We react, and then something else happens, we react, life goes on. Every once in a while we get glimpses into how beliefs form. With a little effort, we can remember important events in our lives and reflect on how they transformed us. We intuitively recoil at the first scenario and feel drawn to the second because many such seemingly ordinary events also shaped us. Many of these events fly under our conscious radar.

Some readers may wonder how this would have played out differently if Samuel already had a tenuous belief about his math ability. In this math scenario, the catalyst for instantly forming or transforming a belief is his uneasiness. If the teacher's comment is consistent with Samuel's fragile belief about his math ability, the belief is affirmed and becomes stronger. If the teacher's comment contradicts Samuel's belief about his math ability, the shock of a surprise statement by an important authority figure might be enough to override his current belief. Whatever the result, the belief is not something Samuel decides consciously for himself through mental deliberation.

A Hardwired Program

The anticipation of events in the environment is a condition of life. If you can't predict, you die. A goal of our central nervous system is to minimize surprise by maximizing our predictability. We have adapted successfully to our environment when life goes exactly the way we expect things to unfold. We can view surprise as an existential crisis, a phenomenological emergency. "Surprise is a concussion for the brain."

Mitchel Bitbol, director of research, applied epistemology,
University of Paris[1]

We are hardwired to make sense of our environment so that it can become a safe, productive, and predictable place. The world is wrought with opportunity and danger. How do we know what to approach and what to avoid? Living organisms only need some form of stimulus-response mechanism that remembers the stimulus and adapts with a response. Organisms that don't move don't need a memory; they can't approach or avoid. Beings that move need intentions: Why move toward this or away from that? Movement requires motivation. If drawn toward danger, you perish. If drawn toward opportunity, you flourish. But you have to remember the difference. First, you need some system for valuing: This is good, and that is bad. We developed emotions to do that for us. To see how this works, let's examine it from a less complex species such as the bumblebee.

Worker bees have a visual apparatus that allows them to distinguish the colors of flowers. After a few visits, they learn which colors are more likely to contain nectar. They do not land on every possible bloom to discover whether nectar is available. After sampling several with different colors, they can successfully predict which ones are more likely to have nectar and land on those of that color more frequently. Bees appear to formulate probabilities that indicate their use of knowledge, probability theory, and a goal-oriented strategy.

Bees have a neurotransmitter system similar to the dopamine system in mammals. When the reward (nectar) is detected, the system alters basic behavior. The motivator neurotransmitter dopamine steers the bee toward the reward. The bee is making a choice, not consciously or deliberately, but by using a hardwired framework that incorporates a preference.

Unconscious emotions also drive human behaviors in much the same way. Like the bees, we also have a preference-making system (approach-avoid) that shapes our behaviors depending on our acquired experiences. This is the essence of learning. Neurotransmitters simply stamp every element of our experience as good or bad. The goodness or badness of situations then shapes our subsequent behavior. Evaluation and shaping are vital to success. Emotions, our guiding urges, are the precursors to beliefs.

For us to attend to something, it must have value. We don't notice the air we breathe unless we suddenly don't have any (panic), it smells nice (approach), or it stinks (avoid). When emotional patterns form, they become beliefs, which guide our behavior, which in turn affirms the beliefs, and this cycle continues.

Imagine that you are an early hominid, and you walk along a riverbank in search of nourishment. You instinctively approach the black-colored berries; they tasted good before. You instinctively avoid green berries; you got a stomachache last time. Sensory data flows in through the senses, and the brain looks for and finds (or creates) patterns and then infuses those patterns with meaning. As sense-making creatures, our brains evolved to use these patterns to explain why things happen.

Beliefs and memories are similar. Memories form in the brain as networks of neurons that fire when stimulated by an event. The more they fire, the stronger the memory becomes. Beliefs form the mental architecture of how we interpret the world. Memories generate automatic responses when dealing with familiar situations. Memories linked together form beliefs.

Our brains make educated guesses about the true nature of the external world. They do this by composing a mental model that makes elaborate assumptions and predictions about future outcomes. Beliefs act as an invisible but intelligent inner pilot, guiding the complex activities of our lives and shaping our understanding of reality.

As memories become more precise and predictive of outcomes, our beliefs, models of our world, provide near-instant explanations of events or information. Bear in mind that beliefs constrain us too. While foraging in the forest you graze on some black berries. All goes well. On a subsequent day, you graze on some unripe green berries and get a stomachache. A belief forms: "Black berries are good, and green berries are bad." Later that summer, someone offers you some ripened green grapes, but you reject them because your belief generalized to "avoid all green berries." Once formed, beliefs impose a view of the world. We become aware of them when we explain our behavior. Do you remember when you formed your impressions of Apple products, people who get tattoos, Corvette drivers, SUV owners, lawyers, hunters, and so on? It's likely that these impressions formed instantly and with no memory of when you first formed them.

We Actively Test Our Beliefs

Imagine you are blindfolded in your own home and placed sitting at the foot of your bed. You're instructed to make your way to the living room to turn on the TV. Also, imagine that the people you live with haven't cluttered your house with potential obstacles and hazards. You might impress yourself by doing this relatively quickly and easily. Relative to what, you might ask. How about relative to doing this same task in my house? (I'd move the fine crystal so you wouldn't accidentally break it.) I place you at the foot of my bed and give the same instructions: Make your way to the living room to turn on the TV. Not so easy, is it? But you could do it, eventually.

In your own home, you have a pretty clear mental model of where things are and, just as importantly, where things aren't (that protruding table corner about shin high). You also know where the stairs are, or aren't. Our brains are constantly active, trying to predict the streams of sensory stimulation before they arrive. Before you even begin, your mind predicts where to turn, when to duck, where to reach, what's the safest or fastest path. These instant predictions help you navigate to the TV remote control. Every time your prediction fails (your outstretched hand reaches the wall sooner than you expected), you instantly adapt. That's learning. Our brains are essentially prediction machines, and their primary function is to reduce surprise by developing an increasingly nuanced model of the world. Even though you don't know me, nor have you visited my home, you would probably succeed because you would instinctively impose your mental model of *a home* onto *my home*. Our brains construct simulations of the world by combining incoming sensory data with existing, mostly unconscious, stored memories, beliefs, and concepts. For example, when you come across a closed door, you'd instinctively reach for a doorknob approximately thirty-eight inches from the floor, the same distance from the ground as your home, and so on. If you inadvertently entered a bathroom, you'd probably just leave without searching for a TV and its remote. (Although this could be an error in my home. Admit it. Who among you has never inadvertently left your TV remote in your bathroom?)

This little illustration demonstrates several key aspects of how our minds work. Our brains are constantly active, trying to predict the streams of sensory stimulation before they arrive. Your brain seems to solve challenges beautifully and silently. It works out the best options and guides you. Here's how Dr. Andrew Clark, professor of cognitive philosophy at the University of Sussex, describes it. "There is always a lot going on in our environment, and our brains are well adapted to live in a perpetually complex environment that frequently provides incomplete information. As intelligent creatures, we don't just passively await sensory stimulation. Instead, we impose our incomplete model on our experiences through prediction and testing. Like scientists, we constantly test our environment to see if our predictions are correct or need adjustment."[2]

Anil Seth, a cognitive neuroscientist at the University of Sussex, tells us how our brains create conscious reality.

> Instead of perception depending largely on signals coming into the brain from the outside world, it depends as much, if not more, on perceptual predictions flowing in the opposite direction. We don't just passively perceive the world, we actively generate it. The world we experience comes as much, if not more, from the inside out as from the outside in.[3]

Lisa Feldman Barrett, who heads the Interdisciplinary Affective Science Laboratory at Northeastern University, tells us why this is. The structure of the brain, she notes, is such that there are many more connections between neurons than there are connections that bring sensory information from the world. From that incomplete picture, she says, the brain is "filling in the details, making sense out of ambiguous sensory input." The brain, she says, is an "inference generating organ."[4]

Since birth, we started forming an idea of how the world works, what psychologists call a "model of the world." We don't just passively learn; we actively engage the world to test our predictions. A baby boy sitting in a highchair drops a fishy cracker on the floor. The patient mother picks it up. The baby does it again, only this time intentionally. The baby laughs and does it several more times. He discovered gravity and delights in more active experiments to confirm it. He also invented a new game: I throw it down, and Mom picks it up. All parents know this game. The game suddenly ends when Mom takes away the crackers. Surprise and disappointment erupt on the baby's face. "Why have you interrupted this grand experiment and ruined the game?" The child instantly learns something, but we don't know what he learned. Did he learn that Mom is cruel, Mom doesn't like games, or Mom thinks he's not hungry (in which case he better wail to let her know)? Mom says, "You mustn't play with your food," but that only brings a pouty face. Moms don't get to tell babies what the surprises mean because babies haven't yet learned language. Just as the child actively tests his surroundings through his little experiments and exploration, Mom tests the child to see if he got the correct message. Mom gives her child another fishy cracker. The baby smiles in delight; the game and experiment are back in play. The baby drops the cracker. Mom considers herself a patient and loving mother. She smiles and says lovingly, "You silly baby." This only delights the child further and embeds his belief even deeper: "Mom loves this game." The baby actively creates his own reality by making sense out of ambiguous sensory input.

As we grow up, our active testing becomes more sophisticated. I was a young teen when I first stole a sip of beer. My parents often savored it, just as I appreciated a refreshing cola on a hot day. Once, when nobody was around, I poured myself a glass of beer. The enticing amber color with condensation dripping down the chilled glass beckoned to me. I checked to see if anyone was watching; then I stole a sip. Yuck! What a surprise. I took another sip almost immediately, thinking my senses had fooled me. They hadn't; it was horrible, and I threw it out. Our active attempts to see if our world is as we perceive it works well in easily tested external reality.

Here is a brief thought experiment for you to try. When picking up a bowling ball, you instinctively fortify your grip and prepare your muscles for a heavy object. If a friend fooled you, and it's really a shiny air-filled lookalike, you'd be surprised when your hands lift the ball so suddenly. You expected it to be heavy. This is the principle used by magicians to perform spectacular tricks. Illusions are only possible because your mind is constantly making predictions. Through these predictions, we adapt our models to new experiences. If you place the ball down and pick it up again, your grip and muscles adapt, and you're not fooled twice. When our predictions are wrong, this is surprising. Did you notice that when you picked up the phony bowling ball, your entire attention focused on that surprising event? Events that surprise us hijack our attention and become isolated from the stream of constant, predicted events around us.

Verifying Beliefs About Ourselves

If I'm surprised by the taste of a beverage, I can taste it again to test my senses. When surprised by the phony bowling ball, you undoubtedly picked it up again several times to test it. You even asked unsuspecting friends to pass it to you so you could delight in seeing their surprise response and subsequent testing. In the external world of our senses, we can often objectively test and verify what we experienced. The personal and subjective world of what we believe about ourselves, our self-concept, takes a far different approach to verification. Herein lies an unappreciated element and essential feature of how surprise events may produce life-changing effects. Internal beliefs affirm themselves by perceiving or misperceiving evidence that supports the now new surprise-generated belief.

If you believe you're a sharp dresser, while walking through the local mall you'll perceive casual glances cast your way as signs of admiration. If you believe you are unattractive, you'll view these same causal glances by passersby as aversion. Michelle started a new job but participates hesitantly because she believes she doesn't have much to offer. One day her supervisor surprises her by commenting, "Wow, Michelle. When you speak at meetings, everyone perks up." Now she speaks confidently at meetings and perceives eye contact from her coworkers as a signifier of thoughtful engagement. Internal beliefs affirm themselves. At first blush, this may seem disingenuous. Upon what evidence did the supervisor base his comment? You don't need much. I once worked with a fellow teacher who radiated a gruff classroom demeanor. Understandably, he was unpopular with the students. One day I told him, "Your ability to connect with the students humorously keeps them engaged." I had no basis for this comment. A few days later, he stopped me in the hallway, and excitedly described how he had cleverly used humor in a recent lesson, and the students laughed. He had accepted my comment and created his own evidence to support it. Using surprise strategically is a blend of science, linguistic structure, and artful timing.

You'll learn much more about the science in chapter 5. I address the structure and timing of these comments in chapters 7 and 8.

Beliefs Evolve from Patterns

We see by learning how to see. Our brains evolved to identify patterns, creating associations by interacting with the real world. It's a survival instinct. In the words of the renowned neuroscientist Dr. Beau Lotto, "The brain didn't actually evolve to see the world the way it is. The brain has evolved to see the world it is useful to see."[5]

Lacking control creates anxiety. The brain looks for and finds patterns to generate a sense of control. It's so adept at finding them that it even finds ones that don't exist (like a face on the moon and animal shapes in clouds). It's much costlier for us as a species to make the mistake of not seeing a tiger than seeing the illusion or pattern of a tiger where there is none. Finding patterns when they don't exist is a relatively minor error built into the system of pattern-making. Sure, we get magical thinking and superstitions, but that's a small price to pay for survival. Superstitions, or false beliefs, are a nonlethal flaw in the system. (I explore the challenges to our beliefs in Section II on bias.)

While we may think our grasp of reality is mostly accurate, our senses and what we attend to can never take in the totality of the outside world. Our senses, memories, and consciousness can envision only a symbolic representation of the world. Accordingly, our beliefs are almost always inaccurate and incomplete. When confronted with others' opinions, we presume that our own perceptions are especially accurate and objective. This subjective feeling functions well for us. The primary task of living is surviving, and since we're still alive, our beliefs must be working. Consider how easily our perception of patterns is manipulated.

Former professor at Harvard and Oxford Jerome S. Bruner conducted multiple experiments that show the illusory nature of pattern-making. In one such experiment, he used a dimmer switch to control a light while a buzz saw hummed in the background. Participants reported that the sound of the saw seemed to rise and fall as he turned the brightness of the light up and down. His research also showed that if you stare at a light while hearing a musical note, then turn off the light and sound, when you turn the light back on without the note you will hear a tone that isn't there. All of our senses play integral roles in providing a coherent and realistic perception of the world, and each of them is subject to misreading or creating patterns.[6]

In the story that follows, Rachel becomes incensed with her coach's angry rant. She responds to him with a scornful stare. The coach mistakes her intense eye contact as a sign of respect.

> I vividly remember this particular moment, unsure at the time that it would be such a memorable moment in my life. It was the beginning of my junior year basketball season. We practiced all year-round, but when the season started, it was nothing but business. Our coach was a very experienced coach and definitely knew what he was talking about. One practice we had done something wrong, something where we were all standing in a circle around the coach. He started yelling his heart out at us. He walked around in the circle angrily. Whenever he looked at me, I looked right back at him and thought, "He has no right!" In the middle of his rant, he looked at me and said, "Rachel has the most heart out of any of you on this team. She will look at me directly in the eyes and isn't looking down at the floor like she is the victim. That shows me that she has respect for what I am saying." And ever since then, I look people in the eyes, whether they like it or not, I just do, to show respect for what they are saying, and not cower away from what anyone is saying to me. It makes me feel like a stronger person for doing so.

The coach misread her impertinent gaze as a sign of respect. Rachel, now surprised, changed her perception of her stare to correspond with his comment. When she initially intended insolence, she now interprets her subsequent use of eye contact as "respect." Her surprise created an openness to accepting this pronouncement, and it changed her mindset (a way of thinking). To make sense of her event, her mind formed it into a story.

In essence, our brains are prediction machines that strive to minimize surprise by recognizing patterns and associating them with other patterns. Since the information we receive is noisy and incomplete, we've adapted to aggressively fill in gaps and generalize from a small set of perceptions.

From Patterns to Story

As pattern-seeking humans, we have experiences, then generate an explanation by joining the dots of the pattern. I remember walking down a trail. A snake slithered across the path in front of me. I jumped. My friend, following several steps behind me, asked why I jumped. I said, "Because a snake crossed the path." I lied. The truth is, I jumped when startled, and then realized it was a snake. If you don't buy this explanation, consider this: Would I have jumped if a gardener, hidden from me by the bushes, had pulled a hose across the path? Yep! Jump first; explain second.

We think we jumped because we saw a snake. That's because our consciousness notes the thinking but doesn't notice the emotion, fear, which came first. The emotional response prompted the jump. The snake (or hose) suddenly moved, we reacted, then consciousness. This is a subtle nuance, but a critical one. During a surprise, we look to the environment for an explanation. We find or manufacture one, then we connect the dots.

Another curious result also occurs. If a moving hose startled us, but we thought it was a snake, we would believe that this trail has snakes. We might even warn others, "Don't go on that trail if you are frightened of snakes." Even if we walked that trail every day for a year and didn't see a snake, we'd still believe the trail has snakes. In the movie *Pete's Dragon*, a logger saw a dragon (positive incident—seeing something) but didn't see it again for the next thirty-five years (negative incident—not seeing something). The logger still believes in dragons. Once we connect the dots, a belief, it remains robust.

Because consciousness is a slow process, whatever has made it to consciousness has already happened. Humans survived a dangerous and chaotic world because of an ability to find order in disorder and put it into a context, what neuroscientist Michael Gazzaniga calls *a story*. Gazzaniga asks, "What does it mean that we build our theories about ourselves after the fact? How much of the time are we confabulating, giving a fictitious account of a past event, and believing it to be true?" Through clever and intriguing research designs, Gazzaniga illustrates how this process takes place, how easy it is to make incorrect patterns, believe them, and then find supporting evidence.[7]

In one experiment, researchers applied makeup to produce a prominent scar on subjects while they observed the process in a mirror. They told the subjects that they were going to have a discussion with another person, and that the experimenter was interested in whether this other person's behavior would be affected by the subject's scar. The subject was to watch for any behavior that they thought was a reaction to the scar. At the last moment, the experimenter said he had to moisturize the scar to prevent it from cracking. What he really did, without the knowledge of the subject, was to remove it. The subjects, who mistakenly believed that the scar was still prominent, then had the discussion with the other person. After the conversation, the subjects reported to the experimenter about how it went.

The subjects reported that they were treated badly and that the other person was tense and patronizing. They were then shown the video of the other person that was taken during the discussion. The video was shot from behind the subject so that they only saw the subject's reaction. They were still unaware that the scar was removed. Subjects were asked to identify when the other person was reacting to the scar. As soon as the video started up, they'd stop it and point out that the other person looked away, attributing this to the scar, and so it went throughout the video. Here you see how the subject's mind grasped the first and easiest explanation it could make with the available information: There was a disfiguring scar, the other person frequently glanced away, there was no one else in the room, and there were no other distractions. They connected the dots, and the pattern indicated that the person looked away because of the scar.

As you already know, people normally glance away during conversations, but it usually goes unnoticed. Except, in this case, the usually unnoticed glancing away made it into the consciousness of these subjects because they were on guard for reactions and primed to notice them. How much of what we believe is created by what we expect and followed by a hypervigilance to find evidence that our expectation is indeed true? Gazzaniga's research results show how our brains take external inputs and synthesize them into stories.

Other ingenious research designs demonstrate that we also take internal input from our bodies and weave this input into a story. In 1962, a group of researchers at Columbia University set out to prove that emotional states are determined by a combination of physiological arousal and cognitive factors.

The hormone epinephrine, excreted by the adrenal glands, activates the sympathetic nervous system, which we commonly call the fight-or-flight response. Epinephrine triggers an increased heart rate, contracted blood vessels, and dilated airways. By doing so, it increases the supply of oxygen and glucose to the brain and muscles. This produces hand tremors, facial flushing, palpitations, and anxiety. Our bodies excrete it under all sorts of circumstances, from the flight-or-fight response mentioned above to other short-term stress reactions: loud noises, environmental stressors such as extreme heat or cold, or getting snapped at by the boss. Excitement, such as seeing your favorite celebrity, or walking on stage before your speech, also triggers epinephrine.

Researchers told volunteers that they were getting a vitamin injection to see if it had any effect on their visual system. Deceptively, they really received an injection of epinephrine. Researchers split the subjects into two groups. Half of the subjects were told that the vitamin injection would cause side effects such as palpitation, tremors, and flushing. The other half were told there were no side effects. After the injection of epinephrine, researchers put the volunteers into contact with an associate researcher who behaved in either a euphoric or an angry manner.

The subjects who were informed about the side effects of the injection attributed their sympathetic nervous system arousal, such as a racing heart, to the drug. As expected, the subjects who were told that there were no side effects misattributed their intense arousal to the environment. The misled subjects with the euphoric confederate reported being elated. The misled subjects with the angry confederate reported being angry. Only the correctly informed subjects generated authentic explanations, that the injection caused the arousal. Deceived subjects connected the dots using clues from the environment, demonstrating our human tendency to generate explanations for events.

When aroused, we are driven to explain why. If there is a quick answer, we accept it. If there isn't, we create one. The first group, alerted to the side effects, accepted the quick answer: the injection. The second group, unaware of the "vitamin" side effects, connected the available dots, mistakenly believing that the arousal was caused by the interactions.

This plays out similarly when we experience a surprise. An intense surprise is an arousal on an immense scale. The startle response during a surprise triggers a neurological burst that creates a need to explain what just happened, to solve the unexpected event. Since we are psychologically most comfortable when the world goes the way we expect, cognitive disease triggers a search for an answer. Sam's story below illustrates just how this happens. Sam, now a teacher, recalls how a surprise comment created a shaping moment when he was an eighth-grade student.

> I had just moved back to Northern Virginia for eighth grade after moving to Germany for three years. I had difficulty reconnecting with my old friends. I was open, vulnerable, and scared. My social studies teacher, Mr. A, made a comment in class one day that greatly influenced me and changed my self-image. After I finally spoke up and answered a short question on some topic, he surprised me and said, "Sam, it is typical that someone with strong empathy for others and solid *smarts* would speak up more and be more engaged in class." It was a quick comment that no one else probably noticed, but it hit me like a stone. He started from a positive assumption. My demeanor and outlook changed after his surprising comment and I began to see empathy and awareness as strengths rather than liabilities. Later, we did a short report on our heroes, and I chose him.

Sam believed that empathy and awareness were signs of weakness. The teacher's comment surprised Sam because it challenged his belief. His surprise caused a reassessment of his mindset. His trust in his teacher, together with the teacher's flattery, worked together as a pattern to connect the dots in a new way: Empathy and awareness are positive attributes. All of this happened outside Sam's conscious control. It was only his mental effort to explain what happened that drove it to consciousness. Just as subjects in the scar research were primed to perceive reactions from others as signs of disgust, the teacher's comment primed Sam to perceive his attributes as strengths.

Beliefs Work Underground

Your mind gathers data through the senses, stamps everything with a value, clusters similar data into "beliefs," then uses these beliefs to make decisions. Imagine looking at an array of thirty donut varieties without a preference. Arriving at a rational choice would be nearly impossible. But you've already collected data from prior visits, and you don't have to look at each one to come up with a reasoned preference. You simply reach for the honey glazed. Prior experiences clustered your preferences and aversions into a simple belief: Honey glazed are best.

In this situation, the donut display activates midbrain dopamine systems associated with motivation toward pleasure and reward. Each choice elicits a different level of activation of pleasure and reward. As you deliberate about which donut to choose, unperceived neural cor-relates precede your decision and action. Your brain is planning ahead and evaluating actions before any conscious thought is initiated. If, in the past, the taste of honey glazed was more pleasurable than other flavors, it prompts the greatest degree of activation of pleasure and reward. Your past reward and pleasure history predicts your behavior. That's just for donuts; what about more complex considerations?

Married couple Fiona and Elroy each spend sixty hours a week at work in their law firms. They fill their recreation time together in active leisure pursuits such as climbing, hiking, biking, and playing competitive sports. In their early thirties, they decide to build a new home. Driving around a neighborhood they've already chosen, they both find houses built by Modern Timeless Construction particularly appealing. They meet with Ronald, the Modern Timeless designer, who gives Fiona and Elroy several design magazines to review over the coming week.

A week later they meet again. Ronald asks Fiona and Elroy some casual questions about what attracted them to some magazine pictures and not others. All the time, highly experienced Ronald makes mental notes about colors, shapes, room size, lighting preferences, room flow, fixtures, and countless other details. As an adept designer, Ronald avoids asking pedantic questions about each element: Do you like this shade of gray for the bathroom, or which of these thirty plumbing fix-tures appeal to you? From experience, Ronald knows that interrupting their free-flowing discussion of "We like this, and we don't like that" would create a distraction and bog them down in detail. Now is the time for the gist, a general impression. Ronald just wants the essence of their inclinations. They agree to meet in two weeks.

For two weeks, Ronald prepares a home proposal. He forms a visual representation of all the preferences he derived from listening to Fiona and Elroy. He also takes into consideration many other elements not directly discussed: why they chose that neighborhood, why that lot, how best to arrange the home for sun exposure, landscaping opportunities, privacy, views, and much more. Ronald also assumes that since they chose Modern Timeless, he can reasonably assume several other tastes not stated explicitly by the couple. He notes where Fiona's and Elroy's notions converge and where they conflict. Using all his industry knowledge, years of experience, and a degree in architectural home design, Ronald spends fifty thoughtful hours preparing his proposal.

Fiona, Elroy, and Ronald meet. The couple becomes giddy with excitement, nodding with delight. They look at each other, smile broadly, grasp each other's hands, and turn in unison to Ronald, saying, "It's perfect. When can you start?" If Fiona and Elroy had tried to do this without expert help, they might have floundered while trying to decide on the pitch of the roof, the width of hallways, types of floorboards, size of windows, and so on. They might find it overwhelming to research window sizes, depths, casings, orientations, materials, framing, and so on. After all their exploration, they would then have to agree. Ronald shortened Fiona's and Elroy's conscious discernment process considerably by making all the formative decisions based on how he perceived their unstated nuanced tendencies and predilections.

The unconscious mind works like Ronald the designer. It logs all the preferences, aversions, subtle considerations, and possibilities. It understands the world because it takes in all available data, filters it through your beliefs, considers likes and dislikes, all while the conscious mind is busy trying to sort out the next case for trial on Tuesday, or focusing on packing for that hike on Saturday. The unconscious mind considers all the necessary details without distracting or overwhelming the conscious working mind. It's like a spreadsheet that collects all the data in the "homebuilding" category and spits out the results.

Your mind does this all day long, instantly combing your beliefs, preferences, and aversions, then sending the summary to the conscious mind in the form of urges, gut instincts. Since your unconscious mind works so diligently behind the scenes, you get to have a conscious life. Most of the time you automatically follow your urges, and that makes sense.

We don't just make most decisions unconsciously; we occasionally make better decisions that way. Using clever experiments, researchers Ap. Dijksterhuis and Loran F. Nordgren provided supporting evidence for the claim that decisions made unconsciously can be superior in quality to those made consciously. The authors predicted that the decision's complexity would dictate whether an individual should employ a conscious or unconscious strategy of thought. To explore the relationships among these variables, the researchers conducted a series of experiments, each of which involved people either consciously or unconsciously making simple or complex decisions.[8]

First, they asked several dozen people to pretend they were car shopping. Half of the participants read brief descriptions of four cars that were termed "simple" (only four features were discussed). Some features were good (decent gas mileage), others bad (little leg room). The second half of the participants read about four cars that were "complex" (these discussed twelve features instead of four). Researchers structured the features to show more positive features for one car, equally positive features for two cars, and less positive features for the remaining car. In the "simple" list, one car was described positively on 75 percent of its features, two cars were good and bad in equal measure, and one car was described negatively for 75 percent of its features. The same was true for the "complex" list.

Half of the participants in each group were then asked to think intently about the cars in anticipation of eventually rating them. The other half were told that they, too, would have to eventually rate the cars, but experimenters immediately distracted them by asking them to solve word puzzles. They did this to prevent buyers from consciously reflecting on transmissions, stereo systems, and other car features. After four minutes of word games, researchers asked them to pick one favorite car or to rank all four cars on a scale ranging from "very negative" to "very positive."

The results were clear. Conscious deliberation helped identify good cars when the cars were relatively simple. However, when the cars were more complex, the distracted people made better choices. They identified the best cars even though their decision-making process took place "below the radar" of their conscious attention as they wrestled with word games. Dijksterhuis and Nordgren followed up with "real world" experiments to see if these findings extended outside the lab. Findings showed that customers who focused intently on a purchase were more satisfied when they bought simple objects. Complex items were enjoyed most by those who did not put a lot of conscious thought into the decision.

But how can this be so? We humans pride ourselves on making rational decisions. Cognitive scientists know that the conscious brain has a limited capacity to keep more than a few elements in mind at the same time. Instead, the mind concentrates on what it thinks are the key elements. Conscious deliberation tends to inflate the importance of certain features at the expense of others. This can distort the results. Consider the "availability bias": a human tendency to overweigh the experiences that are readily available in our memories. For example, if you were car shopping during a very hot day, you might emphasize air conditioning, while conversely, you might emphasize heating if car shopping on an extremely cold day. My wife and I always dreamed of living near the river. The summer we searched for a new home, the city where we lived had record floods. We decided to live on a hill.

The researchers explain it this way: "Conscious thought is like a spotlight on a decision. It illuminates very brightly, but only a particular, narrow aspect of the problem. It has very limited processing capacity. Unconscious thought is more like a child's nightlight, casting a dim light on the entire decision space without focusing in on any one particular thing." Unconscious considerations consider relevant factors more evenly.

Natural selection pushes for nonconscious processes. Conscious processes are cognitively costly in that they require a lot of time and a lot of memory. Unconscious processes, on the other hand, are fast and rule-driven. An ability to work behind the scenes is a huge evolutionary advantage. Beliefs push their agenda, then affirm their results. Because conscious processing is resource-laden, natural selection looks for expediency. In the next chapter, you'll see how this efficient brain of ours creates a disposition to favor believing over disbelieving.

Summary

In chapter 1, the reader learned how we form our beliefs outside our awareness. As sense-making creatures, we are hardwired to form beliefs. They arise automatically from our experiences and perceptions. Beliefs serve as a survival guide to navigate a complex world. They form from patterns in our experiences and our emotional response to events. When aroused, our emotions drive a need to explain why. We usually accept the first explanation if one is available. If not, we make one up to connect the dots to make patterns. All this takes place without any deliberation. These cognitive dispositions make moments of surprise decidedly malleable.

We don't form our beliefs as much as they form us. In the next chapter, the reader will learn how beliefs function and occasionally dysfunction.

CHAPTER TWO

~

How Beliefs Function

We are born with a natural tendency to trust what others say, and we certainly can't take the time to question every bit of information.

Dr. Andrew Newberg in *Why We Believe What We Believe*[1]

One fateful day, when I was five years old, my older brother took me to the store to get a sweet treat. He told me that candy on the floor of the neighborhood confectionary was free. Great. I knocked over a stack of candy. Thrilled, I collected my now-free bounty from the floor and put it in my pocket. The grocer, witnessing my deed, yelled at me, threatened to call my mother, then kicked me out of the store. My brother laughed. To believe my trickster brother was easy. To disbelieve him was unthinkable at the time.

As a social species, we form beliefs by learning from those closest to us. We instinctively accept what our parents and parent surrogates such as teachers, elders, and other trusted leaders tell us. If we were skeptical of everything, we'd live in a constant state of doubt. Constant doubt is a very inefficient way to live on a day-to-day basis.

How did we evolve with a propensity to believe first and question second? Dr. Michael Shermer of Claremont Graduate School, author of *The Believing Brain*, uses the following thought experiment to illustrate the answer.

Imagine that you are a hominid walking along the savanna of an African valley three million years ago. You hear a rustle in the grass. Is it just the wind, or is it a dangerous predator? Your answer could mean life or death.

If you assume that the rustle in the grass is a dangerous predator but it turns out that it was just the wind, you have made what is called a Type 1 error in cognition, also known as a false positive. You believed something is real when it is not. Scientists would say that you found a nonexistent pattern. You connected (A) a rustle in the grass to (B) a predator. No harm. You move away from the rustling sound, become more alert and cautious, and find another path to your destination.

If you assume that the rustle in the grass is just the wind but it turns out to be a dangerous predator, you have made what is called a Type 2 error in cognition, also known as a false negative. You believed something is not real when it is. That is, you missed a real pattern. You failed to connect (A) a rustle in the grass to (B) a dangerous predator, and, in this case, A was connected to B. You're lunch. Congratulations, you have won a Darwin Award. You are no longer a member of the hominid gene pool.

It's better to believe that rustle in the grass is a predator than to think about it. Being safe is the first order of business in evolution. Type 1 errors, believing something is present when it isn't, is much safer than the Type 2 errors. The uncritical acceptance of incoming information, a belief-first disposition, produced a huge advantage for survival. It worked well in our ancestral days before we had the internet and social media. We lived in small communities and trusted our senses, leaders, parents, and reliable others.[2]

And there is another upside to belief as our natural default. In a world where most things fail, a belief that you will succeed, optimism, fosters initiative, innovation, and creativity. Think of young children who witness something outside their capacity: juggling, deft card tricks, playing a musical instrument, agile gymnastic moves, and so on. Young children think they can do it, and eagerly want to try, believing in their inevitable success. They also want you to watch each of their 100 efforts: "Mommy, Daddy, watch this!"

Is Disbelief the Flip of Belief?

Belief and disbelief both provide information that can subsequently inform behavior and emotion. So, if believing is our default, is disbelieving just a negation of a belief, or is it something qualitatively different? Curious researchers set out to see if belief and disbelief are actually different cognitive processes. In 2008, the University of California, Los Angeles scientist Sam Harris performed a neuroscientific investigation of belief. The study set out to determine whether belief, disbelief, and uncertainty could be distinguished as general states of cognitive acceptance, rejection, or indecision.

He put people into a fMRI brain scanner and asked them whether they believed in various written statements. He created questions intended to stimulate belief, disbelief, or uncertainty. Examples included "8 + 7 = 15" (true-mathematical), "Eagles are common pets" (false-factual). They were even asked if God existed. Harris found that statements people believed to be true produced little characteristic brain activity. Investigators saw only a few brief flickers in regions associated with reasoning, emotional reward, and learning. In contrast, disbelief and uncertainty produced longer and stronger activation in regions associated with deliberation, decision-making, and even disgust.

The brain had to work harder to reach a state of disbelief. Uncertainty elicited brain activity in areas associated with error detection and conflict resolution. These results support the idea that belief comes quickly and naturally, while skepticism and rejection are slow and require more considered cognitive processing.

Researchers were surprised to find that acceptance and rejection of ideas as *truthful* appear to be governed, in part, by the same regions of the brain that judge the pleasantness of tastes and odors. This might explain the common term used when someone doesn't like someone else's notion, "That idea stinks." Not surprisingly, our sophisticated cognitive systems that underpin belief formation evolved from more primitive perceptual (including sensate) ones.[3]

Much of the scientific community interpreted these results as further confirmation that the default state of the human brain is to "accept." In other words, belief comes easily; doubt takes effort. While this doesn't seem like a particularly smart strategy for navigating the post-internet world, it makes sense in the light of evolution.

We Trust Our Beliefs

Consider the experience of watching a magic show. Even though you know it's all an illusion, your instinctive reaction, just like it was when you were a child, is that the magician has altered the laws of physics. We want to believe, but as we mature, we learn skepticism and begin to look for other explanations. But initially, if only for a moment, we believe. Think back to when you were a credulous young child, like I was in the store with my brother. Acceptance came easily, while the ability to doubt and reject required more mental resources than you had during your childhood.

Although effortless acceptance comes naturally, we often deliberate consciously. When we purposely contemplate, what is it that triggers this form of thinking? What, if any, system does our thinking follow? What are the drivers of our *reasoning*? Are quick approval and a slower, more measured consideration two separate processes or two aspects of a single mental activity? Do we ever know which one is taking place? Are there telltale signs? What are the factors that determine which process takes place, and when? Thankfully, Nobel laureate Daniel Kahneman already answered these questions.

Quick and Instinctive or Slow and Deliberate

You drive eight miles every day from home to work and then back again. You've traveled that route hundreds of times. It feels automatic, and when you arrive at your destination, you remember little about it. You instinctively make the usual turns, calculate the traffic density, adjust accordingly, travel the appropriate speed, and follow the rules of the road. All this while listening to your favorite tunes. Today, a snowstorm blows furiously. You turn off the radio because you need to focus intently on road conditions. Now vigilant, you drive slowly, brake tentatively, and watch for skidding cars. The usual travel seemed mindless and instinctive. The snowstorm drive feels attentive and deliberate.

In his internationally acclaimed book, *Thinking Fast and Slow*, Daniel Kahneman of Princeton examined how we think and behave.[4] His central thesis is a dichotomy between two modes of thought he named System 1 and System 2. System 1 is fast, instinctive, and emotional. System 2 is slower, deliberative, more logical. System 1 operates automatically and quickly, with little or no effort and no sense of voluntary control. You're in System 1 during your daily drive to and from work. System 2 allocates attention to the effortful mental activities that demand it, including complex computations. System 2 takes over to get you home safely in a snowstorm. (Note that while System 2 now takes command, System 1 still works behind the scenes to produce a firmer grasp of the steering wheel, ready the foot for a quick response to the brake pedal, and so on.)

Think of System 1 as your instinctive responses throughout your day. It's you on automatic pilot. You generally aren't even aware of those countless decisions you make effortlessly during your day. When enjoying coffee with your friends, you are probably in System 1, idly chatting about whatever topic arises. When you are working on a new project with complex computations, System 2 takes over. System 1 multiplies 2×2. System 2 multiplies 64.8×73.19.

You might wonder why he calls them System 1 and System 2 rather than the more descriptive "automatic system" and "effortful system"? When asked, he responded, "The reason is simple: 'Automatic system' takes longer to say than 'System 1' and therefore takes more space in your working memory."

The vast majority of our decisions and judgments look like choices, but they are mostly driven unconsciously by System 1 impulses. The division of labor between System 1 and System 2 is highly efficient. They work together in a complementary fashion to minimize effort and optimize performance. Kahneman states, "The arrangement works well most of the time because System 1 is generally very good at what it does: Its models of familiar situations are accurate, its short-term predictions are usually accurate as well, and its initial reactions to challenges are swift and generally appropriate." System 2 activates when deliberate attention is required, or if a question arises for which System 1 does not offer an answer. This happens when we are surprised.

When surprised, you feel a surge of conscious attention. System 2 activates when it detects an event that violates the model of the world that System 1 maintains. When my brother told me that candy on the floor was free, I effortlessly believed him. That belief prompted my behavior: Bump some candy to the floor and put it in my pocket. The grocer's reaction surprised me, which activated System 2. I had to make sense of this dramatic new development: Taking candy without paying is stealing, and my brother is a trickster. These new beliefs emerged spontaneously and incorporated themselves into System 1. Since then, System 1 prompts different behavior: Be wary of my brother's comments and pay for all merchandise.

System 1 produces a quick-and-dirty draft of reality that System 2 draws on to arrive at explicit beliefs and reasoned choices. Too often, instead of slowing things down and analyzing them, System 2 accepts the easy but unreliable model of the world that System 1 provides. If System 1's impressions remain unchallenged, they are accepted. These unchallenged impressions become the beliefs that drive System 2's conscious considerations when needed.

Incorrect Beliefs Can Form Quickly Without "Thinking"

Which do you believe is more effective for changing behavior, punishment or reward? We often create our beliefs inappropriately because we see them affirmed without thinking why they were supported.

Think of a common classroom interaction. A student misbehaves, the teacher snaps angrily, doles out a punishment, and the misbehavior stops. The teacher's motivator neurotransmitter dopamine raises a bit, signally, "Punishment works. Do it again." The teacher's punishment-is-effective belief appears to work, and this belief garners an instant verification when the misbehavior stops. If the misbehavior doesn't stop, the teacher's belief prompts a harsher punishment. After all, the teacher believes, *punishments work.* Many teachers find themselves trapped in this unfortunate contingency.

So, is punishment effective? It appears to work for the teacher, but if the teacher's job is education, then it doesn't. Here's why. The student experiences punishment as a hostile act, not a correction. If the punished student was timid, the motivator neurotransmitter dopamine level drops a bit, signaling, "Don't do that again. Be wary." Now the student is more anxious in class and less likely to ask the teacher for assistance when needed. After a punishment, the student's attention becomes split between an interest in learning and a fear of being reprimanded again. Research tells us that students who feel emotionally safe in class and those showing a willingness to approach their teachers generally perform better overall.

The causes of misbehavior are often complex and require a thoughtful intervention. Sadly, teachers don't always get the time and opportunity to mediate thoughtfully. Punishment, while ineffective for learning, is often expedient for an overworked teacher. (In later chapters, I offer powerful alternative responses that teachers, parents, coaches, and supervisors can use to counter unwanted behavior to create productive responses.)

Beliefs can form rationally and still be wrong. Unchecked, incorrect beliefs continue. We may not like it in today's complex world, but expedience proved prominent for survival. Checking every belief as it forms would exhaust us.

Shortcuts Trump Accuracy

Imagine that you are buying your first new car and several models line up comparatively well. How do you make your final decision? Your brother tells you, "When everything is equal, get the one with the best maintenance record." Your sister says, "Which one has the best resale value?" Your friend asks, "Which dealer gave you the best bargain?" You recall your father's advice, "Always get the one with the best safety record." They offer you mental shortcuts to ease the cognitive load of making a complex decision.

Our brains evolved to conserve energy. As cognitive misers, we simply can't process all the sensory information that surrounds us. Our brains solve this by making automatic, rule-driven responses to reduce the brain's computational requirements and energy expenditure. Since most of our problems are about uncertainty, these rules-of-thumb judgments drive our intuitions. Our intuitions, sometimes called gut feelings, are tools for an uncertain and complicated world.

Scientists use the word "heuristics" to describe this complexity-reducing, gist-making process that makes the world more accessible. Heuristics develop from our experience and play out as an unconscious form of intelligence. They work as judgmental shortcuts that generally get us where we need to go. Heuristics prove useful because they reduce cognitive effort and simplify decision-making.

Cognitive science shows that we prefer explanations that can reduce complex detailed analysis to rules-of-thumb. When I pitched this book to the publishers, they asked for my "elevator speech." When listening to a long explanation we often wish the speaker would "get to the point." When we paraphrase someone, we simplify and summarize, "So what I hear you saying is." Think of these common expressions: "What's the gist of what you're saying?" "Just give me the essence." "And your conclusion is . . . ?" "What's at the heart of what you're telling me?" All scientific papers start with an abstract, the condensed version. Media specialists use slogans and sound bites to sell their products or ideas. Heuristics make information more accessible, but at a cost.

The downside is that much of what we assume through our hasty and crude assessments is often weak, lacking details, and many times outright wrong. Heuristics are like stereotypes. They are often true, but sometimes they are not. Our everyday reasoning abilities evolved to cope efficiently with a complex and dynamic environment. What's the harm in a few mistakes here and there as long as we survive? Without being alerted, our rational processes see no need to correct a quick response. It seems correct, nobody challenged it, so move on. Accuracy isn't the principal criteria. In chapter 8, you'll learn how to use our inherent preference for simplicity to your advantage with powerful influence messages.

Function Trumps Accuracy

The farmer feeds and protects the turkey. The cautious turkey learns to approach the farmer. It happens again and again. The turkey connects the dots, in its limited fowl brain. The pattern is clear. "The farmer is my friend and protector." This indication functions well for a long time, although it is not accurate. The turkey has no reason to expect what will happen the week before Thanksgiving. Beliefs evolved to be functional, not necessarily accurate.

Cindy was a graduate student in education. She wrote the story below to illustrate a moment that flipped a limiting negative belief about herself into a functional positive belief. The belief is not accurate, but it became critically functional for Cindy. Note that the element of surprise created a brief moment of mindset revision whereby she accepted this comment and formed a new belief.

> All throughout my education, reading and writing have been the most difficult for me. In the second grade, I received an IEP [Individualized Education Plan] for reading and would be pulled out regularly to go to the resource reading class. Fellow students often teased me when I was asked to read out loud. Seeing the teacher reach for the popsicle-stick jar to randomly call on a student to read out loud made me sweat. When we took tests, I felt horribly embarrassed when I was the last one still working. I would begin to rush through to the end, and my scores suffered because of it.
>
> When I was in fourth grade, we were taking a standardized reading test in the computer lab. The librarian Mr. R supervised us. Once again, I got to the point when I was the only one left in the computer lab. I felt extremely embarrassed and stupid. Mr. R came over to me and said, "You know, the people who usually take the longest on a test often do the best."
>
> Wow! This changed my whole life. From that point forward, I never cared if I was the last to finish, and I stopped rushing to the end of my test when I saw that my classmates were finishing up. Now I know that given enough time, I can do anything that anybody else can do.

There is no empirical truth to Mr. R's comment, "People who take longer, do the best," but Cindy wouldn't have any reason to doubt it. To her, the gist of this message, her heuristic, was, "I'm not stupid. I can do anything, given enough time." The act of believing it made it functional for her. The clever librarian crafted a simple, positive comment that captivated Cindy because it surprised her. She accepted this self-affirming comment instantly. Now relaxed and confident, she inevitably took her time and performed more successfully. Even if she didn't experience immediate success, her *expectation* of achievement itself would serve to affirm a successful mindset.

Look at it this way. Initially, she believed she was stupid because she read slowly. This belief produced anxiety and prompted an impulse to give up. Her new belief, "I can do anything, given enough time," prompts perseverance and passion. These are the hallmarks of grit. She now views a lack of success as an obstacle that she can overcome. Psychologists call this a Growth Mindset. I'll discuss this in greater detail in chapter 10.

A surprising comment, if functional, can trigger the transformation of a belief, but generally speaking, our beliefs need to be firmly held. A fickle belief system would lead to emotional chaos and danger. It's better to have robust beliefs that function. It's better to be alive than correct.

Another example of how inaccurate beliefs can function well for us is the "self-handicapping predisposition." Self-handicapping explains why Democrats are convinced that the deck is stacked against them, yet Republicans are also convinced that it is they who have a more difficult job. We all self-handicap. When I went to play golf recently, I told my group, "Don't expect much. I haven't played in two months." My buddies groaned. I believe what I tell them, but they see my comment as self-handicapping. Now if I do poorly, I have a valid explanation. If I do well, all the better because I've overcome the odds against me.

Students say, "I had to stay up late to study for four days. I'm exhausted. I hope it doesn't affect my score." Now if they bomb the exam, it is not because they weren't smart enough. Fans say, "My team has to work extra hard tonight as their star, Marcus, is still recovering from the flu." If their team loses, they still have the better team. If they win, all the more glorious. This looks like the self-serving comment it is. When things are tough, it prods us to notice because barriers to success stand out; we have to overcome them. We hardly notice luck or good fortune because we don't have to fight through them consciously.

Self-handicapping isn't just a way to take the edge off failures or to over-glorify successes. It can create the conditions for immoral practices to flourish. Researchers Shai Davidai and Thomas Gilovich surveyed roughly 100 experimental and non-experimental accountants to see if each group self-handicaps their discipline, claiming the other group had it easier. They found, as expected, experimental accountants thought their discipline faced more obstacles than non-experimental accountants, and vice versa. But to this study, they added a twist.

The researchers then asked them about a variety of what you might call questionable research practices. *Is it okay to take money from a questionable source if the research itself is strong? Is it okay to publish the same paper twice in two very different journals? Can you put your name on a paper as a coauthor if you really didn't do anything?* They wanted to find out if seeing your field and yourself as disadvantaged produces more moral flexibility. In other words, if you see yourself as disadvantaged, is it acceptable to bend the rules a bit to even the playing field? They found that if people feel the deck is stacked against them, they want to make up for that, and they are willing to fudge the rules a bit in their favor.[5]

So how do you combat this inherent inclination? First, knowing that you instinctively handicap yourself is a good start. Remember that function trumps accuracy. Be wary of your self-handicapping. Second, acknowledge how luck and some opportunities helped you along the way. Last, stick to your moral compass if you want to claim moral character.

If We Don't Know What to Believe, We Make It Up

The mind so abhors the mysterious, if it can't find a reasonable explanation, it will make one up to fill the void, and then believe it. Once a belief is formed, it seeks evidence to support itself.

My recent medical procedure required a thirty-hour fast. After the procedure, I ate my regular diet. The following day, I went to the gym and weighed myself, as usual. I put on three pounds. What? The readout surprised me. I go to the gym regularly and a three-pound weight change is extremely rare. I expected that my fast would drop my weight. The number on the scale stopped me cold. I weighed myself again. Same readout. How can this be so? My mind, which loathes a vacuum, instantly formulated an explanation.

I suddenly recalled a passage I read many years ago. It described how humans evolved during times of scarcity mixed with abundance. Our ancient ancestors didn't have effective food storage. Like most animals, we gorged in times of abundance, building fat reserves. We fasted in times of scarcity, living off our fat reserves. We evolved to store fat during times of abundance to compensate for scarcity. Aha! That must be what my body had done. The thirty-hour fast signaled a fat-conservation reaction. Then when I started my regular diet the next day, my body, still in the scarcity mode, stored every single calorie it could. That must be why I put on the sudden weight.

This is what I told myself. It made sense to me, so I believed it. Why not? I went about my workout thinking that my body would adjust after a few days of regular food consumption and my weight would return to normal. It did, so I must have been correct.

Is my explanation correct? I don't know. I believed it because it made sense to me. I'm sure others would invent different explanations and believe theirs. There may even be a sound scientific explanation. This happens throughout the course of our days. We get these micro-surprises, make sense of them based on best guesses, believe our own musings, then go on with the rest of the day. Surprise-Explain-Believe-Repeat. We can't stop and research everything that happens to us. We instinctively explain our way through the day. Would running to the internet to do research help? Maybe, but often not. Here's why. Once we form a belief, we instinctively defend it.

If I investigated my scarcity-abundance-cycle hypothesis, what would I enter in the search engine? Research psychologists tell us that we instinctively look for evidence that confirms our assumptions. Accordingly, I'd probably enter something in the search bar like, "How does metabolism adjust to scarcity and abundance?" Inevitably, I'd find lots of evidence that describes how a diet signals the body to store calories after a fast. I'd then conclude that I was correct after all, strengthening my belief.

But what if I hadn't immediately found something to endorse my hypothesis? Psychologists say I'd keep looking until I did. That's the instinct of confirmation bias at work. (I discuss confirmation bias at length in chapter 4.) My search question itself actually showed a bias right from the start. The very nature of "How does metabolism adjust to scarcity and abundance?" leads me to confirming evidence. I did the search, scanned through the first few titles, and found myself drawn to "Dieting Creates a Scarcity Mentality, Embrace Abundance." Voila. I was right all along. No need to look any further.

This is a glimpse into how our beliefs form, how, once formed, they instinctively validate themselves, and how we use hastily formed ideas to understand the world. Surprise-Explain-Believe-Repeat. Research scientists know this, and that's why they submit their research for peer reviews. They instinctively believe their own explanations. That's why other researchers are better suited to look for alternative explanations and flaws in their thinking.

We do this all day long. It would take enormous cognitive resources to stop and question ourselves all the time. So, if you catch yourself making up your beliefs, act like a scientist and look for other explanations. Run your ideas by your friends, your own peer-review network.

Summary

The first two chapters described the purpose of beliefs and how they form. We learned that beliefs happen as a result of our experience, and we don't get to choose the ones we prefer. Our beliefs evolve from patterns we impose on our experiences. Beliefs not only form outside awareness, but they also work unconsciously by prodding us to act through subtle urges called gut instincts. Believing is natural because we trust our senses; disbelief is hard conscious work. Because of this, once beliefs form, our predisposition to find affirming evidence for them leads to a rigid acceptance of their accuracy. Nobel laureate Daniel Kahneman created a model that explains how our instincts work underground and drive our conscious thinking. In essence, our beliefs drive us by generating rules-of-thumb called heuristics. These judgments work with the primary goal of functioning in a complex world. The utility of our beliefs is based on how well they function for us, not on their objective accuracy. If we can't find a reasonable explanation for events in our lives, we'll make one up. In this next chapter, we explore what makes our beliefs so robust.

CHAPTER THREE

~

Maintaining Strong Beliefs

As we evolved, beliefs, even superstitious ones, allowed our ancestors to make sense out of an incomprehensible, dangerous world.
Their assumptions may not have been accurate, but their beliefs
reduced their fears and imparted values that would facilitate group
cohesiveness.[1]

Andrew Newberg, MD, in *Why We Believe What We Believe*

Beliefs, once established, show a remarkable ability to endure. In 1975,
Albert Bandura and a team of Stanford researchers recruited a group of
undergraduate students for a study about suicide. Participants received
pairs of suicide notes and were told that one was a genuine suicide
note and that the other was falsified. The students were then asked to
guess which ones were fake and which ones were authentic. As with
many psychological studies, its real purpose was hidden: to determine
whether people's beliefs would change after they received the facts.[2]

Researchers then presented scores. Some students discovered that
they had an amazing affinity for the task. Out of twenty-five pairs of
notes, they correctly identified the real one twenty-four times. Other
students realized that they were pathetic. They identified the authentic
note in only ten instances.

After completing the first stage, the researchers revealed that they had lied about the scores. The entire point of the first stage was to make the students think they either did very well or very poorly, though, in reality, their scores didn't reflect their actual performance. Both groups had essentially performed similarly. The students who were told that they were almost always correct had actually only scored average. Their scores were no better than the students who were told they'd done poorly. Researchers then informed students that the actual point of the experiment was to gauge their responses to thinking they were right or wrong; however, this was also a deception.

In the second phase, researchers asked students to estimate how many suicide notes they had categorized correctly, and how many they thought an average student would get correct. The students in the high-score group claimed that they had, in fact, done quite well, scoring significantly better than the average student: the opposite of what they'd been told. They had no basis for this judgment. The converse occurred with those who'd been assigned to the low-score group. They reported that they had done considerably worse than the average student. This conclusion was equally unfounded.

Studies such as these show that even when beliefs are refuted, many people fail to make the appropriate revisions to their beliefs. Back in the 1970s, the contention that people ignore facts was shocking. That ship has long since sailed; we are no longer shocked when we see people "ignore the facts." Numerous subsequent experiments have confirmed and elaborated on this outcome. Why is it that beliefs appear to override reason?

In *The Enigma of Reason*, authors Hugo Mercier and Dan Sperber suggest that having social support is far more important than knowing the truth. Survival required alliances and cooperation. The biggest advantage humans had over other species was their ability to cooperate. They argue that humans developed in the African savanna, and we must understand ourselves in that context. Cooperation, while advantageous, is difficult to establish and sustain. They concluded that reason evolved as a strategic tool for living in collaborative groups as a mechanism to negotiate alliances and persuade the community of one's ideas.[3]

Berkeley doctoral student Emily Pothast illustrates this aspect through personal experience. Like many fundamentalist Christians, she lived in a community where almost everyone she interacted with was also a like-minded Christian.[4]

When faced with evidence that contradicts a core tenet of their religious belief, such as the notion that God literally created the world 6,000 years ago, many evangelicals minimize their cognitive dissonance through *motivated reasoning*. And why wouldn't they? It's far easier to believe that evolution is a lie dreamed up by a faceless "liberal elite" you'll never encounter in real life than to confront the possibility that everyone you've ever cared about in your entire life is wrong about the same thing.

(Motivated reasoning is the use of emotionally biased reasoning to produce justifications or make decisions that are most desired rather than those that accurately reflect the evidence.)

We evolved to believe in those we trust. The logical reasoning of abstract problems served little purpose for our ancestors. From an evolutionary standpoint, social standing and authority were important. According to Mercier and Sperber, "There was little advantage in reasoning clearly, while much was to be gained from winning arguments." Beliefs were based on who and how many of the group held them. Imagine that you hold a "groundless" belief. You convince your friend of your "groundless" belief. You each, in turn, convince another person of your "groundless" belief. This belief is now becoming popular, and opposing beliefs are easily defeated with motivated reasoning because your goal is to earn or maintain your social standing. Winning arguments is pleasurable, and your motivator neurotransmitter dopamine wants you to do just that: convince others of your point of view. The brain rewards us for winning an argument, not for being accurate.

Even though many of our beliefs are incorrect or incomplete, their tenacity is usually quite functional. Stable beliefs provide a sense of order, structure, and coherence to incoming stimuli. If our beliefs shifted in response to each piece of information that was inconsistent, our sense of order and predictability would dissolve. Without stable beliefs, the world would seem too complex, unpredictable, and overwhelming.

Robust, but Not Too Robust

While stable beliefs bring comfort, beliefs become dysfunctional if they are completely resistant to change. Sometimes people acquire incorrect beliefs from others who share them convincingly. Incorrect beliefs can lead to inefficiency, inaccuracy, and sometimes even grave danger (e.g., drinking bleach to kill a virus). Given the potentially high costs of incorrect beliefs, humans developed the ability to assimilate them in response to new information. New beliefs form all the time through experience and persuasion. But once formed, they become instinctively resistant to change. Changing beliefs is categorically different than modifying beliefs. We constantly modify our beliefs through experience and persuasion. When we encounter new experiences or knowledge that complements an existing belief, we easily and instinctively assimilate it, thus modifying or updating existing beliefs. Updating beliefs makes them more complex or stronger, or both; however, changing beliefs is much tougher and less common.

A new experience or powerful persuasion must overcome formidable resistance. If you've ever tried to change someone's belief and had someone try to change yours, you understand the difficulty of such a task. There is, however, a neurological mechanism that gives us a window of opportunity. The emotion of surprise evolved as an instant belief-formation mechanism. Events that surprise us bypass our resistance with a fast track to mindset revision.

While we may want to change dysfunctional beliefs, we don't always want to correct false beliefs if they serve a beneficial role. Remember, the purpose of our beliefs is to guide action and not to indicate truth. Consider Jenna's story. Jenna was a graduate student in my class. Her story illustrates that false beliefs can serve a functional purpose.

> When I was about eight years old, my parents enrolled me in a small private school connected to a community church. There was one teacher for the ten students aging in range from six to thirteen. Before enrolling, I was home taught. Since I couldn't yet read, I joined the first grade. I was excited to learn how to read. My mother read to us children regularly: Tolkien, C. S. Lewis, Wilder, and other classics. My father also read brilliant stories, rich in detail. I knew there were countless books in the world, and I was about to discover the key to this magical kingdom.

Our textbooks for reading were Dick and Jane, and to me, they might as well have been about a brick and a shoe. The common phrase people recognize from Dick and Jane is "See Spot run." And that is about as exciting as it ever gets. So, there I was, a stranger in a strange land with Dick and Jane and Spot and Sally (the little sister), and my troubles with reading began for the first and only time. How those plastic-looking little characters brought anything of interest into the world escaped me.

My teacher and I began to have problems, which would grow beyond my apparent inability to learn to read, and eventually lead to my parents removing me from the school, and resuming my home studies. I was really upset and worried that I would never be able to read well. I knew I was older than many of my reading peers, and that worried me too. I went to my mom in tears, distraught. Would I ever be a good reader?

She told me that she had conducted some research into the matter, and found solid evidence indicating that it is much better to wait to learn to read until after you are nine or ten years old, and in fact, students who learn at a later age end up being better readers than those who learn young and under pressure. She explained that there is a proper order for brain development, and I was right on schedule, not to worry, it was a good thing I had waited this long. She was sure I would learn to read at just the right time, and when I did it would be easy, because I had already done some of the work. Her explanation surprised me. I will never forget this conversation, and how reassured and encouraged I felt knowing that as long as I didn't give up, it was all right there for me. I was so relieved!

My parents decided to give quite a bit of academic freedom the rest of that school year, during which time I poured over *National Geographic*, *Cricket*, and *Ranger Rick* magazines, as well as picture books. A month or so passed, and one day, all of it came together, and I realized I was fully reading and comprehending an article in *National Geographic*. I ran shouting to tell my mom.

I find it interesting how my experience was predicted by my mom exactly, including long-term outcomes. I would go on to consistently rank in the 97th percentile in my yearly state testing for reading comprehension, and, more importantly, I became an avid reader.

This may have been my mom's most brilliant teaching moment. This was not premeditated on her part; she really believed what she told me that day. I now know there is no research to substantiate her claims. What was important is that I believed her absolutely in that moment, and I was able to reframe my relationship with learning to read, which allowed me to move forward without further struggle.

Jenna's mother created fake research to surprise her daughter and create, for her, a false belief that would function for her. This belief bypassed the usual resistance because Jenna accepted the comment as supportive and positive. Note that Jenna's mother, a trusted advisor, referred to "research," which typically carries the weight of proof. Since scientists believe it to be true, it must be true.

It's easy, common, and natural to embrace flimsy evidence to support ill-formed and preconceived notions. We simply can't attend to every bit of sensory information that surrounds us. Our senses are usually correct: That smell indicates flowers, those clouds mean rain, big rocks are heavy, and his smile means he likes it. We generally accept information from those whom we trust, and we eagerly accept statements that affirm our beliefs, flatter us, or give us a benefit. Our predisposition to confirm our perceptions and beliefs affect all of us.

This cognitive process is the same one that generates and affirms superstitious beliefs in primitive cultures. Imagine living in an ancestral tribe. The evenings are dangerous with wild animals searching for prey. Your tribe believes that going out alone at night during a full moon is dangerous. After all, it's easy to find evidence of it. However, when someone returns unscathed after a full-moon outing, villagers naturally attribute the safe return to a special amulet, prayer, or forgiving gods. Questioning their own beliefs simply never occurred to them.

While it's easy to look at this primitive culture and understand their naiveté, the belief in *full moon effects* still continues to this day. Emergency-ward admissions and increased crime are two common myths that persist in spite of empirical evidence that disputes them. The reason superstitions persisted then, as they do today, is the same: the fallacy of positive instances. When an event occurs that confirms our belief, we take special note. In contrast, when an event occurs that counters our belief, we tend to ignore it or reinterpret it as an anomaly.[5]

We literally feel that *we are our beliefs*. Emotions not only help us maintain our beliefs but also defend us against other beliefs that threaten our worldview. When someone comes along with a different belief, what do we characteristically do? First, we dismiss him or her.

After all, our brain has already done a lot of work establishing what we should and should not believe in, and the neural circuits have been set. Our beliefs are what make us unique and that's why we feel threatened when we believe they are being challenged. Occasionally, we may even respond with vigorous hostility. Our emotions fiercely protect our beliefs.

The Enmeshed Affair of Emotions and Beliefs

Our emotions evolved as decision-making algorithms to guide behavior with goals to promote survival, opportunity, and reproduction. To do this, they play a gatekeeper role in cognition. The allocation of attention, working memory, and reasoning outlook is not fickle. We only attempt to solve problems that are emotionally important to us. Think of emotions as a biological thermostat that activates attention, which then activates a rich set of problem-solving and response systems. All driven by our beliefs. Attention is the leader of the brain. Wherever attention goes, the brain follows. A surprise hijacks your attention and demands an instant resolution. You remain attentive until the surprise gets resolved.

When danger or opportunity arises, information from our senses triggers an emotional reaction that informs the rest of the brain that something requires further attention and maybe even some problem-solving. Emotions operate unconsciously, constantly evaluating sensory information from our total environment. When our emotions enter awareness, we call it a feeling, but most of our emotions never pass the threshold of consciousness and merely prompt us to act based on prior responses.

Humans survived for as long as we have because we evolved a decision-making apparatus that is capable of making very quick judgments based on very little information. Psychologists refer to this innate process as "thin-slicing." Scientists and writers don't always agree on what to call this process, but they agree that this process exists. Emotions, below awareness, do an excellent job of sizing up the world, steering us from danger, setting goals, and initiating action in a sophisticated and efficient manner. Neuroscience researcher Dr. Mark Humphries states it humorously.

Many decisions require you to weigh the evidence for different options before you can make a choice. Is that a tiger or isn't it? Do I want the burger or the hot dog? Is that a canoe in your pocket or another item of fiberglass sporting equipment? Your brain seems to solve this beautifully and silently: Without you knowing it, your neurons add up evidence, work out the best option, and tell you how to act. Emotions are not irrational; they are crucial to rapid, life-saving decision-making (and impulse purchases).[6]

Our beliefs don't take direction from our "thinking." The mind operates most efficiently by relegating a good deal of high-level, sophisticated thinking to the unconscious. Emotions come first by setting goals (what Daniel Kahneman calls System 1). If they can't reach them on their own, they will trigger our rational hardware (what Kahneman calls System 2).

Our emotions give us the goals and charge the mind with making the plans to execute them. The emotions decide what to do, and our rational processes decide how to do it. If you prefer barbecue potato chips, you scan the snack aisle, not to examine all the possibilities but to find your selection. Did you feel it, the emotional urge to select barbecue? Humans go through hundreds or thousands of these microdecisions every day. Imagine how exhausted you'd be if you had to think about each one. You'd never have time to get anything important done (or golf).

Even though our beliefs trigger our emotional tone, we typically explain our emotional responses as if our rational thoughts occurred first. We do this because subtle emotional prompting typically occurs outside awareness, while deliberation is a purely conscious act. Consequently, lacking awareness of our emotions, we believe our thinking occurred first. Even if emotions reach the threshold of consciousness to become noticeable feelings, we understand them rationally, once again giving our thoughts apparent priority.

You're excited to go to your favorite pizzeria and watch that new western movie. If you ask your friend about dinner and a movie, she might prefer a different restaurant and even a different movie. You've already made your mind up on the pizza and movie. To ask outright, "How about dinner and a movie?" would mean you may have to negotiate and may even end up disappointed. You don't want this to turn into a long drawn-out discussion or argument. You just want to have pizza and watch the western. So, you suggest, "My mouth is watering for a pizza. I haven't had one for two weeks." Then follow up with, "I saw movie reviews in the *Times* today. The new western gets off-the-chart reviews. Dinner at Joe's Pizza with a movie sounds like the perfect night. What do you say?"

You're not manipulating, only stating your preference. All your friend heard was an invitation to go for pizza at Joe's, then watch the new western movie after dinner. Your friend did not get access to your considerations before hearing the invitation. The instinctive maneuvering you did with your friend is similar to the way your emotions work with your conscious mind. Like your friend who only heard the result of your contemplations, you only get the result of your unconscious urgings, not how they evolved. Emotions keep the urging at an unconscious level so that you take the hint and follow the lead. It's not a discussion, just an urge.

Beliefs rule because they trigger underground urges. Restraining an urge takes much more effort than fulfilling it. Fulfilling it is automatic while restraining it takes measured conscious effort. Hence, we have the term, "fighting your urge." Your emotional urging may direct you to *not* approach that rude and aggressive teenager who jumped in front of you in line. You'd have to consciously overcome that urge to act, fight your urge. Road rage happens when an irate motorist cannot successfully battle the urge to strike out.

Beliefs not only prompt you to act, they also help you focus and select. If I believe that owning a handgun makes me safer, I will instantly accumulate every reason why that is the case. That's also true for a friend who believes that handguns are dangerous, who instinctively gravitates to all the counterarguments. Not only that, our beliefs urge us to note and devalue every point that challenges our beliefs. All this takes place instantly, and we can't believe the other person is oblivious to "reason." I put reason in quotes, because it isn't reason so much as a personal belief with biased evidence.

Emotional signals work outside conscious awareness by altering working memory, attention, and reasoning. By controlling these functions, they bias the decision-making toward selecting actions from past experiences that were most productive. Remembering our past experiences is not as precise as many of us believe. We remember the gist of our experiences through the filter of today's mind. Change today's mind and you change the filter, which, in turn, changes your recollection.

Memories Travel Back in Time to Update Beliefs

Humans continuously monitor their environment, accumulating countless details, ignoring much, and forgetting most. Research team leader Joseph Dunsmoor, a postdoctoral fellow at New York University, researched the question, "Does going through something emotional actually change our memories?" His findings suggest that meaningful or emotional events can selectively preserve the memory of previously encountered information that seemed insignificant at the time. Emotional events can reach back in time and infect prior memories.[7]

Cognitive labs that study emotional intensity often give a gentle shock during the memory exercise. This commonly used procedure is designed to make one category of images emotionally meaningful. The shock sends a message to the brain indicating emotional significance. Joseph E. Dunsmoor's research assistants asked participants to identify a series of images of animals and tools. Researchers then tested the subjects' memories. Approximately five minutes later, shock electrodes were attached to the wrists of the participants, and they were asked to identify a new set of images of animals and tools. In this second round, upon being shown new images—either animals or tools—participants received a mild shock.

Once again, researchers then tested the subjects' memories. Not surprisingly, researchers found that memory for the images paired with a shock was better than for the images not paired with shock. For example, those who received the shock while viewing animal images were better able to recall those images than they were images of the tools, which they saw without the shock.

Remarkably, the researchers also discovered that this emotional learning reached back in time to influence memory for the images seen before the learning procedure when no shocks had occurred. For example, they initially showed Jasmine one group of tools (Tool Group A) and one group of animals (Animal Group A) without any shock.

Five minutes later they showed her a new group of tools (Tool Group B), also not shocked. But then researchers showed her a new group of animals while being mildly shocked (Animal Group B). Not surprisingly, she recalls the shocked set of animals (Animal Group B) more successfully. But here's the fascinating part. She was also better able to recall the original non-shocked group of animals (Animal Group A) more successfully.

It appears that the entire category of "animals" became more emotionally meaningful. The shocked Tool Group also produced the same effect. In other words, subjects improved their recall of ordinary memories because they were categorically linked to newer emotional learning. Newly acquired memories can infect prior memories.

Dunsmoor's research team concluded: "These new findings highlight the highly adaptive nature of our memory system and suggest that our memories not only can travel back in time to retrieve events from the past, but that they can update earlier memories with important new information or details." Researchers noted that this enhanced memory effect was only observed after a delay. They also noted that this delay likely indicates that this retroactive memory enhancement occurs by facilitating long-term memory storage.

This concept is marvelously portrayed in the 2015 Disney animated classic *Inside Out*. The movie tells the story of a young girl named Riley who is uprooted from her happy Midwest life and moved to San Francisco. Her animated emotions, named Joy, Fear, Anger, Disgust, and Sadness, play out the conflict on how best to navigate a new city, house, and school. Riley struggles with school and making friends. In her head, where the animated emotions interact, the character named "Sadness" inadvertently touches a core memory called *Happy Family*. When she does, the core memory of *Happy Family* darkens and turns unhappy. Now the prior core experience is affected by current events of sadness and anxiety.[8]

This doesn't just happen in the lab and animated movies. Consider the classic study by memory expert Ulric Neisser. The morning after the explosion of NASA's space shuttle *Challenger* in 1986, Neisser took a poll of where his students were when they first heard about it. In a subsequent poll three years later, almost all the answers had changed in a variety of ways. Several people had even placed themselves in totally different circumstances and thought they were being deceived by faked accounts of what they had previously written years before. Most of the memory changes seemed to follow a pattern that turned them into a coherent narrative that was told many times, and slightly changed with each telling.[9]

Sadly, we also see this play out regularly with broken relationships. Wonderful memories with a loved spouse will quickly go sour during a nasty separation. It's as if the dark cloud of a contentious breakup travels back in time to cast gloom over the previously pleasing reminisces, making them bitter events. The experiences were not ruined, only the memory of them. Unfortunately, though, the memories are all we have.

The ability of memories to travel back in time is an important clue to be vigilant when something significant occurs. If something traumatic happens to you or you witness it with another, take care to see that the effects of the event are localized to the event itself. Children are particularly vulnerable. If a child stumbles and you call him clumsy, that might stick. If that child stumbles and you comment that he recovered quickly, that might stick too. The following story from a graduate student, Alicia, illustrates what you should do if you witness someone receiving a negative comment about his or her ability.

> Mrs. G was my third-grade teacher. She was a big proponent of parents coming in to help teach the class and run activity centers. I usually got placed with a girl in my class by the name of Jill. Jill was smart. She was the best reader, the best at math, the best at science and history and everything else. Her mom obviously took a lot of time helping her out at home, a benefit that was hard for me because both of my parents worked long hours.
>
> One day, Jill's mom came in to help out with the activity centers, and my table's activity was math patterns. The patterns started out easy, and I didn't have a problem. Joy's mom glowed and praised us all for doing such a good job. Near the end of the activity, there was one number pattern I was having trouble solving. I sat there and stared at my paper, trying to figure out the pattern.
>
> Jill's mom noticed I was falling behind and halted the rest of the group so I could catch up. I felt an incredible amount of pressure at that point and frantically tried to scribble down the numbers. Jill's mom rounded the table and pointed out that the pattern was wrong, "really wrong,"

and that I needed some help. She squatted down next to me and told me to try again, but I was so nervous, my mind just went blank. After a moment or two, she grew very frustrated. Jill's mom snatched my pencil out of my hand and wrote the first number in the sequence for me.

I looked at the number she had written, still unsure how the number was the next in the pattern or how it connected to the number following it. "Do you get it?" she asked me, and when I shook my head no, she got up and walked away. She told Mrs. G that she couldn't help me, and that I needed to be in a different group. I felt so embarrassed that I cried.

Mrs. G took me out into the hallway so I could get myself together. She told me that she didn't agree with what Jill's mom had done, that she believed in me, and that I could accomplish whatever I wanted to, even a "silly old math problem" like the one I had gotten stuck on. We returned to the classroom, I got my piece of paper, and within a few minutes had the rest of the pattern figured out and the worksheet finished.

Mrs. G was so proud that she put a big fat star on it and loudly told me what a good job I had done. All the uncertainty and shame I had before melted away as I proudly looked at my star on the sheet of paper that signified my triumph. I still may not like math, but thanks to Mrs. G, I know that if I work hard enough that I can do it, and that I can accomplish what others or even I think I can't do.

Generally, our mindsets are persistent due to all the cognitive mechanisms that keep it robust. Surprise and other strong emotions can create a moment for mindset revision as it did with Alicia's roller-coaster of emotions. In the first event, Jill's mother surprised her with a destructive comment. It caused a sad outburst by Alicia, but before a subsequent negative mindset could take hold, the adroit teacher took advantage of her soaring suggestibility.

The teacher captivated Alicia with a powerfully positive comment that took hold. The teacher quickly affirmed this new mindset "can accomplish anything" when she put a big star on her paper. Alicia concluded: "I know that if I work hard enough that I can do it, and that I can accomplish what others or even I think I can't do." Some of you might ask what if Alicia had still struggled and didn't earn the star. That clever teacher would have awarded her a star for *Working Hard and Showing Effort*. The result would have been the same, affirming effort, her new and productive mindset.

Once a belief is revised, those same mechanisms that kept it resistant, now take over to affirm it. The new mindset generates accompanying filters that now recall the old memories through these new filters. Little wonder it's hard to believe we once held our prior beliefs. Most of the time we don't remember our shifts; they go by unnoticed, and we adapt immediately. Alicia remembered her story because it shifted vividly during a moment of surprise.

Most of us don't remember our belief shifts unless they leave some dramatic marker such as an extreme emotional response. Belief transformations that trigger a conscious reflection, as opposed to an automatic reaction, can create a memory trace. With Alicia, the emotion of surprise captivated her attention, and she then remembered the events. Now, with this new mindset, earlier struggles won't look so much like failures as successes: "working hard and sticking with it."

The ability for beliefs to infect or "update" memories can happen right in the moment. We can change points of view in an instant. Feeling correct is much more important to our psychological stability than *being* correct.

Beliefs Are Always Correct—At Least Yours Are

Imagine you're a basketball fan and your team barely made it into the playoffs. You watch the first game as they play the league's number one contender. Your underdog team trounces the favorite by a wide margin. Surprised by this event, you instinctively adjust your assessments of the two teams to accommodate this unexpected episode. You don't notice the belief accommodation because it happens instantly. Your mind has been altered by this new perception. You find yourself looking back for signs that you didn't see this coming. And you invariably find those indicators. "There they were. I knew it all along. It really wasn't that surprising." Millions of Americans did not predict former President Donald Trump's election victory in 2016. Many of those millions when asked postelection have since claimed, "I knew it. I saw the signs."

Since new knowledge instantly updates prior knowledge, we are left with the mind's imperfect ability to reconstruct past states of knowledge or beliefs that have changed. Once you adopt a new view of the world, or any part of it, you immediately lose much of your ability to recall what you used to believe before your mind changed. Your instinctive ability to reconstruct past beliefs makes you underestimate the extent to which prior events surprise you.

The tendency to revise the history of one's beliefs, in light of what actually happened, can produce a robust cognitive illusion. We cannot suppress the powerful perception that *what makes sense in hindsight today was predicable yesterday*. The illusion that we understand the past fosters overconfidence in our ability to predict the future.

Nicolas Taleb describes this common process in his popular book *The Black Swan*. He found that expert financial advisors were no better at predicting the stock market when compared to naïve amateurs. He discovered that experts, with all their industry knowledge, were much better at describing *why* their predictions were wrong. In other words, their specialized knowledge only helped them explain an unexpected rise or fall after it happened. When they were wrong, they had a host of cognitive mechanisms in their defensive arsenal. Common explanations included that they were almost right except that they received inaccurate or incomplete information, events happened outside their scope, or some unforeseen outlier took place (e.g., bank collapse in country X). This "almost right" or "right except for" defense mentally absolves them of any blame and keeps their unwarranted belief of superior ability intact. Another popular prediction that eliminates error is, "I'm off on my timing. My prediction just hasn't happened—yet." Once again, we all do this, instinctively, and usually outside our conscious awareness.[10]

Humans are victims of an asymmetry in the perception of random events. We attribute our successes to our skills and our failures to external events outside our control, randomness. It's important to note that when we make a correct prediction, we are rewarded by feeling pleased. This boosts our motivator neurotransmitter dopamine to "do that again." We quickly dismiss, forget, or rationalize missed predictions. Beliefs don't just delude us into thinking we are good at predictions; they *make us better at everything*.

Beliefs Make Us Better at Everything

When something goes wrong, we attribute external causes to these unintentional results: "I fell because I tripped on something," "I spilled the milk because you left the container out," "I was late because the traffic was horrible," "I got the question wrong because you tricked me," "Look what you made me do," and the endless list goes on. When events go as planned, we instantly take credit, because after all, we planned it that way. We explain good results in terms of personal attributes.

Not only are we almost always right, we typically claim success even when we don't have a hand in the results. Famous golfer Tiger Woods experienced scandals followed by physical setbacks. Several years later, he won another major tournament. Several fans stated, "I had faith in him, I knew it would happen. I knew Tiger Woods would come back." That's a safe bet. A comeback means you were insightful, and you could blame the unfortunate circumstance if he hadn't. Essentially, you're always right, or at least always nearly right. The beliefs are correct; it's those confounding circumstances that keep interfering.

This explains our consistent overvaluation of ourselves and undervaluation of others. When things go well for us, it was intentional, we have reasons. When things go badly, it was unintentional, we have causes. This asymmetry in reasoning allows us to over-valuate our efforts. That's why 90 percent of us believe we are better drivers, more trustworthy, better at spotting deception, and so on. And most members of a workgroup typically believe they did most of the work. Have you ever wondered how this can be so? This is a form of confirmation bias. (I discuss this human disposition extensively in the next chapter.) First, we select the most important criteria for measure. Fast drivers may believe quickness is a critical attribute for driving. Slow drivers may believe courtesy or caution is central. Shorter and faster basketball players may believe that play-making is most important, while taller and relatively slower players may believe that rebounding is key. We tend to put ourselves in the best light.

When we do well, it was deserved, intentional, and mostly due to effort. When our adversaries do well, we attribute luck (unintentional causes and luck): "She gets all the breaks." When it doesn't go well for our rivals, we attribute their misfortune to their bad decisions: "What a poor decision. She should have seen the signs." It is so ingrained in us that psychologists call this the *Fundamental Attribution Error*: over-emphasizing personal characteristics and underemphasizing situational factors when judging others' behaviors. Then doing the opposite for ourselves. Comedian George Carlin encapsulated it nicely with his well-known quip, "Have you ever noticed that anybody driving slower than you is an idiot, and anyone going faster than you is a maniac?"

Belief Section Summary

In this section on belief, we learned that we are hardwired to make sense of our environment so that it can become a safe, productive, and predictable place. Finding meaning, order, and control in our lives is so essential that we impose order and structure in our environment. We do this by finding patterns in our experiences that develop into mental models (beliefs) as we connect the dots of events and reactions. Importantly, because danger and opportunity were fleeting in our evolutionary past, we developed a fast-track to belief formation during surprise events.

Beliefs are a way of extracting meaning from a highly ambiguous and complex environment. They work as guiding principles in life, to provide direction and give meaning. This provides the security of empowerment. Beliefs act like internal commands, instructing us on how to interpret what is happening. The mind uses beliefs to form rule-of-thumb guidelines called heuristics. These heuristics save valuable mental resources and help us function successfully. We also learned that we don't choose our beliefs, and many times we are not even aware of them until asked to name or explain them. This lack of awareness makes sense, as our beliefs prompt us to do their bidding through un-conscious emotions.

The pursuit and maintenance of control is a key human motivation. Believing that we can personally predict, affect, and steer events in the present and future produces a sense of well-being. We do this by projecting our beliefs onto our experience, then securing comfort by finding, or creating, supportive evidence.

Believing comes easily because we trust our senses. Our believing nature formed in a simpler world when our lives depended on it, and when trusted authority figures surrounded us. Disbelief is akin to ignoring your senses, and that requires a conscious mental effort. Our beliefs guide us in both impulsive decisions and conscientious deliberations. Stable beliefs provide psychological security in an unstable world; accordingly, beliefs, once formed, become decidedly resistant to change.

As we now know, we are not the rational calculators and logic machines that the Enlightenment philosophers envisioned. We are subject to a vast array of factors that shape our beliefs. Our pattern-seeking predilection ensures that we seek and find patterns in both meaningful and meaningless noise. Our basic sense-making machinery drives us to infuse those patterns with meaning and agency to explain why things happen as they do. These meaningful patterns form the core of our beliefs. Our understanding of reality is dependent upon them. To preserve and protect them, our brains employ a host of cognitive biases that continually confirm our beliefs as true. The next section illustrates how this critical feature of our mind, cognitive bias, instinctively confirms our beliefs to maintain sanity and impose order in a chaotic world. The reader will also learn strategies to recognize and combat unhealthy biases.

These very biases that support and maintain our beliefs suddenly flip during a moment of surprise. They now dismiss the prior belief and endorse the new one, as if it were always present.

SECTION II

~

BIAS

CHAPTER FOUR

~

Who's in Control, Us or Our Bias?

Heavy rainfall cuts channels into the hillside terrain as it rushes down the slopes. Once formed, subsequent rainfall automatically travels down the existing channels. Likewise, thoughts and information naturally fall into our belief patterns and make them deeper. In most cases, this happens with no conscious awareness.

Beliefs. We are unique because of them. Two people can share the same event but gain vastly divergent experiences. These distinct experiences drive the formation of differing beliefs. It's safe to say that our beliefs are as distinctive as our fingerprints. We not only identify with them, we identify *as* them. Threats to them are threats to us personally. To protect ourselves, we must protect them.

Why is it that while we may share experiences, we can produce such divergent interpretations and subjective impressions? We marvel at the *other* person's credulousness. If you didn't already know, these *others* marvel at our gullibility too. That's because we regard our perceptions and reactions as if they are a direct, objective, and genuine reflection of how things "really are" rather than the product of our subjective interpretation.

Information streams through our senses, and we construct our version of reality. But this sensory input is mediated by complex mental processes that determine which information we attended to, how we instinctively organize it, and the meaning we attribute to it. Our experience, family system, education, culture, and the norms implicit in our roles all affect how we process our sensory information.

A scuffle on the playground breaks out. One student feels frightened, another vindicated, a third excited, others saddened. Teachers, the principal, parents, and the media experience it differently too. That same fight might be viewed differently by others in the community, depending on their cultures or political perspectives. The list is endless. We not only view an event differently; we instinctively find evidence to substantiate our view. If we can't find any, we create it.

Think of beliefs as filters to view the world. Bias is the filtering process that only allows confirming evidence to pass through. Our uniquely human tendency to embrace information that supports our beliefs and reject information that contradicts them is called *confirmation bias*. This instinct is so well researched, entire books are written about it. Protecting our beliefs is so important from an evolutionary perspective that we developed a neurological boost to encourage these defenses.

In *Denying to the Grave: Why We Ignore the Facts That Will Save Us*, Harvard researcher Sara Gorman and Columbia neuroscientist Jack Gorman examined cognitive biases. The Gormans claim that these biases have a physiological component. In their book, they cite research suggesting that people experience a rush of dopamine—neurological motivation—when processing information that supports their beliefs. They note: "It feels good to 'stick to our guns' even if we are wrong."[1]

Our cognitive biases help us maintain our beliefs in a complicated world that requires complex navigation. In the previous chapter, we learned how our beliefs evolved outside our control as we interacted with each other and our environment. This chapter explains how our cognitive biases deploy an impressive belief-defense system. But this remarkable armament comes with some baggage. Some of our firmly held beliefs may be irrational, destructive, or flat out wrong.

You might ask, "Who among us are most susceptible to bias?" Research published in *The Association for Psychological Science* set out to find a correlation between confirmation bias and intelligence level.[2] They discovered that intelligence level produced no effect. In some cases, they found that those with higher intelligence were simply better at justifying their beliefs. They convinced themselves with their own eloquence. Psychologists call this the *intelligence trap*. We all fall prey to this inherent disposition.

Beliefs Make Us Unique; Biases Keep Us Unique

Ponder one of the most cited early examples of research from Stanford. Researchers rounded up students who had opposing opinions about capital punishment. Half were against it and thought it did not affect crime, while the other half were in favor and thought it deterred crime.[3]

Researchers asked the students to respond to two studies. They were unaware that the studies were false. One study provided data that supported the deterrence argument. The other provided data that called it into question. Both studies were designed to present equally compelling statistics. The students who had originally supported capital punishment rated the pro-deterrence data highly credible and the anti-deterrence data unconvincing. As you probably guessed, the students who had originally opposed capital punishment believed the reverse. At the end of the experiment, researchers once again asked the students about their opinions. They were now even more firmly entrenched in their views. How can this be so?

Several decades after the Stanford studies, neuroscience research explains these results. University of Southern California (USC) neuroscientist Sam Harris refers to this doubling-down response by these students as the *backfire effect*. That's when new information that contradicts your beliefs blindsides you. Rather than weaken your views, it backfires and strengthens them instead. Harris, with a team of other neuroscientists at the Brain and Creativity Institute at USC, placed subjects in an MRI machine. They asked subjects to consider counterarguments to their strongly held political beliefs. The researchers revealed that when people were presented with evidence that alerted them to the possibility that their political beliefs might be incorrect, they reacted with the same brain regions that would come online if they were responding to a physical threat. One researcher commented, "The response in the brain that we see is very similar to what would happen if, say, you were walking through the forest and came across a bear. Your brain would have this automatic fight-or-flight [response] and your body prepares to protect itself."[4]

While we may not outright ignore data with which we disagree, we can manufacture substantial latitude in how to interpret it. People treat questionable evidence as credible when it confirms what they want to believe, as is the case of discredited research linking vaccines to autism. For example, link-believers regularly cite medical research supporting a link even though this research was almost immediately discredited. Additionally, many of us tend to discount evidence that meets the rigorous demands of science if it goes against what we want to believe. We see this with the widespread dismissal of the scientific evidence of climate change. People often minimize or outright deny viewpoints from the 95 percent of scientists who acknowledge a link between climate change and human activity.

Countless research studies show how we tend to select our own realities by deliberately avoiding information that threatens our happiness and well-being. For example, people on diets prefer not to look at the calories in their tasty dessert, and people choose the news source that aligns with their political views. We are remarkably adept at selectively directing our attention to information that affirms what we believe and at forgetting information we wish were not true.

In the *Journal of Economic Literature*, researchers showed that while a simple failure to obtain information is the most clear-cut case of "information avoidance," people have a wide range of other information-avoidance strategies at their disposal. We tend to block the information that disagrees with what we learned previously and yield to the information that confirms our current approach. We think we are learning, but in reality, we are steamrolling through information and conversations, waiting until we hear something that matches up with our current philosophy or previous experience, and then cherry-picking information to justify our current behaviors and beliefs.[5]

Most people don't want new information; they want information that validates what they already know. Even research scientists, those specially trained in fighting bias, are vulnerable. In his 1962 analysis of scientific revolutions, Thomas S. Kuhn radically proposed that scientists working in a prevailing paradigm typically reject or dismiss contradictory data when they first encounter it. Although received coldly by the scientific community, he was right. Those we typically entrust with objectivity, scientists, were just as defenseless against bias as all of us. For example, scientists used to believe that stress caused ulcers. For decades, funding and research protocols drove the medical community to find effective treatments. We now know that bacteria is the most common cause of ulcers. The medical and scientific community dismissed this research for several years because it challenged long-held beliefs. To prove his point, one of the original researchers ingested the bacteria. He received a Nobel Prize in 2005.[6]

During a radio interview, I listened to the author of the book *Everybody Lies: Big Data, New Data, and What the Internet Can Tell Us About Who We Really Are.* Harvard PhD graduate and Google data scientist Seth Stephens-Davidowitz claims that everyone lies. For him, lying includes embellishing your accomplishments, giving deceptive answers on surveys to look good, telling a fishy story, and underscoring your attributes on Facebook. When asked by the interviewer what he himself lies about, he stated that he was an exception because he was a "compulsively honest person." Shortly after that comment, he described how he changed his picture on a dating website to something more flattering in what he called "lying by emphasis." He claims he did this "because everyone else does." Essentially, he fell prey to his own accusations and then rationalized, as we all do.[7]

We can no more dismiss our confirmation bias than we can see the backs of our heads. If we want to see the back of our head, we can't even see it in a mirror. We need two mirrors and even then it takes focused effort and coordination. Noting our bias is equally difficult and possibly even impossible. Confirmation bias is as natural as walking upright. We like to think, *The objective evidence led me to this conclusion.* In reality, our beliefs led us to the evidence. We must recognize that our view of the world is no more than that, a view, one that is shaped by our vantage point, history, experiences, information from other sources, and personal knowledge.

Sensing Your Personal Bias

Try to consciously note your own biases at work as you read the following composition:

"Sugar and Hyperactivity: Link or No Link?"

Is there a link between sugar consumption by children and hyperactivity? If you give children a heap of candy, cake, donuts, sugary drinks, and so on, will they start climbing the metaphorical walls? What is your gut instinct? What has your experience led you to believe? Form your belief in your head before you continue reading. Pause if you need to. Do you believe there is a link (link-believer) or believe there is no link (link-doubter)? Commit to a position.

When I was younger, my parents would tell me that sugar makes me hyper. I'd eat some sweets and my mother would say, "There he goes, all hyper. It's from the sugar." I never bought into this. I was a hyper little boy, and I never noticed a difference in my behavior after eating candy. I didn't *feel* any different either. Even as a child I always brushed off these comments as nonsense. Like when my mother said, "Look, he's acting up. He's getting tired. It's time for bed." I always thought this was parent-code for "Mom is tired and doesn't want to deal with me anymore."

My nieces bought into this sugar-hyperactivity link too. When one niece eats sugar, her older sister predicts what will happen next with her younger sister, "Get ready! First, she starts giggling, then her voice gets high, then she begins singing." As if on cue, her younger sister starts giggling, her voice gets higher, and she begins singing. It looks like a choreographed scene. Even if she didn't follow the expected pattern, the older sister would inevitably describe her lack of symptoms as an anomaly, delayed. "Just wait for it." Or she'd note some other behavior (e.g., tapping her toes, moving about energetically) as a symptom substitution.

No matter what behavior the younger sister produced, the older sister would attribute it to sugar hyperactivity and knowingly say "See?" I once commented to the older sister that research finds no link between sugar and hyperactivity for the vast majority of children. She looked at me, tilted her head, pursed her lips, and gave me that twisted smile indicating my naivety. After all, her experience tells her differently. And there it is, *experience trumps research.*

Well then, does sugar create hyperactivity in children or not? I think it's a myth, and because I, too, am biased, I'm prone to look for research that supports my belief. In the interest of fairness, I attempted to find legitimate empirical evidence. I entered "sugar and hyperactivity in children" in my search engine. Before I pushed enter, I decided ahead of time that I'd only include empirical research and exclude anecdotal commentary.

Study 1: The results from a critical review of the empirical research (1986)

Milich, R., M. Wolraich, and S. Lindgren. "Sugar and Hyperactivity: A Critical Review of Empirical Findings. *Clinical Psychology Review* 6, no. 6 (1986): 493–513.[8]

"Although the results of correlational studies suggested that high levels of sugar consumption may be associated with increased rates of inappropriate behavior, the results of dietary challenge studies have been inconsistent and inconclusive. Most studies found no effects associated with sugar ingestion, and the few studies that have found effects have been as likely to find sugar improving behavior as making it worse."

Study 2: Nine years later (1995)

Wolraich, M. L., D. B. Wilson, and J. W. White. "The Effect of Sugar on Behavior or Cognition in Children: A Meta-analysis." *JAMA* 274, no. 20 (1995): 1617–21. doi:10.1001/jama.1995.03530200053037.[9]

"The meta-analytic synthesis of the studies to date found that sugar does not affect the behavior or cognitive performance of children. The firm belief of parents may be due to expectancy and common association. However, a small effect of sugar or effects on subsets of children cannot be ruled out."

Study 3: Concluding connection (2016)

Donahue, D. A., F. H. Letterman, H. A. Carson, and D. A. Gobbles. "Hyperactivity: Is Candy Causal?" *Critical Reviews in Pediatrics and Nutrition* 36, nos. 1–2 (2016): 31–47.[10]

"Although most studies to date have found only a tenuous link between high sugar consumption and hyperactivity, a canonical analysis of regression protocol found that the link is immediate for some and delayed for many. Researchers found a robust and causal link between sugar (cause) and hyperactivity (result) when including delayed behavior assessments and boisterousness."

Have you changed your position? Can you feel your own internal bias working? If you can, you are rare, but I prompted you to turn on your radar bias detector. When you started reading the research summaries on a link between sugar and hyperactivity in children, you probably had a belief. With that belief, you probably felt the pull of confirmation bias. If you believed there was a cause-effect link, you probably guessed that I'd attempt to bust it, and your mind instinctively scanned your memories for evidence or experiences to dispute where you thought I was leading. If you were familiar with the research, you might have gotten a sense of satisfaction, maybe even a little dopamine boost of self-affirmation.

If you believe in a link between sugar consumption and hyperactivity in children, you probably reacted to my research citations. I'm guessing that link-believers instinctively looked for ways to dispute the claims: "Hey, wait a minute! This research is over three decades old." You may have focused on the "inconsistent and inconclusive" part: "These researchers can't even agree." Link-believers would surely notice that there is a subset of children who might experience hyperactivity. You may have taken special note of "most in the medical industry." What is most? 51 percent? 99 percent? The term "most" is too vague to mean anything.

Then you read the final "Study 3: Concluding connection." If you're a link-believer, you finally got what you were looking for: supportive evidence. Whew! You noticed that this study used a vastly more complex design of "canonical analysis of regression protocol." Finally, a more powerful research design found the link because it included delayed reactions. The link-doubters are probably thinking, "It was only one study." The preponderance of the evidence claims almost no effect. In the end, it appears, like many other things in life, inconclusive.

The whole point of this exercise is to notice the push and pull of your confirmation bias; it happens instinctively. You can guard against it if you're relentlessly vigilant, but it's immensely difficult and cognitively exhausting to remain watchful. I must apologize. This was an exercise with some deception. My goal was to make you self-examine and notice your instinctual bias. The final report, "Study 3: Concluding connection (2016)," is fictitious. I couldn't find any supportive evidence to support a link, so I had to invent it. What's going on with your confirmation bias now?

After writing this section on the link between sugar and hyperactivity in children, I asked a well-educated friend for his opinion. He reported, "My bias was that there is a link to sugar and hyperactive behavior, based on my recollected experience with my children and their friends." He felt mildly surprised that researchers had not found a link, but qualified this with, "I can believe that is the case, as there is no doubt a social pull when kids have some sugar, as those around them may comment that they are about to go crazy." He finished his assessment with, "Still, it wouldn't surprise me if someone in the medical community found a link at some point. I guess I am hanging on to my bias!" Here we see the human need to make sense of our experience and then justify it with a bias when it doesn't fit the science.

Once beliefs form, the brain automatically looks for and finds confirmatory evidence to support them. When found, we get a small neurological burst (dopamine) for being "correct." This self-affirmation feedback loop boosts our confidence further. Our personal beliefs provide a distinct way of extracting meaning from highly ambiguous and complex stimuli that enters our brains. Firmly held beliefs, right or wrong, impose meaning and a sense of control over an uncertain environment.

Our Experience Makes Us;
Then We Make Our Experience

People intuitively look for support to validate their belief system. It's like seeing the world through narrow keyholes and screening filters. Our beliefs lead us to act in ways that make the belief seem true and also prevent us from encountering or accepting evidence that it is not.

In the story below, a distressed Jill felt stunned by her grandmother's comment. The comment surprised her, creating a moment of soaring susceptibility to a mindset makeover. She accepted her grandma's comment as true. This new mindset prompts her to applaud all her subsequent culinary successes and minimize her failures—confirmation bias.

My grandparents were arriving for a visit, and I wanted to show them my appreciation. Lucky for them I had just begun my teenage summertime baking spree. I followed recipes in my favorite cookbook exactly the same each time I cooked. I decided to bake a batch of Grandparent Appreciation Ultra Chocolate Chip Cookies! I couldn't find my cookbook anywhere. Flustered and distressed, I tossed together whatever my memory would gather and hoped for the best. While they sat on the cooling rack, I noticed something was strangely odd. Something was missing. Oh no!—The Ultra part. They had no chocolate chips!

I gave them to my grandma, who asked why I looked so upset. I held up a sample cookie and confessed, "I can't find my recipe and so I just made it up. I was so worried about getting all the ingredients in the mix that I forgot the most important of them all." She took a bite of the cookie and turned around with a most surprised face. "Jill," she started, "this is the best cookie of my life! You are a wonderful chef. Perhaps you should make your own cookbook." I never thought to make a chocolate chip cookie without chocolate chips. Brilliant!

My mouth dropped open. Then quickly filled with cookie. Behold. The mighty grandparent was right. I had created the best cookie of all time. To this day, I refuse to use recipes. I insist on only reading the list of ingredients and making it up from what I retain. There have been a lot of really amazing dishes gobbled up at the table. And many more have gone to the dogs. But for every kitchen experiment from that moment forward, I had the confidence of Cookbook Freedom.

Jill started as a meticulous cook: "I followed recipes in my favorite cookbook exactly the same each time I cooked." Her grandmother's comment triggered a window for a mindset revision because it surprised her. She accepted the mindset and tried it out. It's important to note that if she hadn't accepted the mindset, she might have made a comment such as, "Yeah, the dough is delicious, but they don't taste as good as real chocolate chip cookies." Such a comment would have endorsed her prior belief that the cookies were a disaster because she didn't follow the recipe exactly. Instead, she thought, "Behold. The mighty grandmother was right. I had created the best cookie of all time." This thought reveals an affirmation of a new mindset. She then finishes by emphasizing the successes of her new mindset while diminishing and ignoring the failures: "There have been a lot of really amazing dishes gobbled up at the table. And many more have gone to the dogs."

She now believes she is a better cook by *not* following the recipe meticulously. Note that no matter what happens in the kitchen, success or failure, both support her new belief. While she used to feel horrified with mistakes in the past, she now views them as inevitable learning events.

Not only does Jill believe she is a better cook when not following recipes, she will also, in all likelihood, find that her dishes really do taste better. That's because our brains are easily fooled. Erik Vance, the author of *Suggestible You: The Curious Science of Your Brain's Ability to Deceive, Transform, and Heal*, describes his own experience while researching his book.

> One of my first reporting experiences, I got electrocuted in this chair for half an hour or so. Every time I got a green light, I got a small shock. Every time I saw a red light, I got a large shock, and this went back and forth. This was by an amazing Maryland researcher named Luana Colloca. I got to the point where that red light would go off and I'd be like, "Oh, my god." I mean, it was a strong shock. My foot would twitch.
>
> On the last round, it felt like maybe the green one had been turned up a tiny bit; it was a harder pinch but not that much. She came in and she said, "Nice job on that last round. We gave you the big one every time." [This was the experimental manipulation.] Depending on which color you saw, I felt it differently? I felt it less [with the green light] and my foot didn't twitch. I mean, it wasn't that I was reporting feeling it less. I really felt less pain. It's because I created expectations for what green and red meant. When expectations didn't meet reality, my brain stepped in and released drugs in order to bring down that pain so that it fits with the expected or at least close to what it expected. That's what's at the heart at a lot of these placebo effects. It's your brain trying to get expectations to meet reality.[11]

Justify to Win

Confirmation bias is distinctively human. In *Why Do Humans Reason*, authors Hugo Mercier and Dan Sperber humorously imagine what would happen if a mouse had the human disposition for confirmation bias. "Such a mouse, bent on confirming its belief that there are no cats around, would soon be dinner. To the extent that confirmation bias

leads people to dismiss evidence of new or underappreciated threats—
the human equivalent of the cat around the corner—it's a trait that
should have been selected against." If we humans evolved to use reason
to lead us to sound judgments, then why would we develop such a serious design flaw as confirmation bias?

The fact that confirmation bias survives suggests that it must have
some adaptive function. Recall from a prior chapter how we evolved
to form alliances and protect ourselves. We're not programmed to seek
truth; we're programmed to win arguments. Mercier and Sperber argue
persuasively that our bias-function stems from this *hypersociability*. To
Mercier and Sperber, reason evolved as a mechanism to explain and
justify our beliefs, not to find truth. Reason evolved as a tool to convince others and get what we want.[12]

While alliances are important in a precarious world, our personal
interests are also essential. It makes adaptive sense to believe someone
you trust with whom you'd like to align. Although survival in our ancestral world was more difficult, it was also less complicated. Align with
those who look healthy and successful. On the other hand, everyone
has their own agenda and instinctively negotiates in their own best
interests. These two conflicting inclinations—align with others, but
think of yourself first—create an inherent tension. Rational hardware
that developed to make alliances and negotiate our agendas is what we
have today.

While confirmation bias appears to be a major evolutionary design
flaw, several advantages exist that make it adaptable. Agreeing with
others, whether their views are accurate or inaccurate, creates social
bonds. We can credit much of our survival to collaboration, cooperation, and alliances. The world of our ancestors was incredibly hazard-
ous, wrought with dangers and fear. An overconfidence in success, or
naïve optimism, allowed our ancestors to innovate and create. The
false sense of security that confirmation bias warrants may encourage
us to forge ahead against immense odds. Imagine what it would be
like if we had no faith in our understanding of how the world worked.
We would face a considerable sense of disorientation, frustration, and
anxiety.

When Beliefs Are Attacked, Switch Roles

People often show substantial latitude in how to interpret information when they can't outright ignore it. If disputing evidence doesn't work, we can change the topic and make it personal. Have you ever argued with someone and discovered you were disagreeing about two separate topics, or two separate aspects of the same topic?

I play recreational old-timer hockey. When a player commits an infraction on another player, an apology typically arises, and we continue. One regular player in our group is notably aggressive and defensive when accused of an infraction. This player tripped me during a game. When he did not apologize, I got annoyed and scowled. He claimed it was an accident. He has a long history of claiming innocence when he is aggressive. I rolled my eyes and shook my head. He then became indignant and aggressive, "Are you calling me a liar?" For me, it's about being tripped: a clear infraction that the other players noted. In his head, he instantly shifted this interaction to an attack on his character, which he will vehemently defend. Now, it's no longer about the infraction; it's about his integrity. He has switched his role from a guilty offender to an indignant victim. He is accusing me of attacking his character and disputing his belief that he is honorable.

Now that he feels attacked, his fight-or-flight responses trigger his limbic system. His elevated emotions undermine any reasonable thought-processing by triggering defensive rationalizations. Frequently, victims give themselves leeway in their behavior. He may even justify, in his head, that I deserved it because I called his character into question. Further conversation is useless because we both see the other as the attacker and ourself as a victim. The "alleged" infraction is now secondary and soon forgotten, while the indignation of implied lying lingers.

Clever politicians know that emotions can outmaneuver rational debate. During the 2016 election, I watched a late-night comedian lampooning Newt Gingrich. The comedian showed a clip of a news anchor interviewing Gingrich. The comedian was incredulous about Gingrich's continual response to the *facts*. In the clip, the news anchor commented to Gingrich, "Statistically, Americans have never been safer. Crime in general, and violent crime in specific, has continued to decline for more than a decade except for one brief spike in 2015." Gingrich replied, "But Americans don't feel safer." The camera returns to the comedian who has a distrustful look and who states to the audience, "Gingrich doesn't even care about the facts—facts don't matter to him." The audience laughs. Back to the news clip whereby the news anchor restates: "Yes. But Americans are safer than ever. Are you disputing the results from the research?" Gingrich: "But American's don't feel safer." The camera flips back to the comedian with a disbelieving look—the audience laughs. Once more that news anchor tries to convince Gingrich, and once more Gingrich gives the refrain: "But American's don't feel safer." Back to the comedian who then rants about the inability of Republicans to listen to facts.[13]

Gingrich was right all along: Feelings outplay facts all the time. We make fun of it when we see others do it. We do it too, but we don't recognize it when we do it ourselves. When someone points it out, "Hey, the facts say you are wrong," we say, "but this is different." Politicians do this and then claim it's unfair when the opposing party does it.

Reflecting on Your Bias

We don't get to decide what influences us in life. Life happens, and we deal with the challenges and opportunities as they arise. Reflection, if it happens, is by its very nature after the fact. Because it is after the fact, and we are usually engrossed in the present, or planning for the future, we never developed a skilled propensity for it. Reflection is uncommon without a conscious effort. Our mental ruminations focus on the here-and-now and what's to come. Our propensity to downplay any prior conflicting beliefs often invalidates reflection as a rational tool for self-examination.

When asked why we behaved the way we did, our explanations quickly rationalize our behavior. We are notoriously bad at acknowledging what influences us. Product sales for items in Super Bowl commercials predictably skyrocket immediately after the Super Bowl. That noted, consumers typically report that the commercials do not affect their purchases. Most of the priming that prompts our behavior takes place outside conscious awareness. The example below is a typical scenario.

Isaiah planned to leave work at 4:30 p.m., but a last-minute phone call from an irate customer kept him late. When he finally arrived at his car, he found a parking ticket on his windshield. Angry at the injustice of it, he pulled out quickly and scraped his fender on an adjacent car. While putting an apologetic note on the windshield, the owner of the scraped car ranted at him. In a hurry on the drive home, he sped and received a ticket. When he finally arrived home late, he saw his son's bicycle in the driveway. He got out of his car, snapped at his son for leaving it in the driveway, then punished him, "I've told you about leaving your bike in the driveway. No media for you tonight." His wife heard the commotion and asked, "Why are you snapping at Joey?" He replied, "I've told him a hundred times not to leave his bike in the driveway!" She thinks, but wisely does not say, "Did you have a bad day?"

How much of Isaiah's decision to punish his son was triggered by his bad day, and how much was the result of his son's leaving the bike on the driveway? Would you say 75 percent bad day and 25 percent bike on the driveway? Would you say 100 percent bike on the driveway?

Consider a better day for Isaiah. He plans to leave work at 4:30 p.m., but his boss notes his hard work and sends him home early. He finds a coupon for a free car wash on his windshield. A fellow worker smiles and notes Isaiah's dashing new sport coat. On the way home, he listens to an outrageously funny comedian who discusses the importance of raising your children in a culture of love and tolerance. Upon arriving home, he has to get out of his car to move his son's bicycle—for the fifth time this week. He snarls at his son Joey then playfully musses his hair. Isaiah instructs his son, "Now go out to the driveway and put your bike on it, walk around the house, then remove it. I want you to do this five times, right now, so that you build a habit." Joey whines, "But Dad." "Don't 'but-Dad' me," Isaiah replies, "Get going," feigning another scowl, and reaching teasingly to muss his son's hair. Joey retreats playfully, shaking his fist.

Most of us can see how both scenarios might play out credibly. While it's easy for us to see how *others* succumb to influence that affects their decisions, we rarely notice subtle or external influences on our own decisions and behaviors. For example, in a Stanford study, the researcher gave a lecture to a criminology class on "Crime Is a Virus." To a separate criminology class, the researcher gave a similar lecture on

"Crime Is a Beast." Researchers then asked both classes to work on so-lutions for fighting crime. The crime-is-a-virus class produced system-atic reform-based solutions, exactly how you would treat a virus. The crime-is-a-beast class generated approaches emphasizing enforcement, exactly how you'd treat a beast. At the end of the study, the researchers informed the participants of the purpose of the study. Even when aware of the researchers' intent, the participants reported that the use of beast or virus metaphors didn't influence their approaches.[14]

Can We, Should We, Fight Our Bias?

> "There are two kinds of studies in the world: those that confirm
> our common sense and those that are wrong."
>
> Attribution Unknown

Who is to say that the way you originally learned something is the best way? What if you learned one way of doing things and better ways ex-ist that are easily accessible? Confirmation bias enslaves us to our old beliefs without us even realizing it. We adopt a philosophy or strategy based on what we have been exposed to without knowing if it's the optimal way to do things. Most times we do things the way we do them because we have always done them that way.

When my wife and I drive home from the same location, we take dif-ferent routes. When I go my way, she suggests her route has less traffic. When she goes her way, I tell her my method is faster. We both have shifting criteria that support our preference. Her predilection is less traffic, and if we encounter heavy traffic, she notes it as an anomaly: "There must be some event here today." If my method bogs down, I will note it as an anomaly or stress some other self-serving interpretation. Neither of us is likely to change routes.

My friend believes she has extrasensory perception. Whenever she sees a deck of cards, she'll ask me to pick a card, keep it hidden, and fo-cus on it. She then attempts to guess its identity. If it's close in number, she says "Ooh, I almost got it." If she gets the correct suit, "Whew! So close." With such weak criteria, she's almost always right. On occasion, because I'm not a believer in her ESP, I get blamed for not focusing on the card hard enough, or actually sabotaging the guess. She can recall many times when she's experienced direct "hits." I mentally note that if you do something often enough, you are bound to eventually get lucky.

This is how psychics, crystal-ball gazers, and tarot-card readers work. People remember the hits and forget the misses. But I'm a scientist, and as such, we have to keep track of the misses, not just the hits. In science, we keep the entire database and look to see if the number of hits outperforms the total number you'd expect by chance. Humans don't usually do an intuitive balance sheet of hits and misses. Hits, such as finding food, avoiding predators, and gaining opportunities had a much bigger payoff, so we notice them exponentially more often.

The examples above are small-scale examples of how bias works in our everyday life. Taking a separate route home, or believing you can guess hidden cards, is hardly dangerous or rife with opportunity. But the same confirmation bias is at work with some critically important beliefs. Does owning a handgun make you safer? Do vaccine injections trigger autism? Does human-produced pollution significantly lead to climate change that endangers our existence? Where you sit on these issues isn't likely to change with more information. More information, if supportive, strengthens your belief. Additional information that challenges your belief becomes diminished or ignored. Remember the backfire effect: Challenging information may make you even more entrenched. Biases both serve us and obstruct us.

To actively attempt to see a more accurate world, we must first acknowledge that biases instinctively distort our perceptions. If you want to combat your own biases, it's a formidable challenge because it's counter to our instincts. It's not like people passing a candy dish when you are on a diet and consciously resisting. In this example, you have a visual stimulus that you can consciously counter. Fighting your instinctive proclivity for bias is vastly more difficult because it happens outside awareness and with no sensory evidence to alert us. That being said, it's worth the fight.

We would all step a little closer to the truth if we unlearned a tendency that comes naturally to all of us—the tendency to assume that our gut hunches are correct. As a general rule, you should consult research evidence, not your intuitions, when deciding whether a scientific claim is correct. Although our first instincts and gut impressions may be helpful in "sizing up" people or in predicting our long-term emotional preferences, they're typically inadequate for evaluating scientific claims about the world.

Intuitions, Right or Wrong?

During an interview at the World Business Forum with Nobel Laureate Daniel Kahneman, the interviewer asked if we should trust our intuitions. Kahneman defined intuition as "thinking that you know without knowing why you do." To show how easily intuition can lead us astray, he asked the attendees to guess the GPA of a college senior he called Julie. He told the crowd one fact about Julie, that she read fluently at a young age. He then asked them to judge how good of a student she had been.

From prior research, Kahneman knows that most people guess that Julie has around a 3.7 GPA. He tells the crowd, "You might think that this is a good answer," he said. "It's a terrible answer. It's an intuition, and it's absolutely wrong. If you were to do it statistically, you would do it completely differently. Actually, the age that people read is very little information about what student they will be twenty years later." According to Kahneman, this is an example of an intuition that we generate automatically with high confidence, but it's wrong statistically.

He believes that our intuition *may* be wrong unless we meet these three conditions. The first is that there must be some regularity. He uses chess and a long marriage as examples of regularity with engrained patterns. He also notes that the stock market doesn't have enough regularity. Avoid intuitions here for sure. The second condition is "a lot of practice." Here we see where the chess master and long marriage partners excel again. The third condition is immediate feedback. You must know immediately if you were correct or incorrect. The chess master learns quickly if a move was successful.[15]

Caution: Even though you now know that you should question your intuition, remember it's better to make a Type 1 error: false positive, believing something is real when it isn't. For example, what should you do if you find yourself traveling late at night with an urge to go to the toilet? You pull up to a lone gas station. It's dark and foggy. You hear the eerie sound of a flickering sign as it swings on a creaking hinge.

This is not the time to question your intuitions. Get the hell out of Dodge.

Living Effectively with Bias

Psychologists often draw an analogy to explain the difficulty of fighting our biases. It's based on an understanding of the Müller-Lyer illusion. If you haven't seen this illusion, any you call to mind will do. Most of us have seen the two parallel lines with arrows at each end. One line's arrows point in; the other line's arrows point out. Because of the direction of the arrows, the latter line appears shorter than the former, but in fact, the two lines are the same length. Even after we measure the lines and find them equal, and we learn the neurological basis of the illusion, we still perceive one line to be shorter than the other. In the daily world of dealing with people and situations, we don't get this benefit.

Learn and practice skepticism. Advertising agencies know that the mere frequency of a claim, or implied link, often becomes believed simply due to repetition. This is how branding works. Hearing a claim repeated over and over again doesn't make it correct. Many beliefs spread by "word-of-mouth" are nothing more than urban legends; therefore, we shouldn't assume that widespread beliefs are accurate.

An important first step in achieving wisdom, a balanced, considered judgment, is by recognizing that bias is how we are built. It can distort our views as much as others' views. It's part of being human. Confirmation bias is such an important cognitive threat to our beliefs and understanding that the CIA trains its operatives to fight against it. In his book, *Why We Believe What We Believe*, Andrew Newberg lays out eight strategies that the CIA uses to teach its intelligence-gathering analysts to think more wisely and open-mindedly. This is achievable and good advice for all of us. Here is the list.

1. Become proficient in developing alternative points of view.
2. Do not assume that the other person will think or act like you.
3. Think backward. Instead of thinking about what might happen, put yourself into the future and try to explain how a potential situation could have occurred.

4. Imagine that the belief you are currently holding is wrong, and then develop a scenario to explain how that could be true. This helps you see the limitations of your own beliefs.
5. Try out the other person's beliefs by actually acting out the role. This breaks you out of seeing the world through the habitual patterns of your own beliefs.
6. Play "devil's advocate" by taking the minority point of view. This helps you see how alternative assumptions make the world look different.
7. Brainstorm. A quantity of ideas leads to quality because the first ones that come to mind are those that reflect old beliefs. New ideas help you to break free of emotional blocks and social norms.
8. Interact with people of different backgrounds and beliefs.[16]

Are you mentally exhausted? Awareness is a great first step. While it's immensely difficult to notice and challenge our own biases, it is child's play to see them in others. Though it's easy to spot biases in others, pointing it out inevitably triggers a defensive posture. You've just threatened their identity. Arguments among those with strongly held convictions seldom come to a resolution. Firmly held beliefs defend themselves against challenging information. The usual strategy of bombarding people with information that challenges their cherished beliefs is more likely to engender defensive avoidance than receptive processing.

When Do Beliefs Change?

So how can we form new beliefs and channel different thinking? Traumatic events can break down an existing pattern and build a new one. I watched an affable comedian with a stutter. In an interview, he told viewers that he used to be a self-centered jerk with an air of entitlement. That is, until a freak accident left him with a stutter. Since then, he learned to support those who struggle with challenges. Using trauma strategically to change someone's beliefs comes with ethical and moral challenges.

Immersion in a culture with a different point of view can force beliefs to change through the sheer weight of conviction. The popular

Canadian sitcom *Schitt's Creek* illustrates this theme. The fabulously wealthy Rose family suddenly find themselves destitute. They move to a small town that they had once purchased as a joke. This endearing comedy lampoons how this once-entitled family slowly changes into upstanding, regular, and generous citizens. It took six seasons, so it's not a fast enlightenment.[17]

What's left? Surprise. While changing beliefs is a monumental task, we are all susceptible to spontaneous belief revision during moments of surprise. The emotion of surprise evolved to instantly defeat the armaments surrounding a current belief. The very biases that work to keep our beliefs robust are bypassed during a surprise event, then instantly recruited to support this new belief. This all takes place instantaneously, with no conscious control, and often with no awareness.

Summary

This chapter described how cognitive biases, particularly confirmation bias, traps us in our beliefs. While our beliefs make us distinct, this distinction is often based on flimsy evidence from a fast-acting pattern-making cognitive proclivity. Our distinctions often reflect our errors in thinking. Easily seen in others, uncovering our own biases takes considerable effort. We learned that with focused thoughtfulness, we can see our biases at work, but that kind of vigilance is rare and requires immense conscious effort. Our conscious effort is a valuable resource that evolved to look for danger or opportunity, and then make plans to strategically avoid or approach the situation. The vast majority of our beliefs function just fine, even if inaccurate. If we battle our instincts to "reflect" upon our beliefs, the reflection itself remains biased. We have a vigorous armature to maintain our functioning beliefs. Fighting our biases, while counterintuitive, leads us to a clearer picture of who we are and the world at large. The battle, while tough, is worth waging, and the final section of this chapter provided tested tools for the effort.

SECTION III

~

HOW SURPRISE WORKS

CHAPTER FIVE

~

Surprise

The Revision Reflex

Five-year-old Carol was enjoying a horseback ride with her family and a trail guide in the rolling hills of Wisconsin. At the top of a knoll, with the stables in view far below, her mother dropped her scarf. The guide quickly turned to get it, causing Carol's horse to bolt. It took off at a full gallop down the long hill toward the stables. Carol recalls, "This trail horse was going at lightning-speed with five-year-old me on his back. I pulled on the reins as hard as I could, but to no avail. I hung on for dear life." Her father and the guide tried to catch her, but this only spurred on her horse. "The horse that I was riding thought the race was on and ran faster. The stable hands ran out when they heard the yelling, and they forced my horse to stop." Carol credits this next moment as a life-changing event. "I briefly noticed the terror in their eyes, but that was quickly wiped out of my mind when I heard their words: 'Wow! You sure are some horsewoman!' and 'You're a real cowgirl!' I beamed proudly, barely noticing the sweat on my dad's brow and the sight of my mother fighting for composure when she caught up a few minutes later. What could have been a terrifying memory with the potential of obliterating my love of horses and riding, instead became a story I wore as a badge of honor because of the ranch hands' words. I returned home and started riding my older brother's bigger and more spirited horse sometimes, and though I continued to ride and love my sweet old horse Dakota, I have preferred a horse with an edge ever since."

If Carol's story had ended when she arrived at the stables after racing recklessly down the hill, behaviorists, like most of us, would have predicted the origin of a fear of riding horses. The stimulus, an uncontrollable horse speeding down the hill, triggering a response of fear, is what behaviorists label classical conditioning. Instead, the opposite occurred. She now views herself as a mighty cowgirl and prefers horses "with an edge." How did what looked like terror end up with a positive result? Surprise. Surprise differs from classical conditioning because it contains a cognitive component that is not present in the behaviorist's models. The perception of the recipient shapes the valence (positive or negative) of the surprise, not the event itself. It's this perception that we can manipulate, strategically.

In this chapter, I unpack how a surprise event creates a neurological storm that opens a momentary window for a belief revision. The reader learns how our normally robust belief systems, with all their inherent defensive structures, get rattled and reassembled. Like a phoenix rising from the ashes, surprise creates an opportunity for rebirth.

A surprise, when something unexpected occurs, exists in many forms and degrees. You may be surprised to see your hometown neighbor while relaxing on a beach in a foreign country. You may be surprised how quickly you learn a new skill. You may be surprised when the doorbell rings at 3:00 a.m. You will definitely be surprised if you win the lottery. Surprises can be negative too, like unexpectedly losing a promotion you anticipated or being bitten by your neighbor's dog. While these events fit into the category of surprise, I focus on those surprises that disrupt our self-concept, what we believe about ourselves, and how we fit in the world in which we live. These are the core beliefs that serve as a basis for screening, categorizing, and interpreting our experiences.

Self-concept and self-esteem describe two critically different constructs. Your self-concept is enduring to a large degree. It is built from your fundamental beliefs about yourself, and it comes with a robust set of built-in defense mechanisms. Self-esteem is a different notion. Self-esteem reflects your ongoing self-rating, is changeable by nature, and fluctuates due to many situational variables. Your self-esteem may be high with friends but low with adversaries (social). It may be higher when winning and lower when losing (achievement). It might be high with golf, but low with math (endeavor). Self-esteem can also change your mood. The changes I discuss in this text focus on the life-changing ones that transform your self-concept.

I also include surprises that dramatically affect our outlook, our perception of the world. Witnessing a flying squirrel chasing your cat will not dramatically influence your perception of the world, while learning that "the world is an oyster and all you have to do is open it to discover the pearls" can prove life-changing. While the oyster expression is cliché, it can strike a chord during a moment of surprise, as it did for Catherine.

> I grew up in a tight-knit community with a strong school and keen classmates. During my sophomore year, my parents decided to move to California, telling me it would be a great experience for me, and I'd get to go to the high school where my father had graduated. That was all well and good until I looked up the school's ratings and test score averages. I started freaking out because, on paper, the place looked terrible. I confided to my advisor about the situation. I worried my education would suffer because I was going to a school that, in my opinion, was subpar. I never cry in front of people, but I found myself openly crying. That's when he stunned me with a comment that I carry with me to this day. He said, "If you don't like how things are, change them. I know you're the kind of person who can influence a change and turn even the worst situations into a positive one. Take it as a learning opportunity at the very least." From that moment I started looking at everything differently and there aren't any real "negative outlooks" that I have in my life. Everything is a learning experience or opportunity for growth, and it's made my life so much brighter.

Her parents tried reason to convince her of the opportunities. It didn't take. The surprise comment (she used the term "stunned") from her counselor bypassed any conscious resistance to make a dramatic impact. Now empowered, she sees herself and the world differently: full of possibilities.

What Surprise Is Not

"Eureka," Archimedes exclaimed after he had stepped into a bath and noticed that the water level rose. He suddenly understood that the volume of water displaced must be equal to the volume of the part of his body he had submerged. This epiphany, or "aha" moment, illustrates the sudden and unpredictable solution to a problem.

Epiphanies, such as the one Archimedes experienced, are the breaking of a mental impasse. They are positive realizations in the sense that you figured something out. A surprise differs from an epiphany because it is always initially experienced as a negative emotion, if only fleetingly—as a disruption. This disruption demands an immediate interpretation, "Is this good or bad?" Subsequent emotions follow: joy, fear, anger, disgust, or sadness. Carol also experienced a sudden realization while horseback riding, but it differs because the unexpected insight was not the solution to a problem she was considering. Her perception changed how she saw herself, not the solution to a problem she was pondering. Whether what you figured out was positive (people are funny) or negative (people are mean), we experience any act of insight as beneficial, a better understanding.

A personal epiphany occurred several years ago. After studying formative moments for decades, I suddenly realized that most of them were triggered by a surprise. This sudden realization sparked years of research and the writing of this book.

A surprise is a brief cognitive and emotional state experienced as the result of an unexpected event. It can trigger neutral, pleasant, unpleasant, positive, or negative experiences. Surprise occurs when our expectations are suddenly violated, and it can occur in varying levels of intensity. The sudden awareness of this violation triggers a window to new knowledge.

It's also easy to get the terms *startled* and *surprised* confused, but they are distinctively different concepts. They can happen together or separately. If you hear a sudden bang while walking, (e.g., a car backfiring), it will both surprise you, "What just happened?" and startle you. You'll recoil fearfully. If you see your favorite celebrity at a grocery store, you'll be surprised—*I didn't expect that*—but you won't be startled, flinching defensively. Both *startle* and *surprise* capture our attention and demand an immediate explanation.

The startle response is a primitive, physiological, defensive reflex to sudden or threatening stimuli. It's most common with a sudden noise or a harsh movement. It typically triggers tightened muscles, hunched shoulders, and eye blinking. These autonomic reflexes evolved as survival strategies. If a gust of wind slams a door, your eyes will blink and your muscles will tighten because the loud bang startles you, but wind slamming doors is not surprising. You didn't learn anything. If it happens again an hour later, you'll have the same reaction. The purpose of surprise is to gather more information, to adjust our incorrect expectations.

Surprises are tied to expectations, while startles are not. You reach to pick up a large pink ball, expecting it to be hollow. It's a ten-pound exercise ball. Surprised, your eyes opened wide as you tried to see what it is about this event that violated your expectations. If you pick it up again in five minutes, you won't be surprised again because you learned; you adjusted your expectations.

Surprise often accompanies novelty, which may be the reason the two concepts appear related. Novelty is about learning something new. Surprise is about changing what you thought you knew. A familiar observation may feel surprising in a context in which something else is expected. For example, you can be surprised at finding your car door locked when you thought you had just clicked the unlock button on your key fob. That might surprise you, but it wouldn't be novel. A friend shows you an innovative way to format a document in Word. It's novel, but not surprising. If that friend bursts into song when you've never heard her sing, that will be novel (new, different, unusual). But if that friend, who usually sings poorly now suddenly sings gloriously, you'll feel surprised. The magnificent singing, while novel, also contradicted your expectations.

Novelty is based on memory stores and the processes that determine if an item is, or is not, in memory. Surprise, on the other hand, is based on expectations from systems capable of predicting, the process of generating such expectations, and the process that compares the expectations with what is actually experienced. Novelty supports the acquisition of items by memory, while surprise plays a key role in improving the capacity of the system to predict.

Surprise also differs from amazement. Feeling amazed by a magic show typically elicits a positive emotional response. In these cases, we expect to be astounded. While we commonly label the viewing of remarkable acts as moments of surprise, they are more correctly labeled as astonishment. In these shows, we *expect* to be amazed.

The Cognitive Structure of Surprise

Surprise is a feeling that signals an error in one's cognitive processing, a general alarm. It is the automatic reaction to a mismatch between an incoming input and our prior knowledge. The popular sixties television reality show *Candid Camera* started a craze that continues to engage us. It was the original show to capture people in their most unguarded, spontaneous, and natural response when they are tricked. A popular radio show preceded the early television version, which didn't translate very successfully. Critics accused *Candid Camera* of being mean-spirited and sneaky.

The host, Allen Funt, knew he had a gem and continued to tweak it for years. During a typical segment, a person, the foil, would be fooled. A classic example shows someone given a thimble-sized cup of coffee but charging them full price. In early shows, when the foil would get upset, Funt would leave him alone. Funt decided to attempt a new approach, which turned out to be a brilliant piece of psychological showmanship.

In his new adaptation, as the person is about to get upset, Funt grabs the foil and points to the hidden camera. The person now sees the hidden camera. In that initial moment, the person looks confused and out of sorts. Funt often restrained the person from looking away, so the camera could capture that one unguarded raw moment. The person is angry, embarrassed, ashamed, confused; they don't know how to feel. Right at that moment, Allen Funt says the magic words: "Smile! You're on *Candid Camera*." And smile they do. Suddenly, everything is solved. The familiar music and jingle play: "Hocus pocus. You're in focus. It's your lucky day. Smile. You're on *Candid Camera*."[1]

Surprise motivates us to solve inconsistency, to prevent possible dangers due to a now-apparent lack of our ability to accurately predict our environment. It invokes and mobilizes resources for a belief revision to cope with a potential threat or a golden opportunity. Our beliefs drive our perception, expectations, and behavior. Surprise is a belief-based phenomenon. If we had no beliefs, we would not be surprised. The main effect of surprise is instant belief revision; our prior knowledge base is wrong and needs updating.

Initially, surprise increases processing depth to prepare for cognitive adjustments. It does this by instantly allocating attention mechanisms to focus on the surprising stimulus. Researchers at the University of Iowa found that surprising events manifest the same brain signature as the outright stopping of cognitive processes. They refer to such an interruption of ongoing cognition as "attentional reorienting." This interruption frees up cognitive resources and reallocates them to event analysis. The sudden alert signal, cognitive disruption, and reallocation of resources gains consciousness as the *feeling* of surprise. This often takes the physiological form of freezing, as our senses gobble up incoming data for event analysis and instant learning. Once surprised, all senses pique to quickly ascertain danger or opportunity.[2]

We experience the interruption as negative, and shortly thereafter the response unfolds to other emotional states depending on the nature of the stimulus. Time is thus a key factor to understanding surprise and distinguishing it from its consequences. In her innovative doctoral dissertation, Dutch researcher Marret Noordewier showed that studies of surprise need to take the temporal dynamics of sense-making into account and to distinguish surprise from the emotional state that follows it. Of special importance she notes, "Surprise is known to amplify the state that follows it." That's why we like to surprise our friends at special events. A joyful surprise (like your best friend, who is out of the country, unexpectedly shows up at your birthday party) creates a greater degree of excitement than an expected happy event.[3]

Surprise creates the uncomfortable cognitive result of disorientation, creating a momentary alarm. This is why the police, the military, and criminals like to use surprise strategically. Surprise momentarily hijacks your attention. You must stop whatever you are doing to make sense of the surprise. This moment of sense-making gives the surpriser a brief window of disruption and a strategic advantage.

The Valence of Surprise

We associate most emotions with a clear-cut valence: positive or negative. Fear feels bad and joy feels good. Until recently, a surprise wasn't so clear, and many researchers portrayed it as a kind of emotional chameleon depending on the cause of the surprise. It could be positive (a glowing compliment) or negative (a raging criticism). We now understand that surprise is neurologically experienced as an error signal—negative—although the intensity is short and not as negative as fear or sadness.

Because surprise is such a short-lived emotion, we blend the experience of surprise with that of the emotion that follows. In essence, unexpected events trigger a surprise emotion (fleeting negative valence), but once the event is understood (positive: glowing compliment or negative: raging criticism), the emotions related to that event take over. Given that surprise induces arousal, this residual arousal remains after the surprising event is understood, and the initial emotion of surprise has dissolved. It's this additional arousal that usually leads to more intense experiences of the subsequent emotion. For example, surprise gifts typically lead to greater joy than for those we expect.

Researchers now consider big surprises as two-stage events. First, we respond to the surprise (negative valence), then to the event itself as we initiate sense-making. Responses then unfold contingent on the meaning of the event. The meaning of the event is contextual, malleable, rife with opportunities to be manipulated. Herein lies the critical point, and it deserves emphasis: *Surprise creates the opportunity for a crafted experience.*

When you break it down, it works like this. Surprise happens. *Oh my goodness. My beliefs about the world don't work. I need to immediately discern what just happened!* At this initial moment, you don't know if it's good or bad, nor what it means. All your attention mechanisms focus on finding out, including a soaring receptivity to any solution that eases this psychological crisis. This is when an agent can take control of your perception.

Dopamine: The Surprise Signal

Most laypeople think that dopamine is our "reward" system. The University of Manchester neuroscientist Dr. Mark Humphries tells us that the lay understanding of dopamine is mostly wrong, and that if we change "reward" to "outcome" we have a much more accurate understanding. Dopamine doesn't give us a reward so much as it predicts reward possibility, steering us toward a rewarding outcome or steering us away from a probable loss. Think of it this way. Many of us are motivated to go to the gym for a hard workout. That's our dopamine motivating us by "predicting a reward." The reward might be looking trim, fit, or an opportunity to enjoy a calorie-rich, guilt-free treat. Envisioning ourselves looking fit feels good and enjoying that treat tastes good. Both are rewards.

But dopamine can change quickly or slowly, and each manner produces significantly different results. Humphries explains it this way.

> We usually have a consistent level of dopamine in our system. Our goal is to keep it constant. An unbroken level means our experience is going pretty much the way we expect it; no surprises. When levels of dopamine change, it's either fast or slow. Fast changes are an error signal. Slow changes are a motivation signal. These correspond to two different ways dopamine is released. One way is a precise, short, large spike in the amount of dopamine, in a small region of the brain. The other way is all the time, creating a constant, low concentration soup of dopamine sitting around in many regions of your brain.

The role I'm mostly interested in is the fast-changing large spike, the neurological broadcast signal signifying surprise. Humphries states, "It [dopamine] rapidly and simultaneously tells huge regions of the brain, 'Something really important just happened.'" This sudden spike of dopamine alerts you that your expectations are wrong and need fixing. Then, the burst is over. Now you have to make meaning of the surprise. He adds, "Your brain needs to discover what actions caused that outcome, and then glue the outcome to the action by strengthening the link between them."[4]

So, what happens after the surprise, the sudden and fleeting spike of dopamine? Cambridge neuroscientist Wolfram Schultz states it this way.

> It [the dopamine spike] subsides in a few tens to hundreds of milliseconds when the neurons identify the object and its reward value properly. Thus, the neurons code salience only in a transitory manner. Then a second, selective response component becomes identifiable, which reflects only the reward information (a reward prediction error). From this point on, the dopamine neurons represent only reward information.[5]

I'll break this down for you. Once the brain has signaled an error, surprise, it needs to discover what caused the surprise and then, as Humphries states, "glue the outcome to the action by strengthening the link between them." It needs to make sense of the surprise so it doesn't get surprised again. Here's how two-phase dopamine works (called *phasic* by scientists). Phase one is a sudden but transient spike signaling surprise, that something important is going on (what psychologists call *salience*). Phase two is a long-lasting change in the dopamine concentration, tagged to the cause or outcome. This can be a drop in dopamine, signaling avoid, or an increase in dopamine, signaling approach. The indication of positive or negative is what psychologists call *valence*.

Here's an example of how this might look. Compare these typical scenarios.

1. You sing well at your concert recital, and your friend says, "That was great." You feel pleased. Dopamine is a reward-predictor, and it usually appears with the reward. Note that dopamine does not cause the good feeling (other feel-good neurotransmitters do this) as much as it accompanies the good feeling as a message to "do it again." You expected a supportive comment. Because you weren't surprised, you don't receive a spike in dopamine.
2. You sing well at your concert recital and your friend says, "That was awful." You expected a supportive comment but received horrid criticism. The unexpected comment triggers a dopamine spike (salience: something important is happening) followed by

a drop in your general level of dopamine for singing, less motivation (valence: avoid this).

3. You sing well at your concert recital, and your friend tells you,
"That was great." You expected a supportive comment (no spike
in dopamine) and feel pleased. Your friend adds, "Your ability
to hold your high notes shows attention to detail." You didn't
expect that. You receive a burst of dopamine. Now, you instinctively pay attention to your high notes and hold them proudly.
You learned instantly.

4. You sing well at your concert recital and expect your friend to
give you a glowing appraisal. Instead, you see a look of displea-
sure on her face as she says, "You've got some work to do." You
expected a supportive comment but received a look of concern
with a criticism. *Surprise—Alert!* Your friend adds, "Swinging
your head from side to side with the beat distracts the audience.
Other than that, it was awesome." You just experienced phasic
dopamine. The unexpected facial expression with the comment
triggered phase one: salience, something important just happened. Phase two tells you to learn instantly. The comment that
followed specifies what to learn. The overall general concentration of dopamine remains for singing but drops for head-swaying.
You still enjoy singing, but are now vigilant and motivated to
avoid swaying your head.

Compliments are great, and we love to receive them. *Quick tip*: If
you use surprise, you can make remarks immensely more powerful. In a
very real sense, you can strategically manipulate the comment's impact.

Manipulating Perceptions

Researchers from the University of British Columbia set out to study
the reaction of middle-aged men while crossing a long, narrow, fear-
arousing suspension bridge. The wooden planks and wire cables tilted,
swayed, and wobbled 230 feet over the Capilano River in Vancouver,
Canada. An attractive young woman approached each man and asked
if he would complete a short questionnaire. After finishing the survey,
the woman gave each man her telephone number with an invitation to

have her explain the research in more detail. Here is the experimental manipulation: The woman approached some men before they crossed the bridge and some after they completed the harrowing crossing. Results showed that the men approached after the crossing were significantly more likely to call for more detail.[6]

The researchers concluded that the men who met the woman immediately after crossing the shaky, swaying, suspension bridge were experiencing intense physiological arousal, which they would normally have identified as fear. But because they were being interviewed by an attractive woman, they mistakenly identified their arousal as sexual attraction. As best-selling author Daniel Gilbert quipped in his reference to this study, "Apparently, feelings that one interprets as fear in the presence of a sheer drop may be interpreted as lust in the presence of a sheer blouse—which is simply to say that people can be wrong about what they are feeling."[7]

It's easy to manipulate perceptions. Bodily sensations can be labeled in different ways; it's possible to get confused about exactly what it is we are feeling. While our environment might appear to trigger one emotion, we might end up perceiving the feeling of another. Writers and philosophers have noted this for centuries. Ovid, a Roman poet who lived at the time of Christ, gave his contemporaries the following advice on the art of love: "To stoke the ardor of wives or mistresses, attend gladiator contests. They produce strong feelings of arousal that lend themselves to feelings of lust." Ovid anticipated modern-day research that shows how easily our emotions can be mislabeled.

In their book, *The Wisest One in the Room*, Thomas Gilovich and Lee Ross note that contemporary versions of Ovid's advice for igniting sexual arousal "include scary movies or roller-coaster rides at the amusement park, or even the local gym, where the combination of elevated heart rates, sweat, and lightly clad bodies offer excellent possibilities for similar mislabeling. This is one of the reasons that 'makeup sex' following an intense quarrel often proves to be so passionate and gratifying."[8]

Experiments like the Capilano bridge research show that the experience of arousal can be ambiguous and therefore misattributed to an incorrect stimulus. Individuals seek to make sense of an internal state and may misattribute the actual cause of the increased arousal to something else that seems plausible. Once a misattribution takes place, our biases and self-confirmation programs kick in to affirm our perception. In essence, our explanations change the nature of our experiences.

The physiological clues associated with emotion can be relatively diffused, leaving our experience open to the influence of situational cues and labels. We often attach the label "nervous" to the arousal we are experiencing when there is something in the environment we regard as daunting (e.g., public speaking, taking a test, performing, attending an interview). Similarly, we apply the label "excited" to the arousal we experience when we see or hear something we are especially willing to encounter. Neither of these arousal signals have neurological signatures. We label them as either nervous or excited according to the context. This leaves a window of interpretation for those astute enough to sense this constructive opportunity to create a positive perception.

It's not just our physiological arousal that is easily manipulated to generate new expectations. We are easily fooled. Renowned MIT researcher Leon Festinger wanted to create a situation in which individuals were led to experience conflicting "cognitions." And both cognitions had to be highly resistant to change. To do this, he had participants wear prism goggles that made the edge of a door appear curved. He then asked them to run their hand along the apparently curved edge. Festinger presumed that participants would experience dissonance between these two perceptions: the visual one that indicated the door was curved and the tactile one that indicated that the door was straight. Much to his surprise, they experienced no dissonance but instead had the illusion that the door was in fact curved. This research suggests that cognitive inconsistencies can create misattributions in order to reduce dissonance. Festinger suggests that we do this unconsciously and automatically to make our experiences consistent and easily grasped.[9]

To a large degree, the manipulation of expectations partially explains hypnosis and the placebo effect. Both subjective and physiological responses can be altered by changing people's expectancies. Acclaimed Harvard placebo researcher Irving Kirsch suggests that the effects of hypnosis and placebos are based upon the participant's beliefs. Kirsch hypothesized that placebo effects are produced by the self-fulfilling effects of response expectancies in which the belief that one will feel different leads a person to actually feel different.[10]

When testing a new drug, medical research always includes a placebo group. The new drug being tested must outperform the placebo to be considered effective. Those who think that a treatment will work display a stronger placebo effect than those who do not. Expectancy also explains why larger placebo pills have a larger effect. Placebo pills can take many forms: differences in color, size, and shape. To boost the placebo effect, scientists occasionally give an "active" placebo; that's active in the sense that it produces a small inert effect, like tingling fingers. The intent is to get the recipient to notice the effect and *misattribute* it as a signal of efficacy. This misattribution enhances the expectations and significantly multiplies the placebo's success. *I can feel it working.*

Expectations Drive the Brain

Expectations drive the brain. Your expectations, what you anticipate will happen, play a critical role in your experience. They shape how we think and move in the world. They dictate how we respond to events, how we experience food, and how we communicate. Our brains spend most of their time processing what they have already experienced in order to figure out what's about to happen next. Expectations, driven by beliefs, are the expedient way that our brains have developed to get through life without stopping every few moments to think things through. If we change our expectations, we change our experience.

Imagine that you and your friend are casually walking through a park when you encounter a large black Labrador retriever. You see a friendly animal that you would like to pet. Your friend sees a threatening animal and starts to feel anxious. Our prior experiences generate our beliefs and determine our present perception. You expect a friendly dog, pet it, and feel affirmed. Your friend expects a potential bite, shies away from the large teeth, and feels affirmed.

Hundreds of studies reveal how easily our expectations drive our experience. Stanford researcher Thomas Robinson found that the branding of foods and beverages influences young children's taste perceptions. Children were separated into two groups and given the same food. The researchers told one group the dishes were from McDonald's. Since children generally expect food at McDonald's to taste better, it led the McDonald's group to experience it as significantly tastier than ratings from the control group. Robinson commented, "If you want your children to eat more vegetables, tell them they are from McDonald's." Manipulating expectations in adults also works well. Adults give higher ratings to the taste of wine if it's poured from an expensive bottle. To them, it actually tastes better. Our expectations don't simply change our experiences; they can influence others' experiences too.[11]

Website managers for the online dating service OKCupid tested their site's algorithm by telling poorly matched couples that they were, in fact, good matches. Remarkably, the couples behaved accordingly and engaged in more extended e-mail conversations. Couples expected compatibility, and that's what they experienced. This shows that our expectations don't just guide our perception and behavior; they influence others because expectations create a dynamic that signals reciprocal responses. If I expect to get caught, I'll look sheepish, and others will look at me and wonder why I'm acting guilty. They will then interrogate me. My expectation generated a corresponding response. This is undoubtedly what happened with the dating couples. Expectations of harmony triggered reciprocal behavior in each of them.[12]

This dynamic reciprocal process was magnificently illustrated in the famous Pygmalion experiment published in 1968. Robert Rosenthal and Lenore Jacobson's study showed that leading teachers to expect enhanced performance from students created enhanced student performances. While students were randomly assigned to classrooms, researchers led teachers to believe that some classes were comprised of "high performers." Teachers then viewed students in these so-called high-performance classes differently, classifying student work as superior, and ordinary student behavior as "more academic." Not only did they see the students as stronger academically, the teachers actually behaved differently.[13]

Researchers hypothesized that the elementary school teachers subconsciously behaved in ways that facilitated and encouraged each student's success. Students responded accordingly to this expectation with their corresponding raised expectations in a mutual, teacher-student feedback loop of success. Rosenthal argued that those manipulated expectancies created self-fulfilling prophecies for the students and the teachers. Clever teachers use this strategy intuitively, as was the case with Erin, who teachers fourth-grade students. Note how she changed a student's expectations by initially changing her expectations about that student.

In preparation for my batch of students, a colleague told me that I have a wonderful group, except for Johnny. She said she continually struggled with him to get his work done last year, especially in writing. This teacher commented that I would be lucky if I could get him to write more than a sentence or two.

This new information did not sit well with me. She gave me this pre-conceived notion that this student was already being set up to fail before I even had an opportunity to work with him. I decided at that moment that I would be the changing factor in this child's life.

On the first day of school, I gave my students a short writing assign-ment. I asked them to write down what they would like to learn in the upcoming year. I then moved around the classroom, talking with my students about their ideas. When I got to Johnny, I saw that he had only written one sentence, and my feeling of elation started to disappear, ever so slightly. Instead of allowing that to overcome me, I knelt down next to Johnny and whispered, "I see you are thinking very hard about what you would like to write about." Johnny sheepishly nodded his head, and I continued by saying, "That's wonderful! I know you have wonderful ideas and I would love to know what they are. By writing down your ideas, you can share them with the world." I gave Johnny a quick smile, stood up, and moved on to the next student. When I circled the room again, I was amazed at how much Johnny had written. He gleamed as he showed me a half of a page of written ideas, and I responded by smiling back and saying, "I bet you are very proud of your work!"

Over the next couple of days, I asked my students to write on various topics. When they completed their writing, I would ask for volunteers to share their writing. I was elated when Johnny raised his hand to share one day. He had written a story over two pages long and was beaming from ear to ear.

Erin strategically changed her expectations, then fought the impulse to regress to the prior teacher's prediction, even though it initially ap-peared that Johnny was not going to write much. She cleverly reinterpreted Johnny's reticence to write as "thinking very hard about what you would like to write about." Johnny, accustomed to the prior teacher's struggles with him, probably felt surprised by this turn of events. We see this in his sheepish smile. Johnny's nod also indicates that he accepted this crafty reinterpretation. With this renovated mindset, Johnny became a proud and productive writer, just like Erin predicted (expected) in her surprise pronouncement to the student.

In the anecdote above, note that Johnny was probably already experiencing stress when Erin arrived at his desk. Previous exchanges with prior teachers were struggles, and he undoubtedly expected more of the same. Stress alone can raise suggestibility; the addition of a surprise catapults it immensely.

Stress Raises Suggestibility

Changing someone's expectations changes their experiences in a fundamental way. During a surprise event, we have a brief window to make a suggestion that may trigger a new expectation that in turn may generate a self-fulfilling prophecy. Momentous stress itself increases suggestibility by creating psychological uneasiness that drives the search for an adaptive response. A surprise can magnify the suggestibility even more. High stress followed by a teacher's surprise comment produced a life-changing moment for Susan.

> When I was in high school, I loved my foreign language classes (French, German, Russian), and my mood improved every time I entered one of the classrooms. One year, our French class had to memorize a poem, and I chose "Il Pleure dans Mon Coeur" by Paul Verlaine. We had to recite it in front of the class and were graded on pronunciation, memorization, and interpretation. After I was done, my teacher said, "Susan, that was fine. Can I see you after class?" I was devastated. I worried that I had completely trampled it and expected to get scolded for not doing well enough. After class, Mrs. A. said that she was blown away by my recitation and asked me if I would please enter an upcoming statewide contest. That moment cemented my belief in my ability, and since then I've never doubted myself when it comes to languages. I went on to major in French and taught it for a couple of years at a small private school. I still know the poem, too, every word.

Susan described her reaction to the initial teacher's comment as "devastated." She stewed in her stress response for the rest of the class, until the teachers surprised her with a glowing comment. Her already high suggestibility shot up another notch with the surprise, and she eagerly embraced the teacher's comment and its life-changing effect. In this event, surprise magnified an already heightened suggestibility.

Once surprise triggers the cognitive revision process, we are prone to accept updates from reliable sources. So then, what makes a reliable source? Credibility arises from a variety of sources, not just traditional authority figures.

Agents of Belief Revision

Agents of influence appear in many guises. A young child's comment carries the weight of unadulterated observation. I witnessed a young child ask a plump female friend of mine, "When is your baby due?" Peer comments during the impressionable adolescent years can create life-long influences: "Wow! You sure have a flair for fashion." Comments from loved ones, with your best interest at heart, can go either way. Accepted because they are said with love, or dismissed because we expect positive comments. Sometimes, even a passerby without a vested interest can make a comment that captures your attention. While dancing at a wedding, another guest shares, "You have masterful control of your body." It might be easier to make a list of those we instinctively don't trust, such as politicians, lawyers for opposing parties, salespersons who try too hard to woo our interests, and those with vested interests in influencing us for their benefit.

In the following anecdote, Kara recalls a momentous comment, made by a new acquaintance she'd just met while hiking. This particular influence carried the conviction of a stranger with no ulterior motive or vested interest.

My husband and I were hiking the Runyon Canyon trail in West Holly-wood. For anyone who hasn't done this specific hike before, parking is impossible, and navigating through the trail is like a game of Frogger, not due to rocks, or logs, or streams, but because of the amount of foot traffic and baby strollers. We always ran into someone we knew when we hiked Runyon. This time we ran into my husband's friend Dave. Dave was dating a stunt person, and they were hiking with a bunch of her colleagues. These ladies had just finished training, and they were telling me crazy stories about standing on horses running at top speed and running through fire. These were just two tales in a whole host of impressive stories. These women were the real action heroes in the movies. I was in awe of them.

Then, one of them turned to me and said, "What do you do? You're a dancer, right?" WHAT? ME? A DANCER? Did she know she was talking to a person who punched herself in the face during the one and only hip-hop class she ever took? I was doing a lot of yoga at the time and I was in my yoga/hiking outfit, so I was in pretty good shape, but a dancer? That was definitely not me. Or was it? I do love to dance, but I never considered myself a good dancer, until that moment. I kept thinking about it. This beautiful and powerful stunt person sized me up and thought I was a dancer. It made me feel good! And from then on, I guess I felt a lot less self-conscious when I danced.

Years and years passed. Recently my sisters said that they love the moves I bust out. They tell me I'm a good dancer, too. Yep, that's me! I'm a dancer!

Before that moment, Kara thought she was a clumsy dancer. That surprising comment, from someone she only knew briefly, shows how broad agents of influence can be. Her new belief drives her expectations to "bust great moves." It also drives her interpretation of these moves. What she used to think was reckless flailing (like when she punched herself in the eye), she now accepts as the cost of a bold dancer, self-perpetuating. This story shows that any unpredicted comment, even from a passing contact, has the potential to create a window of momentary belief revision. Trace back the origin of your personal moments of inspiration. Many of them were triggered by surprise comments.

Teachers hold a special place in our authority hierarchy. As such, many of the stories of influence in this text depict teachers as agents of mindset revision. When we started school, these creatures replaced our parents as absolute authority. What parent hasn't been overruled by a teacher's comment? "But Mom, the teacher says, 'You don't need to eat all your vegetables all the time.'" While the parent may win the battle at the dinner table, the teacher often won the battle of *knowledge* source. Such challenges indicate the replacement of the parent by the teacher as the knowledge dispenser.

Although the delivery of a suggestion by an authority figure is usually more powerful than by a peer or subordinate, exceptions exist. During moments of high suggestibility, we instinctively assign authority to any agent that produces a suggestion with some conviction. It is the conviction itself that is the key. This is the reason that adults often fall prey to children's comments. We attribute honesty and transparency to young children because they haven't yet learned social graces and political correctness.

A friend of mine teaches fourth grade. She recently changed her hairstyle from conventional to bold, spending an inordinate amount for the special treatment. When she walked into her classroom, a bewildered student asked, "What did you do to your hair?" According to her report, other students just looked at her hair in stunned silence. All her polite and supportive colleagues told her the new hairstyle looked marvelous. The next day she arrived with a more conservative cut. Conviction, regardless of your status, born of honesty, carries its own authority.

Agents of influence can be anyone, at any time. Agents in any guise increase the likelihood of a message's success when delivered with conviction, but only if the recipient is receptive. Surprise creates receptivity; however, surprise comes in many degrees.

Surprise Comes in Degrees

Surprises vary in magnitude. Seeing a blue-striped frog in your yard elicits a small surprise. Seeing it during a snowstorm is more surprising. If it asks you to come inside to warm up. . . . The intensity of the surprise signals that things are not going as expected and your knowledge needs to be reconsidered. Generally, wrong beliefs lead to mistakes or poor performance in fulfilling our goals. But, it is not convenient for our survival to update or reconsider our beliefs every time a new fact is perceived. Reassessing our beliefs after every perception would interfere immensely with our day-to-day lives and use valuable cognitive resources needed to achieve our goals.

Regarding learning, legendary researcher Jean Piaget focused on how we adapt to new information. He divided this adaptation into two processes, which he named *assimilation* and *accommodation*. For Piaget, assimilation is the process of fitting new information into preexisting cognitive schemas (loosely translated as mental models.)[14] For example, you see a shark for the first time, and you fit it into your schema for fish. The first time you saw a dolphin, you probably also tried to assimilate it (incorrectly) into your fish schema because it seemed to fit. Your parents then told you it was a mammal, but it didn't fit into your schema for mammals: four-legged furry creatures. Now you have to totally renovate your mammal schema. Changing your schema (mental model) is called accommodation. We instinctively assimilate because it's easier and automatic to squeeze new information into a current way of thinking (think Kahneman and System 1). In contrast, accommodation requires considerable cognitive resources (think System 2). We have to consciously consider the new knowledge and then renovate the entire model in which it belongs.

Like the child who tries to incorrectly fit the dolphin into the existing fish schema, we are prone to assimilate. Driving down the highway, I'm passed by a speeding, older-model coupe. I instantly think it's probably a young male in a hurry, an insurance industry stereotype of a reckless driver. I assimilate by assuming the driver fits my model of "speedy drivers." When I catch up to the car at the exit ramp, I notice that the driver is a gray-haired senior female. Do I assimilate by squeezing her into my existing model of speeding drivers and say to myself, "She sure drives like a young male?" If I do, I keep my model intact by squeezing her into my existing model as an outlier. Or do I accommodate by changing the model, "I guess my model for older women drivers needs adjusting?" A week later, I see a speedy driver and assume it's a young male. My model didn't change; I must have assimilated instead of accommodated. We impose our understanding of the world on events and interpret them according to our understanding. It's natural. A surprise to our self-concept, if intense enough, disintegrates that portion of our self-concept schema, and we instantly build a new one: accommodation. An intense surprise fast-tracks belief formation.

In the following story by Cory, she challenges her teacher, bordering on insolence, but she finds herself surprised by his response. This surprise creates, in her words, a self-fulfilling prophecy. She could have assimilated the experience, accepting it simply as praise. Instead, the surprise created a receptiveness to build (accommodate) a new and self-fulfilling concept of herself.

One day in high school, I walked into my econ/American government class to find a substitute teacher. I was mildly disappointed that I wouldn't be able to enjoy the lesson from the regular teacher (one of my favorites). To my surprise, the substitute asked me if I was prepared to teach the day's lesson. I was in shock as the substitute explained that the teacher had informed her that he had spoken to me and I was to teach today's lesson. He hadn't spoken to me about anything; in fact, all the information I had to go on was the substitute's words, a handout the teacher had prepared explaining to the rest of the class that I would be teaching that day.

Thankfully, the class was understanding, and I fumbled my way through the lesson as best I could. The next day I arrived at school angry at the teacher for putting me in such an uncomfortable situation; how could he be so thoughtless? Shouldn't he have asked first? I felt that the trust, respect, and safety I experienced in his classroom had been shattered. I felt betrayed. I quickly made my way to his room and said, "What was that all about yesterday? You should have told me I was going to have to teach the class." I worried that I was on the verge of being disrespectful.

He gave me a goofy smile and told me, with absolute conviction, that something unexpected forced him to be absent, and that out of all my classmates, he was positive that not only would I take on the challenge despite my discomfort, but given my drive and my intellect, I could only help but excel at it.

I'm not sure if my nature or my intellect is really at such a level that I can excel at anything, but ever since that day I've always readily accepted challenging uncomfortable experiences (perhaps even sought them out). I always say to myself that not only will I be able to handle them, but I will also do so with flying colors. This attitude has become a self-fulfilling prophecy for me because, having set the goal of doing well at anything I undertake, I work with all my energy to make it so. I don't know if I really excel in these situations, but I *feel* successful.

Generally, we accept new information that fits coherently with our intact system. This explains why we like our favorite news sources; they generally share our biases and we accept their points of view readily. We also tend to accept small updates incrementally as it takes little cognitive resources. The really big surprises, the ones that stun and shock us, are the ones that create a one-shot learning feature.

One-Shot Learning

Humans display two prominent and distinct learning strategies for identifying the relationship between a cause and its effect: incremental and one-shot learning. With incremental, we gradually acquire knowledge through trial and error. The experience of repeated pairings between a stimulus and a consequence drives this form of learning. You learned how to write incrementally, like most subjects in school. However, we sometimes encounter unfamiliar situations, and if deemed important enough, we need to learn rapidly in order to survive. In these circumstances, we need a mechanism to learn instantly.

One-shot learning is learning from a single pairing of a potential cause and a consequence. Scientists have long suspected that one-shot learning involves a different brain system than gradual learning, but they could not explain what triggers this rapid learning or how the brain decides which mode to use at any one time.

Researchers at Caltech recently discovered that uncertainty in terms of the causal relationship is the main factor in determining whether rapid learning occurs. Good presenters and educators try to induce uncertainty when they teach. To open a class on self-esteem, I ask my adult students to estimate the correlation between a student's self-esteem and the student's school success. Most students guess that it's a positive relationship, somewhere in the strong to very strong range. I then ask, "Did you go to school with fellow students who were ridiculed because of their weight, clothing, complexion, and so on? Did any of these students do well in school?" They all raise their hands. This example challenges their guesses. Next, I ask, "Do you know any students who think they're great, love themselves, but didn't do well in school?" Another example that challenges their assumptions. Now that I've created uncertainty, most of them adjust their initial estimates. They eagerly await my answer. I tell them, "It's complicated." They collectively groan, but the uncertainty I produced prepares them for my subsequent delivery of incremental information.[15]

In the boardroom and classroom, raising uncertainty piques our interest and drives curiosity. We see this plainly in the world of external knowledge. Learning about the relationship between self-esteem and school success doesn't hit the threshold of *critical information*. It's just not that important. But what is more important than your identity?

Uncertainty spikes during a surprise: "What just happened?" Uncertainty focuses our attention on learning the relationship between stimulus and outcome. Researchers found that the degree of causal uncertainty instructs the brain to dramatically adjust the learning to engage one-shot learning when required.

This activation works like a switch: all or nothing. Researchers found that the part of the brain associated with complex cognitive activities, the prefrontal cortex, evaluates causal uncertainty and triggers instant learning if warranted. Importance is a designation our emotions determine. Once triggered, the brain recruits the hippocampus to regulate the emotions and initiate long-term memory storage. If not recruited for immediate learning, the hippocampus remains silent. The authors stated, "Like a light switch, one-shot learning is either on, or it's off." Although we know little about what level of emotional stimulation we need to trigger one-shot learning, we do know it works as a switch, as an all-or-nothing activation. While other routes to one-shot learning may exist, the immense emotional burst of a surprise to your self-concept is a definite trigger. As long as the surprise is important.

Not all surprises require belief-updating. You're watching orcas swim gracefully in the ocean with their fins appearing time and again. Suddenly one swims under the boat, and you get a clear view. While surprised, you don't need to update your beliefs. Here we see the difference between expected surprise and unexpected surprise. That orca under your boat surprised you, but it was predictable. No phasic dopamine. A great story, but that's it. Phasic surprises facilitate synaptic plasticity; that means they prepare to accommodate a belief revision.

Learning is most visible during curiosity. Curiosity is a drive, and it is most acute during a surprise event. It's important to note that during a surprise event, we don't consciously register curiosity. During a surprise experience, the event takes place instantly and the search for a solution to the unexpected is automatic and experienced as critical. Nevertheless, studies in conscious curiosity can inform us about learning during surprise.

Curiosity

When something surprises a baby, like an object that doesn't respond the way it is expected to, the baby not only focuses intently on that object but ultimately learns more about it than from a similar yet predictable object. This continues throughout our lifespan. We know from neuroscience that we pay attention to things that do not match our predictions about the world. Little bursts of dopamine, triggered by the novelty of unpredictability, signal what to focus on in our environment.

Curiosity is the desire to gain information once we become aware of a gap in knowledge in something we want to understand. It motivates our attention to close this gap. Curiosity is understood as aversive because it frustrates people's desire to understand their environment with a sense of predictability, certainty, and structure. In line with this, Dutch investigators using brain-imaging research (fMRI) found that by inducing curiosity they activated brain areas related to conflict and arousal, while resolving it activated areas related to reward. We experience the discovery of new information as rewarding because it helps reduce the undesirable state of uncertainty.[16]

Although viewed as aversive, our experience of curiosity can be pleasurable or unpleasant. When walking into a museum we are naturally curious to see new exhibits that entice and inform us. Filling out a tax form and finding that the balance doesn't work raises our curiosity to find out where we made the mistake. Both forms of curiosity motivate us to gain information. It's the anticipation of gaining the answer to our gap in knowledge that stimulates us. The anticipation of discovering the outcome weakens the negativity of being deprived of information. We feel curiosity as pleasurable when our anticipation of learning the answer (reward) outweighs the price of not knowing.

Researchers at the National Institute of Health linked curiosity to the motivator neurotransmitter dopamine.[17] They found that the act of wanting and desiring new information directly involves mesolimbic pathways of the brain that activate dopamine. Researchers found that the brain treats the solution to curiosity as a reward. They explain that in the presence of uncertainty, the brain anticipates there will be available information for clarification. In other words, when we need a solution, our dopamine activation system readies for new information, to then stamp it as a reward. When I created uncertainty about the relationship between self-esteem and school success, the students' dopamine levels increased, motivating them, predicting the reward of learning the answer.

Curiosity studies also show us that the brain releases higher amounts of dopamine when the reward is unknown and the stimulus is unfamiliar. This is what happens during a surprise. In other words, during a surprise event, a substantial amount of dopamine is preparing to disperse once the solution to the surprise is reached. The longer it takes to solve the surprise, the more discomfort and sense of urgency; hence, we get a greater amount of dopamine buildup. The first reasonable solution to arrive wins the relief-and-motivation sweepstakes, getting neurologically stamped as the "solution."

We Typically Accept the First Solution During a Surprise

We typically grasp at the first solution that appears to solve our curiosity gap, even if it's not the best or accurate. Knowledge-seeking studies show that people feel discomfort when they do not know something and even prefer knowing negative outcomes as opposed to remaining ignorant. Our need to solve our curiosity is so deeply ingrained in our genetic architecture that we'll accept anything that reduces this discomfort. A delay in the gratification of knowing makes us reach impulsively for the reward of knowing, even if it's inaccurate. Think of this analogy. You suddenly experience excruciating tooth pain. You'll accept *any* solution to stop the pain. Our need-to-resolve drive works on an exponential scale during surprise.

Neurologically, dopamine stamps the first solution as effective. From a cognitive view, accepting the first solution also works. Have you ever asked yourself, *Why is it that I always find what I'm looking for in the last place I look?* It's because once you find it, you stop looking. That's why, in most cases, we quickly accept the first solution to our confusion after a surprise. Dopamine is our motivator messenger. Once the solution is discovered, our motivation plunges, and we are not compelled to look further. Researchers in the airline industry demonstrate this human disposition.[18]

A major factor in aircraft incidents and accidents is that pilots are failing to keep up with technological changes, resulting in surprise and confusion for the pilots. Aeronautics and Air Transport researchers Amy Rankin, Rogier Woltjer, and Joris Field studied how pilots reacted to unexpected events in the cockpit. They wanted to examine how they made sense of events after a surprise. They refer to this process as sense-making: a response to experiencing a surprise when there is a discrepancy between what is observed and what is expected.

The researchers created situations to confront pilots with abnormal events in the context of a training scenario, checking to see how quickly the pilots recognized and carried out solutions. Researchers found that once trainees made a hypothesis, they quickly set out to confirm it (confirmation bias), often leaving alternate causes unexplored. Researchers noted that this can lead to critical events going undetected. "The problem of getting stuck in one frame and failure to see inconsistencies or look for alternative explanations [is] described as fixation error." Just because something works does not mean it is the best solution. Also noted as fixation error was the pilot's tendency to rationalize anomalies to make them fit the current frame.

Consider a mouse in a maze. The mouse searches for a route to find the reward, a piece of cheese. Once it finds a path to success, the mouse remembers it, and the next time it goes into the maze it quickly reaches the cheese. While the mouse is successful, it may not be taking the best route, only the one that worked initially. Once the goal is achieved, the solution is accepted and reaffirmed. The pilots, like the mouse and the rest of us, typically accept the first solution to a problem and eagerly attempt to affirm it, ignoring other alternatives.

A surprise indicates decreased confidence in our current beliefs. As a result, new observations receive more weight than previous observations. This implies that the speed of learning will increase when we encounter uncertain predictive relationships. That's what European biomedical researchers discovered in 2015: We value information received after a surprise as superior to information preceding a surprise. They found that a simultaneous increase of newly acquired information after a surprise led to a faster adaptation of belief modification. It may sound mundane now, but it was big news then. New information, after a surprise occurs, often overrides our old beliefs. It's simply viewed as vastly superior.[19]

The human brain's dogged tendency to stick to the first solution that comes to mind and to ignore alternatives is called the Einstellung effect. Einstellung literally means "setting." This human propensity was described as far back as 1620 by English scientist Francis Bacon: "The human understanding when it has once adopted an opinion . . . draws all things else to support and agree with it." In his 1942 classic experiment, Abraham Luchins was the first to clinically demonstrate how mindsets can hinder the ability to solve novel problems. In his frequently cited research, he showed that participants used methods that they had used previously to find the solution, even though quicker and more efficient methods were available. He used the non-continuity theory, our tendency to maintain a specific behavior until it fails to work, to explain this behavior. Do you know anyone who continues to do something the same old way, even though better ways exist? Yes. All of us.[20]

We see this effect regularly in hiring practices. Interviewers who find a candidate physically attractive regularly perceive that person's intelligence and personality in a more positive light, and vice versa.

This propensity happens to all of us, even those trained to avoid false conclusions. Researchers found that radiologists examining chest X-rays often fixate on the first abnormality they find and fail to notice further signs of illness that should be obvious, such as a swelling that could indicate cancer. When those secondary details were presented alone, radiologists saw them right away.[21]

Once you hit on a successful method to peel an onion, there is no point in trying an array of different techniques every time you cut up a new one. The trouble with this cognitive shortcut, however, is that it sometimes blinds people to more efficient or appropriate solutions than the ones they already know.

Our propensity to accept the first solution from some authority, even if unsuitable, is magnified exponentially during the neurological blitz of a surprise event. This is likely the reason that so many of us have self-defeating or debilitating beliefs. Consider the story of Sunny. She was "shocked" by a comment from her father, and it created a self-defeating mindset.

In high school, Sunny no longer wanted to play on the volleyball team because it wasn't fun anymore and it felt stressful. She quit the team. Her father loved sports, and she dreaded the response he might have when she told him. She hoped he'd show compassion.

> The first thing he said was, "I'm not mad at you, I'm just really disappointed. I feel like you quit when things start to get hard." Hearing that came as a total shock to me. I thought he would've seen how clearly upset I was about it and understood, but he didn't, which not only caught me off guard, but made me even more upset.
>
> Ever since then I feel like when things get overwhelming, I spiral down and give up. I don't join clubs because I'm afraid of signing up for anything that involves a commitment. I'm worried it would be something that causes stress and I wouldn't want to do it anymore. I don't consider myself driven or motivated, or a very hard worker, no matter how well I do or how many goals I set. I know I'm a strong person who has accomplished a lot, but ever since this experience, part of me has seen myself as weak, afraid, and lazy.

She expected sympathy but received criticism, which surprised her. This made her hyper-receptive to the comment from her father, an authority figure. Sadly, she now misses a lifetime of opportunities because her new mindset dictates that she may quit and disappoint not only herself, but others as well. This could have gone much differently. A positive and supportive comment might have created a more productive mindset. What if he had hugged his daughter and said, "Good for you. You know when to move on"? No surprise. Just a simple affirmation of love.

Summary

In this chapter, you learned how a surprise event creates a neurological storm that opens a momentary window for a belief revision. Surprises signal a cognitive crisis, informing us that our understanding of ourselves and our worlds don't work. To deal with surprises, our brains instantly focus our attention mechanisms on determining the reason for the surprise. Our earnest need to solve this psychological crisis generates a predisposition to accept the first viable solution. Big surprises, deemed important, trigger a two-stage process whereby the first stage is received as negative, as an error signal. This initial negative valence is followed immediately by a second stage whereby we perceive whether the stimulus of the surprise itself is either positive or negative. It is this second phase, the meaning-making stage, that creates an opportunity to craft a positive suggestion. This chapter also showed how easily and frequently the attribution of a surprise and perceived meaning can be manipulated.

Entertainers, comedians, writers, and movie directors regularly use surprise as a mechanism to engage audiences. The next chapter describes how all of us can use, and in some cases create, moments of surprise strategically to create positive lifelong influences for those whom we wish to sway.

CHAPTER SIX

~

Surprise Is All Around Us

Surprise happens everywhere, at any time, and to all of us. We regularly use it intentionally ourselves. Who hasn't planned a surprise party, gift, or appearance? Most of us understand that surprises magnify the emotion that follows, although few of us would describe it that way. A surprise gift always seems more exciting than one that is expected. We often feel a giddy delight in preparing to watch the surprise response of the receiver. News shows often end with a feel-good moment: the surprise when someone who serves in the military makes an unexpected entrance. The downside is equally amplified. A surprise disappointment stings more intensely too. Anticipated setbacks just don't carry that penetrating bite that comes with a surprise disappointment.

While most of us use surprise intuitively, performers and professionals in media recognize its power and use it more methodically. Comedians intentionally set up humorous punch lines to surprise us with a twist. W. C. Fields famously said, "I cook with wine. Sometimes I even add it to the food." Jokes you've heard before become less funny to you because the punch line no longer surprises you. Punch lines force us to reexamine our faulty assumptions. The greater the faulty assumption, the more we laugh because the emotion from the surprise multiplies the emotion of enjoyment from solving this dissonance: getting the joke. "He's so modest, he pulls down the shade to change his mind." You may not have laughed, but you recognize this as humor. We expect the change to be a change of clothing, yet the shift of reference violates our expectations. That's why computers don't *get* humor. They compute that a shift in reference is an error. Humans recognize the shift as humor and laugh because we "get it." We solve the unexpected.

Professor Jeffrey Ely from Northwestern University noted the following about the use of surprise in cinema: "We view the construction and the development of suspense and surprise and other aspects of entertainment as basically optimally economizing on a scarce resource, which is the ability to change someone's beliefs." Directors use suspense as the anticipation vehicle that prepares us for a belief change. The surprise initiates the change.[1]

Lisa Cron writes about neuroscience in literature. In her book, *Wired for Story*, she tells us, "Surprise is the only thing that matters in setting up a narrative structure. You have to set up an expectation, and then you have to violate that expectation." As you already know, dopamine is our motivator neurotransmitter. Surprise is a story's way of releasing dopamine, creating uncertainty, and setting up anticipation of something unexpected. She writes, "When we actively pursue new information—that is, when we want to know what happens next—curiosity rewards us with a flood of dopamine to keep us reading long after midnight because tomorrow we just might need the insight it will give us." This is how trailers work; they set up surprises to induce curiosity, triggering dopamine-motivation for the reward of solving curiosity. Even the evening news does this, "Stay tuned. After the break, we'll tell you what happened at City Hall. You won't believe it." Our dopamine signals a reward, "right after the break."[2]

Network television broadcasts a vast amount of unscripted shows often called "reality TV." While much of it remains unscripted, it's almost always strategically choreographed. To secure their viewers, trailers show twists, moments of surprise. At the end of every segment, a promise for an upcoming surprise keeps us tuned in. The immensely popular variety show called *America's Got Talent* uses surprise masterfully. Clever producers know that strong performances are even more electrifying when they are unexpected, because surprises enhance the emotions that follow. To do this, they carefully edit interviews of exceptionally talented performers before their live performances in front of the judges. These interviews often try to produce low expectations in the viewer. Then we, the television audience, feel surprised, and instantly revise our beliefs about the contestants.

Advertisers are sophisticated manipulators of surprise and wield it to impress us with their brands. For instance, consider the acclaimed Mane 'n Tail shampoo commercial from the eighties. It starts with a bathroom scene. We hear the sound of running water and see a close-up of a bottle of Mane 'n Tail shampoo. As the camera pulls back from the bottle of Mane 'n Tail, you see a father washing his little boy's hair. The camera continues pulling back, and we see the father turn to his left as he also washes a sudsy Shetland pony. The surprise produces an indelible impression. The message: If it's soft enough for children, and strong enough to soften a horse's hair, imagine what it would do for you.

Sales soared immediately after the commercial played. The clever use of surprise in marketing helps us accept the message uncritically. It's much stronger than a simple slogan. That favorable first impression, dramatically enhanced through surprise, boosted sales. If you were to ask users why they purchased Mane 'n Tail shampoo, they probably wouldn't refer back to that commercial; rather, they would laud the shampoo properties of "soft but strong." Nevertheless, significant sales increases link directly to that commercial. That was the definitive moment that branded Mane 'n Tail.

Branding

We construct many impressions instantaneously without giving them much thought, typically unaware of the impression we just assessed or how that impression was first formed. Do you remember when you became branded by Apple? What are your impressions of Harley-Davidson motorcycles, Corvettes, hybrids, or Monster trucks? What about men in sleeveless t-shirts or three-piece suits? How about women with tattoos or high heels?

Brands have considerable power over the brain. I have a conservative friend who wouldn't dare purchase a Subaru because "That's what liberals drive, and I don't want people to think I'm a liberal." Apple computer buyers often think they are more creative. We assign value to a multitude of different things every single day without barely a conscious thought. The media brands many of our impressions through such vehicles as movies, books, advertising, TV, politicians, and, of course, the news. Think of branding as an imposed stereotype, a widely held and oversimplified image or idea. Once we accept a brand, and much of this happens below conscious awareness, we apply it indiscriminately.

Although professionals in industry and entertainment intentionally use surprise to create branding, powerful but unintentional instances of surprise-induced branding occur in schools, medical facilities, places of employment, and within families, teams, and other groups. We can learn from them. The strategic use of surprise, timed tactfully, can spark a mindset makeover. In the following story, Monica recalls this life-changing story from her youth.

> When I was younger, I was heavily involved in competitive gymnastics. My coaches were like my second and third sets of parents. When I finally decided to retire from the sport, my coach Martha took me aside. I was already very emotional, as was she. She looked me in the eye and told me that she knew I would do well in life because I was "golden." I was taken aback by the word at first, but the more we talked and the more I thought about it years later, it really resonated with me. I try to embody being "golden" in nearly everything I do now, and my dream is to brighten people's lives and bring light and warmth wherever I go, no matter what I do.

The coach branded Monica as "golden." That comment surprised her: "I was taken aback." Her already heightened emotional arousal neurologically boosted her surprise: "I was already very emotional, as was she." Many years later, Monica continues to "brighten people's lives and bring light and warmth wherever I go, no matter what I do." She embodies the brand the coach gave her. This is what advertisers do to increase brand recognition, to increase sales.

Their goal is more than selling the product. They seek to create an image that sells their *idea*. Can you place an organization with the following slogans: *Just Do It; Breakfast of Champions; Like a Rock; It's finger lickin' good; I'm lovin' it; They'rrrrr Great!; Like a good neighbor __ __ is there?* We hear or see these slogans so frequently that they incrementally imprint on us, much like a song that we can't get out of our heads.

(Answers for above: Nike, Wheaties, Chevrolet Trucks, Kentucky Fried Chicken, McDonalds, Frosted Flakes, and State Farm.) Slogans can also brand us with a clever one-shot commercial that we see during a special event such as the Super Bowl. Advertisers pay several million dollars for commercials that last less than a minute. Yes, it's an idea they are selling, not a product. Award-winning film director Morgan Spurlock describes it this way:

> But, you know, and I don't think we're just seduced by brands. I think we're seduced by the imagery that surrounds that brand. It's that these pants are going to make you slimmer. This drink's going to make you hotter. This perfume is going to make you sexier. It's like everything that comes with that brand and the messaging around it. You know, we buy into the dream that surrounds that product much more than we buy into the product. And then once we start using it, we start to believe in the dream of what that product does for us in a lot of ways. You know, I still believe Guinness gives me strength every time I drink a pint.[3]

Lucky Monica was branded "golden." Branding can happen incrementally when we repeat the same message consistently with someone. Positive: "You're brilliant." Negative: "You're an idiot." It can also happen instantly, during a surprise. As you already know, it's not the surprise itself that is positive or negative, it's the context following the surprise that determines the valence.

Branding messages can be powerful. Even when not intended as negative, we may perceive them that way. The context following a surprise often determines the valence. Regardless of the intent, the meaning and valence (positive or negative) are determined by the receiver. Now an adult, Lenore recalls just such a detrimental event when she was five and how a friend's father made a lasting impression with an off-hand comment.

Like many children, Lenore felt intimidated and nervous when meeting her friend's father for the first time. Accordingly, she didn't speak up. The father teased her by calling her "Silent Sam." Reflecting on that moment, she recalls, "I felt so impacted by that comment that I pondered it for quite some time and never forgot. I thought it meant that I should talk more, but I didn't know the right things to say at the right times. I started to feel uncomfortable with my quietness."

These events happen to all of us. The comment surprised her, and she was already nervous. These two neurological events combined to create a robust impact. The valence could have swung either way. She could have perceived it as a kidding jest and teased back. Developmentally though, young children are typically unable to decipher such complex intentions, and certainly not while emotionally aroused. They accept pronouncements literally. As an adult, Lenore shows considerable insight into this branding comment as a formative event. Stories such as these caution us to carefully consider our casual comments to children, especially when they are already nervous.

While more visible with children, these events are common with adults too. As a high-school dropout with a GED, Doris felt insecure, yet hopeful about her opportunities. During a college advising appointment, she expressed an interest in becoming a paralegal and eventually entering law school. She recalls how the counselor looked her straight in the eye and stated, "Perhaps someday I will watch you being appointed to the Supreme Court and they will call you Justice Almando." Doris called that moment a turning point. The advisor's conviction and belief in her ability changed her belief in herself. She also recalls how he continued to refer to her as "Justice Almando" whenever they passed in the hallway.

This unexpected message produced the intended neurological effect. It stunned Doris into a receptive mental state. The clever advisor created this formative moment and capped it off with a brand that he could reinforce strategically on a regular basis. As noted above by director Morgan Spurlock, "we buy into the dream that surrounds that product much more than we buy into the product." Not all new beliefs trigger a sudden realization.

Surprises that trigger a belief-formation *may* initiate an epiphany. The epiphany doesn't cause the belief change. Just the opposite. The epiphany reflects the cognitive assessment of the belief that has already changed. Contrary to conventional wisdom, we don't reflect on whether or not we want a new belief; the reflection *follows* the change that already took place.

Epiphanies, Reflections, and Surprises

Not all life-changing events trigger a sudden realization, an epiphany. To clear up any preconceptions about this topic, let me tease out the nuanced differences in epiphanies and how my work on surprise differs. I use the term epiphany to denote a *sudden realization* or *understanding*. It's that definitive moment when you finally *get it*. Hopefully, while reading this section on the difference, you'll suddenly say to yourself, "Aha. Now I get it." That's an epiphany, but it didn't change you or trigger a new belief. This is also my intention for writing this book: I hope readers discover countless "aha" moments that lead to a new and fruitful understanding of how surprise creates an opportunity for mindset revision.

The Merriam-Webster dictionary defines epiphany as a "usually sudden manifestation or perception of the essential nature or meaning of something." Epiphanies reflect the surprise, like when Archimedes displaced the water in the tub and discovered a principal of volume and famously exclaimed "Eureka!" The water displacement didn't surprise him; the sudden realization triggered the surprise. This epiphany didn't change any internal personal belief about himself. It changed how he understood that element of science. In a recent class, I triggered one such moment in Lauren, one of my graduate students.

At the end of one of my classes, she approached me with a complaint. She told me that my reading assignment lacked clarity, and, as a result, she read two chapters because she didn't know which one was the required one. She stated defensively, "Did I have to read both?" While I don't remember this conversation, she reports that I replied, "You didn't have to, but whoever learns the most wins." She told me that her view of coursework changed instantly at that moment. In her words, "I understand that I am not doing the assignments just to do them, but because they will genuinely help me become a better teacher and more well-rounded individual."

She expected an apology for "unclear" instructions, but I surprised her with a positive spin. She now reads and studies with a different mindset. While I intended such an outcome, like most of us, we can never be sure we get a strike unless we're lucky enough to be told about it later. I cast statements like these regularly, similar to throwing a line in a stream and hoping to lure a bite. The epiphany, her new understanding, reflects a sudden realization of the meaning she made from my remark. Another student in the class may have experienced that same statement differently.

A sudden realization for me may not be a meaningful insight for you. In the following example, Danna's experience shows us how messages are received differently depending on the receptiveness of the listener. She heard what was for her a captivating comment while sitting amid a class full of fellow college students. Many of the other students would likely not remember this phrase and some might even dispute it, but Danna embraced it as an epiphany with liberating significance.

She doubted her intellectual ability because of struggles with spelling. That is until one day when her science professor matter-of-factly commented, "Spelling is *not* a sign of intelligence." She recalled how that simple cast-away comment stunned her. She told me, "It was as if a weight I hadn't realized I had, was lifted from my shoulders. I could still be intelligent even if I couldn't spell."

Danna was a middle-aged student, doubting her endeavors in search of a second career when she heard this affirming comment. Danna's sudden insight continues to inspire her.

We can experience epiphanies without a surprise. Suzanne told me about a sudden realization that she had when she was seven years old. "I threw a tantrum at dinner because I did not want to eat what was being served. My parents told me that if I did not eat what was served, I would not be eating, which I settled for. Later that night, my dad called me over to come and sit on his lap while he read the newspaper. *The Daily News* cover story showed two children in Vietnam eating cakes of grass and dirt for food. He explained to me that the food we eat is a luxury, and there are places where people are literally eating dirt and grass. The picture drove it home. It was the first moment I realized what privilege was, and that I had it."

Surprising comments don't always produce sudden realizations. Sometimes they initiate deep, conscious contemplation as the recipient of the comment works to make sense of it.

Surprises don't always come with a solution or clear-cut message. Occasionally, they create open-ended reflections whereby we try to find the meaning of the surprising event. What is it that needs revising?

In the next story, Ron expected a shameful scold but received a warm, receptive, and encouraging message instead. It surprised him, and changed the trajectory of his life. The meaning only became apparent with later reflection (not a sudden realization). Although his mindset changed immediately, the realization took longer.

As a student with high-functioning autism, he had the opportunity to take tests in a separate room with extra time. He recalls an instance when a fellow "regular" student commented that he wished he also had such an opportunity. Ron lashed out defensively, "Is that really what you want? Do you think it's cool having autism? It's not cool at all. It's embarrassing!" The teacher asked Ron to step outside in the hallway to calm down. Shortly thereafter, she approached him. He remembers bracing himself for the imminent detention and reproach. Instead, she surprised him with compassion and a remark that immediately changed his belief in himself. She said, "You are so hard on yourself sometimes. You should be proud, not ashamed. Your experiences and work ethic show that you are a sincere person. You shouldn't be afraid because you have so much to offer the world. I believe in your ability to change it for the better."

He thought about those words a lot over the coming years. He credits her surprising response for his realization that he needs to make people aware of what autism is like, and expose his situation to help people understand it, and help the autistic community. Years later, he decided to become a teacher. He wanted to educate the next generation, and do for them what she did for him.

Occasionally, a surprising event that changes a personal belief may not trigger any conscious realization at all. The story that follows illustrates why many transformative events probably go by unnoticed. I first met Natasha as a university senior studying music. She asked about my research, and I told her I study surprise. I then asked her how she first became interested in music. She paused thoughtfully, then told me about a time when she was eight years old.

After the recent death of her grandmother, Natasha went with her mother to her grandmother's home. Her mother told her to play in the yard and forbid her to enter her grandmother's bedroom. With no one to play with, she soon grew bored and entered the house to explore. As she wandered around, she eventually came to her grandmother's closed bedroom door. Curiosity overcame her. She peeked inside, then entered. Distracted by all the pretty things, she quickly adorned herself with beautiful lacey scarves. Upon noticing a harmonica on the bedside table, she picked it up, then began twirling around while playing a tune. Suddenly, the door opened. She froze. Her mother gazed at the jumbled room, then softly said, "You play that beautifully. You have an ear for music. Your grandmother would have loved it." She smiled and walked away.

Natasha expected a reproach, but received inspiration instead. That's a surprise. Natasha then told me, "That's funny. I hadn't connected that moment with my love for music until just now. I guess that's where it started." As you can see, not all surprises come with epiphanies. New beliefs can happen outside our conscious awareness. Her epiphany happened *thirty years later* while talking to me, and she may not have had one at all if I hadn't prompted that story by talking about the element of surprise. If you ask others about their formative moments, you'll find, as I did, that many were triggered by a surprise.

Most of our formative moments fly under our conscious radar. It's only those few that make it to consciousness that gives us a glimpse of what happens during a surprise event. Can you describe all your formative events? Probably not. They happen, we adapt, and then move on with our new perspective. In the next chapters, you'll learn how to use surprise intentionally. I use the brief preview that follows to show you how a surprise-driven formative moment may go undetected in the recipient. You might also note that in many cases we want our enriching comments to go undetected so that they don't trigger a conscious resistance.

Imagine that your employee worries that she doesn't learn her protocols quickly. Call her to your office. She will be nervous, expecting criticism. Surprise her instead by saying matter-of-factly, "Your ability to carefully learn new protocols thoroughly makes you a valued employee. Have a nice day." While at first blush this looks like a simple affirmative statement, and if it was just that, it might be excepted as flattery, dismissed as empty praise, or outright ignored. But, if the comment authentically surprised her, there's a great deal more going on. You'll learn more about the nuances and structure of intentional surprise in chapters 7 and 8. For this section, it's only important to note that if she experiences this as a formative moment, she's not likely to recall it as such. It's not like someone is going to ask her, "So when was it you first recognized that you learn protocols so thoroughly?" and she will be able to answer that question. As far as she now knows, she's always learned them thoroughly. She just didn't know it until her supervisor pointed it out.

Once we tune into how surprises work, we get to enjoy them, but they no longer trigger new beliefs in ourselves, outside our awareness. Then, we can consciously experience them as they unfold and become the true architect of our belief system. Here's an example of what I mean.

I spoke at TEDxSalem in January 2019.[4] I thought the talk went well. My only self-criticism was that I thought my pauses were too long. (Belief: I don't use pauses well.) Several months later, I read *Leading by Coaching* by Nick Marson, an engaging book about effective leadership in the business world.[5] We conversed back and forth about our common ground, exchanging ideas about how to use the element of surprise in the world of business. At the end of one correspondence, he wrote a note at the bottom: "I look forward to reading your book, I think you are onto something! I liked your TED talk. You use silences well." Surprise! I felt the neurological surge and smiled. He turned my presumed deficit into a powerful asset. (My new belief: I use pauses effectively.)

I immediately wrote to tell him how his comment triggered a formative moment for me. That new belief drives a new mindset. Before that comment, I used pauses hesitantly, rushing through them, feeling anxious with the silence. Now, I use them confidently and deliberately. I even watch how others use silence to make their messages more engaging. This all took place consciously because I have *surprise radar*. You do now too. That means you can accept the positive ones, and if you receive a negative one, you can dismiss it. Now when I speak . . . I use my pauses strategically. After all, . . . I am the master of the pause.

My formative moment only affected my public speaking. While localized to one aspect of my identity, if was formative, because as a professor and presenter, speaking is a sizable piece of my professional life. Sometimes, a surprise-driven belief change generalizes to a whole new outlook. Natalie's story below illustrates this.

She entered the dance studio full of excitement. Natalie was about to begin work with her dance idol. Despite years of dedicated hard work, she worried that she was not graceful enough, light enough, or feminine enough to be a dancer. When she apologized for these apparent shortcomings, her idol commented, "That's just a story you have about yourself in your mind. We build up these negative ideas about ourselves, but you choose what to accept to be true." Those words had an immediate impact. Natalie told me, "I will never forget that session and I have continued dancing unreservedly ever since."

While Natalie's reflection on the comment took very little time, her receptiveness, boosted by the surprise of the comment and an already heightened emotional arousal, helped produce a new perspective that she instantly affirmed by dancing unreservedly. In the full version of her story she concluded, "I have taken her words, 'That's just a story,' into every aspect of my character, examining what traits about me I believe to be true as just stories projected by others that I've accepted, and what traits about me I want to accept as legitimately true." This reflection shows how a simple, yet powerful, comment generalized to all areas of her life.

Natalie's reflection seemed immediate. It resonated with her quickly, and she accepted it as her new "truth." Surprises that spark uncertainty often take more time to digest, and they usually dominate rational processes until a solution is reached, until the sense-making finishes. Janine describes just such an event that illustrates a much longer process until she arrived at a conclusion.

While riding the school bus in seventh grade, laughing casually with classmates, she jokingly called her friend a "retard." The bus driver gave her a look of disgust and sternly commented, "That word is unacceptable on this bus. I do not ever want to hear you say that again. Do you understand the effect that word has on some people? My daughter has Down-Syndrome, and that word really offends us when it is used negatively." Initially, Natalie felt indignant about being called out. Later, upon reflection, the words finally hit home for her. Since then, she's never used that word as an insult or in a joking manner.

The surprise of the pronouncement made an indelible effect. Her instinct, like most of us, was defensive, but the comment inspired reflection. Eventually, she made sense of the driver's outburst, and she changed her behavior. When a surprise causes confusion that can't be solved with an immediate solution, reflection takes place until a resolution is reached.

Emotional Arousal Can Magnify Receptivity

When surprises are intense enough to create heightened arousal, a window of influence momentarily opens. When physiological arousal is present, it gives a surprise a neurological boost. Many times, spikes in emotions are simply intense, unspecified, general arousal, a heightened state in need of a description and context. At this time, a clever agent can name that emotion to create a positive valence. This happened to Lucas when he was ten years old, riding horses with his grandfather.

His grandparents owned horses, and he'd grown up around them his entire life. To prepare for their annual camping trip, he got assigned to a new colt. He was excited to be the first to ride the pony.

> When it was time to go on the ride, my papa told me that if anything bad happened that I should just jump off the horse. After a nice long ride, we returned to camp. My papa got off his horse and a branch snapped! That scared my colt, and he started to run around recklessly. I no longer had the reins in my hands, so I held onto the saddle horn for dear life. I remember my papa yelling at me to hang on. While we were running all over the place, I kept looking for a place to jump off like Papa had told me. Somehow, he calmed the colt down and I got off. I was so scared that I didn't want to ride anymore. But my papa looked at me and told me that I had done great and he was proud of me. From then on, I loved riding horses that had a little spunk.

Lucas's grandfather, Papa, acted quickly to reinterpret Lucas's arousal. The bolting colt produced a burst of neurological arousal. Worried that Lucas might respond with fear, a clever Papa quickly changed Lucas's experience to one of excitement and then pride. If his Papa had not intervened to reinterpret the emotion, it would have continued as distress, and Lucas would likely have developed a fear of spirited horses, rather than a preference. The window to name generalized arousal is usually brief.

In Lucas's case, the arousal soared suddenly. Sometimes arousal begins slowly and crests into eager anticipation, a readiness for influence. In another example, ever since Daniel was young, he wanted to sing. In his twenties, on a whim, he scheduled a lesson with a voice coach. After the lesson, he nervously waited for the instructor's proclamation. Daniel recalls his exact words, "This is a gift of yours, and you can do it if you work at it. There is no doubt in my mind you have this gift." He recalls feeling dumbstruck. Daniel said, "I was completely emotionally vulnerable, and I accepted his statement uncritically. His words, said the way he said them, burned themselves into my psyche. Now I know I can do it, if I am willing to put in the work."

Daniel's anticipation of influence elicited heightened emotions. While his emotions soared with self-doubt, Daniel eagerly awaited the coach's pronouncement. It could have gone either way: "You have a gift" or "You just don't have the basic talent." The pronouncement stunned him. As a poet, he lyrically stated what this declaration did for him; the words "burned themselves into my psyche." Daniel worked himself into a neurologically aroused state of anticipation, and the addition of a surprising comment (he worried he might not be good enough) cemented the uncritical acceptance of the coach's remark. In some cases, a hot-button topic itself can trigger arousal. Public speaking and bodyweight are two such topics.

Bodyweight and Public Speaking

What weight and public speaking share in common is a fear of being judged negatively, shamed, or ridiculed. Another commonality is that both concerns are prevalent in youth. Adolescents notoriously worry about body image, and school classrooms swell with demands for student presentations. These conditions create a perfect storm for moments of substantial influence. Add surprise to these conditions, and "buckle up."

Angela wrote this reflection as an adult, recalling an episode when she was twelve years old. A surprising comment made by her mother started a negative self-image that continues more than two decades later. This insensitive comment created the susceptibility characteristic of surprise. Angela was expecting sympathy, but instead, she received sarcasm.

In the summer of my twelfth year, my family visited my great-grandmother in Eureka, California. It was a particularly warm and humid day, and we'd been walking through the sticky air along the coast for over an hour. I was wearing a light, flowing summer dress. Consequently, my legs rubbed together until an uncomfortable skin irritation developed. I began to lag behind. "Hurry up! You're walking too slowly," my mother called from up ahead. I replied that it hurt to walk and showed her the distressed skin. Instead of displaying sympathy, her initial reaction was ridicule. She said sarcastically, "Your thighs rub together? Already? I had had four babies before my thighs rubbed together." Underlying the statement was the assumption that it was not a good thing for thighs to do so.

Her comment, though not striking at the time as I was more concerned with the stinging pain, shifted my entire image of myself. From that point on, I felt like something was inherently wrong with the way I was built since I was bigger at twelve than my (much taller mother) had been at thirty. I was not overweight. Short, yes. Solid, yes. Athletic, yes. I was a dedicated dancer in several classes, and I spent more time running, hiking, and playing outside than anything else.

Despite my level of fitness, I developed an incredibly negative body image and a sense of helplessness that there was nothing I could do, that no amount of exercise could fix what was wrong. While negative body image is not uncommon in youth, and such things are often brought about by the media, I believe I was fairly unaffected by them. But what ushered in the self-doubt was that the idea came from someone who I looked up to. I was talking to my sister over a year ago about my struggle to regain physical fitness, and the memory of my mom's comment just spilled out. I recognized it as having fundamentally altered my perspective. Once I realized that, I was better able to give my mind a less self-deprecating routine. It feels odd to share this as it is rather personal; however, it is one of the most noticeable moments of influence I have ever experienced.

Until that moment, she was unaffected by body-image messages. She credits this comment as a monumentally negative influence in her life. She was extremely active and athletic in her youth, but now struggles to regain fitness because that would mean "bigger thighs."

Seemingly simple comments can not only create excessive concern, they can even initiate mental illness. Elise, now a mother, told me she was unaware of her weight until a comment by her grandmother when she was eleven. It created unforeseen devastating consequences. It all happened one Christmas, when at age eleven, her parents gave her a silver ring with a small ruby in it. Proudly, she rushed to show it to her grandmother, to share her excitement. Her grandmother commented, "That ring would look better on a finger that wasn't so chubby." Elise told me, "That single comment altered my entire self-perception, and I suddenly felt enormous." Since that remark, she became overly self-aware of her body. She eventually developed an eating disorder in high school. Even now, as an adult, she still struggles to come to terms with her weight.

Elise was excited to share her excitement with her grandmother, expecting to share a moment of delight. Unexpectedly, her grandmother crushed her with sarcasm and created a self-defeating spiral into mental illness. Weight is an extremely sensitive subject, particularly for youth. However, sometimes a comment about weight can produce a positive effect.

I don't recommend comments like the one in the following story about Mason, but I share it because it created a positive result. When I first met Mason, he was a college football player in excellent physical condition. I would not have guessed that he had struggled with weight as a youngster. The story he recalls took place when he was a chubby eight-year-old.

During a lunch break, his childhood rival made a lasting comment while Mason munched hungrily on his chicken, "Eww! You like the skin. That's all the fat. That's why you're so fat!" Since that comment, Mason started eating carefully with healthy choices and became a self-proclaimed fitness addict.

How did this "fat" comment create a positive result when so many weight comments create adverse effects? Mason's anecdote differs from the two prior stories in a subtle, but critical way. In the first two, the comments implied that the recipient of the message was fat. Their weight was part of their identity. The surprise comment in Mason's story stated declaratively, *You are fat, and this is why.* In other words, *you can change your size.* Mason's realization: *I'm fat because of what I eat, and I can change what I eat.* Life is in the details. You'll learn the nuances of powerful and effective linguistic strategies in chapter 8.

The comment ended up positive because it empowered him. Negative comments about weight are rife with the potential for dangerous consequences. Don't give them. (At least until you read chapter 8.)

Public speaking can heighten arousal in most of us and our attraction to, or avoidance of, speaking in public is often traced to those vulnerable teen years. Most adolescents just want to fit it, and if they can't fit in, they often just want to become invisible. Others enjoy standing out. Regardless of what category they belong to, doing a school presentation in front of your peers can make even the coolest kid in class a sweaty mess. Classmate ridicule and laughter regularly create public-speaking phobias that last into adulthood. As Jerry Seinfeld humorously quipped, "The number-one fear in the U.S. is public speaking. The number-two fear is dying. So, if you were at a funeral, you'd rather be in the casket than delivering the eulogy." Occasionally, surprising moments can counteract this common phobia as it did for Corinna.

As a youngster, I used to have an intense fear of public speaking. If I had to give a speech, I would practice many times beforehand but would still stumble and rush thorough my speech due to nerves. At the beginning of my junior year in high school, my business class teacher asked me to spend three minutes to prepare an impromptu speech. After giving my speech, my teacher looked at me and said, "Wow, you are a natural presenter." After that day, I viewed myself differently. I became a much more effective speaker simply because I gained confidence in my abilities. That same year, I competed in a persuasive speaking event. I won first place at the regional level and then earned a second place at the state level. My teacher built me up at a time when I was nervous and vulnerable. I have him to thank him for my current heightened self-efficacy in public speaking.

Initially, Corinna experienced an intense fear of public speaking. Her heightened emotions during the impromptu speech readied her for influence. She got a "Wow!" with a comment about being "a natural presenter." This transformed those plastic emotions into pride and excitement instead of anxiety. The surprising comment happened immediately after the presentation, when the arousal emotions were still operating. No doubt, the delighted look on the teacher's face when she exclaimed, "Wow!" made a strong impression.

I'm often asked if a written comment can also produce a powerful surprise moment. Absolutely. Whether you're a supervisor giving an employee a personal memo, a teacher writing a comment on an assignment, or a coach doing an evaluation, written comments, if presented immediately, can produce dramatic results. This happened with Melissa.

Melissa's biggest fear was public speaking. Despite careful preparation, she typically felt very nervous. On one such occasion, her nerves were so rattled that her English teacher turned down the lights to help calm her nerves. Near tears and trembling, she managed to get through it and recalls, "As traumatic as the situation was, it turned out making a really positive impact in my life." I asked her how this could be so. She replied:

> This is because of the note that my teacher left on my grading rubric. She said that I was a great example to my classmates of what courage is, and that she was proud that I presented my speech, despite my fears. I was definitely in a highly emotional state, and my teacher's response surprised me because I was feeling so bad about standing up in front of the class. I think about this comment every time I have to present a speech, and I have gotten better at giving presentations.

Melissa received the feedback on her rubric immediately after her speech, while her emotional arousal was still high. She now describes that traumatic event as "positive." What surprised Melissa was that the comment focused on her courage, not her speaking ability. So now she feels courageous as a counter to her speaking anxiety. Whether it's in the classroom or the boardroom, all of us can find something positive to say at the end of presentation jitters. While immediate positive comments are ideal, delayed positive comments are still valuable, especially if they surprise the recipient. This happened to Rylie.

> When I was in fifth grade, my teacher often assigned creative and fun projects. I remember clearly that we once had to write a small book and present it to the class. I wrote mine about a boy who turned into a dragon slowly after being adopted by dragons. The concept was okay, but the execution was terrible. And oh my, did I ever get mocked for it by

my classmates! They all hated it, and a couple laughed at me for it. Later that day, my teacher pulled me aside and told me that she thought the idea was wonderful. She told me that even if no one else liked my writing, she thought it was great. Since that day, I have been writing stories about fantastical characters, and have improved my writing skills. I hope that one day I can positively influence a child like this.

While feeling sorry for himself, filled with self-doubt, the teacher's comment abruptly changed Rylie's mindset because it surprised him by countering his emotions from embarrassed to proud. When a clever teacher, coach, supervisor, or parent sees someone stressed over a performance, it's the perfect time to counter that anguish with a surprise positive comment, delivered with conviction.

Conviction May Seem Greater When We Overhear Comments

As a young boy, I'd often brush off positive comments from my parents or teachers. After all, they were *supposed* to say something nice, so where is the conviction in that? When my spouse says something flattering to me, I accept the comment in a similar vein, smile, and say thank you. But if you overhear something, the comment seems to carry more weight. It was expressed without a demand for social grace or vested interest. If it is a surprising comment, that revision impulse can create a whole new mindset because of the seeming truthfulness.

Turner is a middle-aged, outgoing, and spirited teacher who is eager to help others and show initiative. She used to be a timid youngster until one fateful day. She overheard a conversation when she was a child, and it changed how she viewed herself. As a nine-year-old child of a single parent, she spent much of her time at school and helping at the daycare. She didn't like the daycare because she thought the women working there didn't like her. Accordingly, she stayed quiet and helped wherever she could. They never gave her any compliments or positive feedback. It all changed in a surprising moment.

One day I was sitting behind a bookshelf quietly reading when I overheard three teachers talking about a student they loved. They spoke about her helpfulness and her enthusiasm, about her bright smile and intelligence. They each told a funny anecdote about her and laughed warmly. Just as the conversation was wrapping up, one of them said this dream student's name—It was me! Since then I have felt like I am doing well and am well-liked, even if there is no proof. My self-understanding altered forever in a very positive way that day.

Turner longed for validation as an enthusiastic and intelligent helper. If she had received them in person, as she had hoped, such comments would simply endorse her fragile eight-year-old self-assessment. She might even have brushed them off as "That's what they are supposed to say." However, overhearing a conversation among teachers, sharing stories warmly about her, cemented her identity with conviction. She even commented, "Since then I have felt like I am doing well, and I'm well-liked, even if there is no proof." She learned in that moment that a self-assessment and doing good deeds trump the need for positive comments. That's pretty sophisticated for a youngster: *Good deeds are their own reward.* We see evidence of that in her final phrase, "even if there is no proof."

The conviction inherent in overhearing a surprising comment can also create negative effects. Even though many comments are not intended to create debilitating mindsets, it depends on how a message is received and not how it is intended. Garner, a graduate student in education, recalled a conversation he overheard between his mother and teacher during a parent-teacher meeting in the third grade. At that time, he thought of himself as a goofy kid with a tendency to make jokes and act silly. Despite his antics, he thought he was a thoughtful and courteous student. That changed suddenly one day when he overheard the teacher express a concern. She thought Garner was becoming the class clown. As a child, he was unable to process the broad meaning of such a comment. He immediately became withdrawn, a disposition that remained well into his adult years. It wasn't the words of the comment so much as the tone. The same words with an approving tone would make a different impression. Sadly, when I talked to him about this, he told me that he preferred the way he used to be.

I finish this section with a warm story from Laurie. She overheard her mother's friend's comment, and it brightened her life forever. The comment changed what she thought was a negative feature, one that troubled her into a positive feature that she now embraces. Stories like these lead one to consider, "Should we intentionally speak to be over-heard, to generate influence?" This story leads into the next chapter, where I address that very question.

> When I was eleven, I was very skinny and awkward, like a new colt. I always felt ungraceful and odd looking. I was sure that I was not, and never would be "beautiful." I was too odd. By the time I was thirteen I was growing to be less stick-like and gangly, but my mindset stayed the same. One night, a friend of my mom's housemate came to visit. She was a singer and also a belly dancer. She was full of confidence and quiet power. I don't know how the conversation came about, but she told my mom that I was exotic looking. It stuck with me, and I grew up embracing my differences and seeing them as strengths.

Summary

Surprise events are ubiquitous with pervasive effects. This chapter showed how some professionals use elements of surprise strategically to garner attention and generate mindset revisions. Most of the non-professional examples explored in this chapter illustrated the intuitive or haphazard uses of surprise as a mechanism for moments of sudden influence. I also explored how moments of heightened arousal may increase the neurological power of surprise as a belief-revision reflex. The next chapter synthesizes what we have learned so far and puts this precious knowledge into a framework for strategic use: the how, when, and where to create life-changing events.

~

SURPRISE AS A TOOL

CHAPTER SEVEN

~

Using Surprise Strategically

This chapter explains how to use the mechanism of surprise to create opportunities and build personal resources in our children, students, athletes, team members, employees, and others. I teach my graduate students how to manufacture, then strategically use, surprise to generate productive mindsets. The brief story below illustrates how high-school teacher Karla changed a student's self-concept.

> I teach junior English. Jeremy, a quiet student with low confidence in his ability, misses a lot of school. I learned recently that he works at a computer shop with his father, repairing and assembling all sorts of electronic equipment. He has impressive skills that I'll never possess. One day he arrived late while students were already in working groups. I assigned him to a group. He asked if he could go to the resource room because he didn't think he was smart enough to contribute to the group. Typically, I feel sorry for him and acquiesce. I decided to surprise him. I told him in a matter-of-fact tone, "Are you kidding me? You're one of the smartest kids I know. Anyone who can do what you do with computers is brilliant." He joined the group and participated. Since then, his attendance, while still low, vastly improved, and he doesn't ask to go to the resource room anymore.

Karla demonstrated the strategic use of surprise to create a mindset revision for Jeremy.

While teachers aren't the only ones who can use this strategy, they are the most expedient to train and critique. Classes of teachers in graduate school or those in preservice training make up a readily accessible group to learn, practice, and report on the uses of surprise. Accordingly, many of the examples presented here will focus on teacher-student interactions.

These dynamic principles transfer easily to settings other than classrooms. Strategic uses of surprise are available for everyone, particularly parents and also professionals in the business of influence: physicians, healthcare workers, coaches, and employers. The list is endless.

As a psychologist, I've used surprise to create constructive mindsets for my clients. I've also used surprise strategically as an athletic coach and academic advisor. As a parent and grandparent, I've used surprise to trigger healthy mindsets for my family. Many professionals use surprise as a tool in their toolbox, but they do so intuitively, usually lacking a scientific foundation: the purpose of this book.

For instance, Marine Corps General Charles Krulak intentionally instituted a training rule that instills the use of strategic surprise by his drill sergeants. He instructs them to only compliment people on things that are unexpected. He trains his drill sergeants to "Tell the wimpy kids that they did a good job running" (indicates determination) and "Compliment shy people who take a leadership role" (indicates initiative).[1]

You can use the element of surprise strategically by recognizing when it occurs naturally or by intentionally producing it methodically (chapter 8 discusses several methods to trigger surprise intentionally). On your journey to master this powerful skill, you'll discover how to recognize opportunities to create powerfully positive beliefs. To start this journey, I'll begin with several real-life moments of surprise that inadvertently produced adverse effects. Learning missteps is instructive. Seeing mistakes provides clarity by contrasting correct methods. The act of spotting *what not to do* typically stimulates the ability to generate your own creative possibilities.

The following section illustrates several scenarios whereby an external agent of influence initiated the development of a negative mindset during a moment of surprise. When you read these scenarios, look specifically for the following elements: the surprise trigger, the statement that induced the negative belief, and what you could say instead to prompt a more productive mindset.

What Would You Do?

The first story is about Paul, who aspired to become a professional singer. He performed well in talent shows and choir performances, receiving frequent praise and commendations. While chatting with his aunt about his career ambitions, she suddenly asked him to sing for her. The demanding request caught him off guard and he told her about this nervous hesitance. Her surprising response instantly changed his ambitions and self-assessment. He recalls:

> She said, "If you can't perform on command without hemming and hawing about it, without making a big production about it, then you're not a real musician." The comment surprised me and left me feeling a little disappointed with myself as I came to realize that she was right. With that said, I decided that singing, and music in general, would never be a suitable career aspiration for me. I now only do it for personal enjoyment.

Her unexpected reaction to his nervousness catapulted his suggestibility to a higher level. He then equated his hesitation to *sing on-demand* as a sign that singing professionally was outside his grasp. In his vulnerable mental state, he accepted this unsubstantiated pronouncement immediately, and confirmed it with, "I decided that singing, and music in general, would never be a suitable career aspiration for me."

The relationship between performance anxiety and a performance is complex. Many professional entertainers experience it regularly and put on masterful performances. What would you have said? Note that you don't need the weight of evidence to support your claim to have it believed; his aunt didn't offer substantiation. Because of his highly suggestible mental state, Paul would have accepted any surprising comment said with conviction. (If you want to formulate your own intervening comment, pause now and do so. I offer mine next.) In this situation, seeing the elevated arousal from nervousness, I would have said, "Wow. You already show the signs of seasoned professionals by reflecting thoughtfully about your preparation." I labeled his physiological arousal and hesitation as "thoughtful consideration" and related it to veteran professional entertainers. It may not make him a better performer, but it keeps the potential impediment of nervousness at bay; indeed, it describes the inevitable arousal as common. A skilled influencer uses whatever stimulus is available (physiological arousal and hesitation) and relates it to the goal (professionalism).

The second story describes how Nicole's surprise event initiated the beginning of her math anxiety. She herself wonders how this apparent anxiety might have played out differently if not for this formative event. She became branded with the "bad at math" moniker. Nicole recalled a time when she was a second-grade student, struggling with a math task. The teacher had her stay after class to get some extra assistance. On that fateful day, the teacher seemed frustrated and gave Nicole a comment that continues to haunt her.

> One day she just gave up and told me that I will always struggle in math and that I should work really hard at the things that I am good at so that it could make up for my downfall in math. From then on out, I decided that math just wasn't for everyone and it wasn't for me. It became a joke in my family, and it was understood that I was just terrible at math. I remember using my fingers and being embarrassed. I still have to count on my fingers today. In high school, math continued to be a nightmare, and I needed help every day with homework. When I decided to go to college, the obvious choice was to pick a major that had nothing to with science and math. I now wonder if my view on math would have been different if I'd spent less time fighting it and more time accepting the challenge in trying to understand it.

While not stated explicitly, we can safely presume that Nicole was already nervous during this time while she was receiving help from a frustrated teacher. We might also presume that when a trusted authority figure, like a teacher, gives up on you, you will be surprised or at the least extremely emotional. As a young child, Nicole was incapable of challenging the presumption of this authority figure; hence, she accepted the teacher's pronouncement uncritically. As an adult, she wonders if her math anxiety would have played out differently with a more positive comment.

What would you have said? How could you use her state of arousal as a catalyst for forming a positive mindset about math? While you formulate your answer, note that the teacher in this scenario was probably well-intentioned. But who's to say where math prowess lies at the tender age of eight. (If you want to formulate your own intervening comment, pause now and do so. I offer mine next.) This comment might foster the opportunity to develop a success mindset: "Your willingness to work extra hard with these math problems will help you get more comfortable with math." Such a comment describes her frustration as *working hard* and links it to a result, *comfort with math.*

Coaches hold considerable influence over their athletes due to their powerful position as leaders and mentors. As an avid runner, David won a position on his college cross-country team. The team he joined had just won the National Championship, and he looked fondly to the coach for guidance and instruction. As an aspiring coach himself, the event he describes below taught him how *not* to behave and how not to treat his future athletes.

He worried that his new coach didn't care about him until a teammate informed him, "Our coach makes you work for his praise and does not hand it out like candy." Hearing that, he pushed harder to succeed. One day, he pushed so hard that he tripped during a hurdle drill. He felt embarrassed because he had tried intently to impress the coach. On that particular day, the coach had filmed the drills.

The coach announced to the team, "If anybody wants to see David eat it on the hurdle, come up to my office and I'll show it on the big screen." "His coaching style did not work for me," explained David. "It did however show me who I didn't want to be when I become a teacher and coach. Now, as a head coach myself, I give descriptive praise to my athletes and tell them how they improved each day."

David's emotional arousal from embarrassment added to the emotional spike from the unexpected comment. Note that while this event didn't change his view of himself, it changed his view of the coach, and helped him clarify what kind of coach he wanted to eventually become. Even though it wasn't an influential moment for his performance, a clever coach, one schooled in the art of strategic surprise, could have made it seminal.

In David's case, he was embarrassed about tripping on the hurdle. An astute positive coach might say something like, "This guy works so hard, he doesn't care if he fails. He gets up and keeps going. Now that's grit." Comments such as that cultivate encouragement rather than discouragement and stimulate the potential to create a formative moment. Whatever you see, you can use, as long as you recognize the signs.

Recognizing the Signs

As the story goes, there was a flood in a small town, and they were evacuating. The rain continued to fall as the water level rose dangerously. Reverend Joseph helped evacuate the needy. As the last car was leaving, its driver offered, "Jump in, Reverend. I can make room for you." The reverend replied, "Don't worry about me. Take some other needy soul. God will look after me." The water rose to waist level. A man in a canoe was leaving when he noticed the reverend. "Jump in. I've room for you with the cats and dogs." Reverend Joseph waved him on and said, "Don't worry about me. Save some other needy soul. God will look after me." The water continued until only the roofs were visible. A helicopter flew over the church where the reverend waved, clinging to the steeple. The pilot cried out, "I'll drop a rope ladder. Crawl up and I'll save you." The reverend replied, "Don't worry about me. Save some other needy soul. God will look after me." Sadly, the reverend perished. While entering the pearly gates of heaven, he questioned God, "I looked after your flock selflessly for thirty-five years. I put their needs before mine, all my life. I fervently believed that you would look after me in my time of need. Why didn't you save me?" God replied, "I sent a car, a canoe, and then a helicopter. What more could I do?" Like the reverend, we have to be able to read the signs.

Artful influence agents read the signs of opportunity and instinctively use moments of elevated arousal in a surprise as an opening to follow with a constructive comment. This is good practice for everyone, especially teachers, coaches, parents, employers, and supervisors. Most influential moments, like the one that follows, frequently pass unnoticed in spite of their powerful effect. When prompted, many of us can remember events similar to Jamie's. She sat nervously at the middle school parent-teacher conference, worried about the assignments she hadn't completed and what the teacher might say about them.

The teacher told my mother that I may have difficulties turning in homework through the course of the year, but that I was a strong finisher and he was not worried about me finishing this year with strong grades. Wow! I was so thankful, relieved, and honored that he spun my conference into such a positive light. Mr. F turned my tardiness into a strength and complimented my abilities to finish strong. I internalized his comment and made it come true. It has bubbled over from academics to sports, and my work ethic in general. I pride myself on being a hard worker and strong finisher to this day.

In this story, the wise teacher recognized the student's apprehension. Seizing this moment of heightened vulnerability, the teacher understood that an unexpected twist could lay the foundation for a new mindset. He turned the notion of tardy assignments into a sign of a "strong finisher." This mindset even generalized to other areas of the student's life. When we hear stories like these, we get glimpses of how to strategically structure moments of influence. Whether you're trying to capitalize on already-heightened emotion, or trying to trigger a surprise response, it's important to recognize the signs. Clever influence agents also understand that emotional arousal is malleable.

Distinguished emotion researcher Lisa Feldman Barrett tells us that "emotions are your brain's best guess of how you should feel in the moment. Emotions aren't wired into your brain like little circuits; they're made on-demand. As a result, you have more control over your emotions than you might think."[2] When we have an emotional response, many times it's just that: heightened general arousal. Naming an emotion and putting it into a positive context can create long-lasting effects. In the following example, Jordan experienced aroused emotions in the context of stage fright. A wise music instructor controlled the situation by naming the experience as "normal," thereby reducing his fear.

As I approached the stage, I noticed my hands were shaking, and I had a curious feeling of butterflies in my stomach. As I seated myself in front of the piano, I froze. I felt like crying, and I did not know what to do. Suddenly, I felt a warm hand touch my shoulder; it was Mrs. S. She then said something to me I will never forget, "It's all right, what you're feeling is normal, and I get the same feeling each and every time I perform. I believe in you." Her keen ability to recognize my emotions turned what would have been a negative moment in my life into a positive one. With her wise words of advice, I played my piece, got stuck only once, and bowed to a cheering auditorium. I am so thankful for the positive influence Mrs. S. had in encouraging me to overcome my stage fright. I will always remember the moment my piano teacher inspired me.

This perceptive music coach recognized the boy's emotional arousal as a malleable moment. This young musician started the day eager and excited. The coach's well-timed comment relabeled what he felt as *impending fear* back to *eager excitement*. Branding his experience as normal liberated him from a debilitating fear, resulting in a successful performance. Emotions are subjective; either good or bad. When the teacher labeled it as normal, the young musician recaptured his excitement and changed his experience back to enjoyable.

Most of our behavior is a response to events as they unfold in our lives. Generally speaking, we spend little time reflecting on our moment-to-moment actions, thus allowing our underlying beliefs to guide us below the radar of our awareness. Unless our instinctive and automatic assessment of our behavior or perceptions is challenged, we make the assumption that we are correct. But remember, our experience and perceptions are malleable. Whether teacher, parent, coach, or supervisor, if you, as an agent of influence, plan to create powerfully positive moments, you'll become a crafty expert when you learn to work with whatever you get (behaviors, intentions, circumstances, context, reactions, thoughts, or just about anything). Learn to recognize the tools at your disposal. These tools are the event itself, any behavior, or the accompanying emotion. Note that the behavior can be implied or observable. For example, noticing that someone is "thinking thoughtfully" is only implied and not necessarily observable.

Be creative. Use what you get. If an athlete trips on a hurdle and feels like a failure, then walks away instead of trying again, you can label the *walking away* as *showing reflection* and *mental preparation*. If your coworker makes a big mistake, you can comment on how a *willingness to fail shows an eagerness to improve*. You have an immense wealth of opportunity at your disposal.

Working with What You Get

In the movie *Field of Dreams*, an Iowa corn farmer hears voices and interprets them as a command to build a baseball diamond in his cornfield. He does, and the 1919 Chicago White Sox team arrives and plays ball. He hears mysterious voices whisper, "If you build it, they will come."[3] In my adaptation of that well-known expression, I propose, "If you notice it, they will exhibit it." But you have to notice it, read the signs, and then use whatever you get.

In this example, Danielle recalls a simple comment made by a classmate in the third grade. While this happened many years ago when she was a young child, she still remembers how it created a moment of influence. This illustrates that what is noticed tends to be repeated, and often emphatically.

> Until third grade, I had terrible, illegible handwriting. My parents wanted to have me tested for some sort of dysgraphia. But in third grade, we started doing proper cursive handwriting, and my writing began to improve by leaps and bounds. One day a classmate of mine complimented me on my writing, and I didn't think anything of it. But ever since then, I have made this huge conscious effort to practice my handwriting, to try and improve it even more, to gain the admiration of others. To this day, I still have pretty wonderful handwriting, and if given the chance will practice writing words and phrases on the sides of my papers, just because I still have this need to improve.

She started her recollection by referring to her parents' concern that she exhibited dysgraphia (a learning disability that affects writing abilities). In this context, an unexpected comment from an unlikely source probably produced a surprise for Danielle. If it was a meaningless comment, she likely wouldn't have remembered it. The classmate renamed what Danielle previously thought was a weakness as a prized asset.

When an attribute someone considers a weakness becomes described as a strength, the unexpected perspective inevitably stirs a surprise response. My colleague Sarah told me she used to worry that her inability to focus on tasks at work would eventually lead to her downfall. That is until her director commented one day that her "ability to let her mind wander gave her a creative edge." She now expresses her innovative ideas proudly. The reframing of *inability to focus* to *ability to let her mind wander* changed its valence from negative to positive.

I first met Samantha in a graduate class. She didn't say much, but when she spoke, it was usually deliberate, informed, and coherent. She talked with an authority that commanded attention from her fellow students. I noticed this in class and commented on it during her participation. She informed me that it wasn't always the case. She used to consider her reluctance to speak up as a weakness that interfered with her ability to make a positive impression. She told me how that all changed several years earlier when her swim coach surprised her with a formative comment.

During her senior year of high school, her coach named her as one of three captains of the swim team. One cocaptain was loud and assertive, while the second was bubbly and friendly. She didn't know how she fit in. Samantha had never considered herself a leader, nor aspired to lead in any capacity. When the coach called a team meeting to explain his reasons for selecting captains, she "dreaded" what he would say because she hated being the center of attention. He said this.

> "Your last captain is Samantha. She may be quiet, but when this girl says something, you're going to want to listen." It was definitely a moment I will never forget. What he said about me took what I was most nervous about—not being a good leader, not finding a way to be a good captain, being too quiet—and relieved all those worries. He gave my voice value. This made my "quietness," which was noticed or even mocked at times, an asset instead of a negative thing. He portrayed me as a thoughtful and worthy person.

Describing an apparent weakness as a positive attribute is a powerful strategy to surprise someone. (I'll detail this strategy further in the next chapter.) It triggers a susceptible moment to inject a powerfully constructive message. When it comes to dispositions, who is to say which ones are beneficial attributes and which ones are destructive? Spinning a potential deficit into a valuable tool shows the artful ability to intervene with positive prowess. This is what happened for versatile actor-producer-writer-comedian John Leguizamo. A surprising comment made all the difference in his life and career.

Leguizamo loved cracking jokes in school, playing the role of class clown. One fateful day his math teacher pulled him aside. He awaited the usual scolding; however, this time his teacher surprised him and said, "Listen, instead of being obnoxious all the time—instead of wasting all that energy in class—why don't you rechannel your hostility and humor into something productive? Have you ever thought about being a comedian?" Stunned, he found himself speechless, without his regular smart-ass retort. He describes that comment as the turning point in his life. He says, "Everything kind of converged, you know? The planets aligned." By finding something positive in apparently disruptive behavior, the teacher created a surprise event that fashioned a lifelong positive mindset. Finding the inherent resources in behavior requires thinking past initial impressions.[4]

All behavior is potentially resourceful if you can name the underlying assets. I'm not suggesting that you ignore destructive behavior, like relabeling sexist comments in the workplace as an ability to express yourself openly. I believe, though, that discovering underlying assets in someone's behavior can prove empowering, like labeling failure as a willingness to learn. I teach my graduate students to identify the underlying assets of a behavior. Their goal is to identify features of their students' behaviors as resources to employ to empower their students.

Remember the following: All behavior, good or bad, contains underlying assets to be named and enlisted as strengths.

All Behavior Is Resourceful

While delivering an address on linguistic structures, I stated to the audience, "Your careful attention to detail *makes* you an excellent leader." Most of the audience nodded in agreement with this self-evident remark. I then asked them to comment on my statement. They quickly listed numerous ways that paying attention to detail enhances leadership: "It ensures that everyone gets to be heard," "It helps by avoiding problems in the long run," "It's the little details that make things run smoothly," and so on. I then stated the complete reverse: "Your careful attention to detail *interferes* with your leadership abilities." The audience found it equally easy to list numerous ways leadership could be hindered by paying attention to detail: "Losing sight of the overall picture," "Becoming insensitive to people," "Forgetting long-term goals," and so on.

This exercise shows how easy it is to direct someone's thinking by leading their thoughts down the path of my choosing. Associations between abstract concepts such as *leadership* and *paying attention to detail* are vague. We all employ leadership during our lives, even if we do it infrequently. We also pay attention to detail at various times. When someone implies a relationship between two concepts, as I did with attention to detail and leadership, we automatically scan our experience for evidence to determine if we agree or disagree. In other words, in order to understand a statement, we must first test its validity, tacitly accepting it, before deciding if we fully accept it. The mental act of making sense of the comment subtly invests us in the plausibility of the statement itself.

Think of it this way. A friend remarks that you move like a cat. To understand this comment, you have to know how a cat moves, and mentally form an image of it. You then have to mentally form an image of your movement and juxtapose it with a cat's. Then you have to agree or disagree. It's easier to find similarities because that's what was stated. Now, while it probably took fifteen seconds to read this passage, your mind did it in milliseconds. So fast that you didn't even notice.

In the following story, Michael tells how his prior belief in a lack of mathematical ability flipped when a thoughtful community college instructor created a new belief for him. The instructor labeled Michael's behavior as *an ability to proficiently explain ideas* and then linked it to *mathematical aptitude.*

> I thought I was "mathematically challenged" until I got to Debbie's class at community college. She told me, "Your ability to clearly explain how you arrived at your answers shows that you have mathematical adeptness." This unexpected comment was a real confidence booster for me, and I remember thinking, "And all this time I thought I wasn't a math person."

The cognitive act of making sense of a comment predisposes us to acceptance. Remember that our default position is *to believe*, and that plausibility trumps truth. Pondering the meaning of his professor's statement invested him in the acceptance of it as the truth. This is especially true when you hear an unexpected surprise comment. Surprise triggers a readiness to accept the first plausible explanation.

Some of the richest people I know don't have any money. Some of the smartest people I know didn't go to college. Most of us find it easy to accept these apparently contradictory statements. It's easy to make these statements true. Notice that each interpretation leads in a positive direction. The act of interpreting a message subtly invests us in it. Our unconscious scans our memories for positive instances, finds or creates them, then instantly concludes, "It must be true because my experience bank generated examples." Psychologists use the term *psychological closure* to name our predisposition to find positive instances in order to verify assertions. How we approach a situation influences the meaning we make of it and the subsequent emotion that emerges.

When we hear subjective statements, "Men take too many risks," we each create our own interpretation, consistent with our model of the world. We individually determine exactly how the statement best fits within our unique framework of understanding. Vague comments stated in an active voice (X makes Y) orients the listener's mind toward constructing an interpretation that suits him or her best. We can all think of times when men took too many risks, but they will each have different meanings for us. If instead, you had read, "Men always choose the easy path," you could have found evidence or thoughts to verify that too. In a very real sense, each listener receives a challenge to produce a personalized thought.

In the end, is attention to detail beneficial, detrimental, or indifferent to leadership? Like a lot of things in life, it depends. Our beliefs drive us. Everybody pays attention to some details and not others. Whether it works as an obstacle or a benefit depends on what we believe. If I believe attention to detail enhances leadership, I will pay attention to detail boldly and confidently, incorporating these modes as a conscious part of my leadership style. If I believe attention to detail hinders leadership, I will pay attention to detail hesitantly, anxiously, and privately. Who is to say which of these opposing behaviors serves as a resource for which goal, and at which time? The point is, we all achieve our goals in different ways by calling upon our unique personal resources. We can enlist almost any behavior as a resource if we believe it to be one. Sadly, we can also enlist almost any behavior as an obstacle.

The following story illustrates how a young boy changed his belief about why he struggled at school. Until age ten, Max worked very hard in school as he had to overcome a reading disorder and attention deficit disorder. Despite linking his lack of success to his learning challenges, he continued to produce impressive efforts. That all changed with an outburst by a teacher in his elementary classroom.

On that auspicious day, a frustrated teacher confronted Max about taking too long for what seemed to be a mundane task: copying notes from the board. Max responded by simply telling the teacher that it was hard for him. Here's how Max described what happened next:

> The teacher responded by saying, "Hard? This is an easy warm-up. All you're doing is copying words down from one place to another. You're just making excuses for being lazy." I didn't expect that, but the words *easy* and *lazy* really stuck. He unknowingly gave me a convenient excuse for not trying at things that were hard for me. It was much more comforting to think that this "easy" task isn't hard for me because that would imply that I'm stupid, it's just because I'm too "lazy" to complete the task at hand. After that moment, I pretty much gave up on most assignments that gave me even a little trouble. Each time I did this, I ended up reinforcing my character and self-image as a lazy student. These bad habits lasted until grad school. Now I know better; I'm actually quite industrious again.

Prior to the teacher's statement, Max linked his *learning disabilities* to his *schooling difficulty*. The unexpected and convincing comment made by his teacher created a new link, a new belief. He then linked being *lazy* to his *schooling difficulty*. This won out, probably due to a compelling and unexpected pronouncement during Max's heightened arousal. When in a receptive mental state, and a link seems plausible, it inclines us to accept it. How we phrase a comment can make a world of difference to the receiver.

The following two statements are both true: "Delegating authority can enhance or impede leadership" and the opposite, "Centralizing decisions can enhance or impede leadership." Imagine the following scenario. You would like to tell your associate that he causes confusion among his staff by delegating authority. Which of the following two comments would produce the best result? "Your delegating of authority causes confusion among your staff," or "Your centralizing of decisions fosters clarity among your staff." Both comments address the same issue; yet, one names an obstacle and the other a resource. Noting someone's resourcefulness empowers that person. The recipient will also instinctively scan their experiences for validating evidence and make it true. Naming an obstacle may elicit a defensive posture whereby the recipient instinctively defends and affirms his or her position. In the end, we all overcome obstacles by using our resources.

We accept plausible comments because they fit into our existing framework for understanding. When you create a plausible link—"Your centralizing of decisions fosters clarity among your staff"—it creates a goal outside our awareness, what is called nonconscious. Distinguished neuroscientist Jeff Hawkins describes thinking as the precursor to predicting, which generates brain commands to fulfill the prediction. He writes, "Thinking, predicting, and doing are all part of the same unfolding of sequences moving down the cortical hierarchy." Think of predictions as an active form of expectation.[5]

Expectations as Nonconscious Goals

When you expect to do well at something, you behave much differently than when you anticipate doing poorly. When you expect a poor outcome, you are more likely to exhibit behavior consistent with a poor result. If someone asked you to sing the national anthem at an event, and you have a self-image as a poor singer, expectations of doing poorly, while embarrassing yourself, will interfere with your performance. Your anticipation of a poor performance triggers a physiological response. Your autonomic nervous system sends adrenaline surging through your body, giving you the sensation of butterflies in your stomach. You interpret this as anxiety, which then escalates, sabotaging your performance by interfering with proper breathing, correct posture, and voice projection. You warm up with a note. It sounds off key and hesitant, which confirms your fear and also raises your anxiety one more notch. On the other hand, if you anticipate doing well, you will breathe deeply, stand erect, and project your voice effectively, thereby enhancing your performance. You warm up with a note. It sounds off key, but you brush it off as a necessary exercise to find your tone. You interpret your physiological arousal as excitement. In essence, your expectations enlist corresponding responses and perceptions.

Our understanding of the world screens our experiences and determines what behavior is appropriate for any given situation. This screening process generates expectations that elicit corresponding behaviors and produce self-fulfilling prophecies. Expecting to sing poorly not only increases the likelihood of a poor performance, it also elicits hypervigilance for expected errors, an inclination to interpret arousal as anxiety, followed by the likelihood of a poor self-evaluation. In this sense, your expectations activate your present behavior—your (anticipated) future predicts the present. Our expectations unconsciously direct our senses to search for confirming evidence that we were indeed correct in our anticipation. Thinking of something is literally the start of doing it.

Think of your expectations as nonconscious goals that drive your behavior automatically throughout the day. These nonconscious goals instinctively tap into the reward structure of the environment. Hypnotists know how to manipulate expectations. Consider the case of the nervous singer. Think of a typical hypnotist's show. Imagine that Mel is a poor singer, but he accepts the suggestion that he is indeed a magnificent singer, and that an eager audience awaits his powerful rendition of the national anthem. In these shows, the typical result is that Mel will probably amaze his friends with an impressive performance. The suggestion changes Mel's expectations to conform to an anticipated excellent performance. By manipulating the expectation from *poor singer* to *promising singer*, the hypnotist shifts singing from a negative valence, avoid, to a positive valence, approach. Approach tendencies lead you instinctively toward your goal by enhancing positive attitudes and motivation. You are more likely to pursue goals where you expect to be successful or if it brings enjoyment.

In the story below, Christina's willingness to talk openly to her parents transferred from negative valence to positive in one moment of surprise. With a new, optimistic mindset, instead of fearing a conversation with her parents, she warmly approaches open discussions.

At sixteen, having just earned her driver's license, she was driving with friends. While pulling out of a friend's driveway, she mistakenly put the car in drive instead of reverse, and jolted into the garage door. She recalls calling her father while being barely able to hold the phone with her trembling hands.

> My dad answered and I broke into tears. I stuttered to say what happened and was utterly confused when I heard him laugh. "Was anyone hurt?" he asked with a chuckle in his voice. I told him no; just awful damage. He always told me he would never get mad for accidents, and to always call when my siblings or I needed help. However, in this case, I was certain he would be livid. My dad continued to laugh and told me as long as his kids are okay, he could care less about his cars. I felt so relieved and shocked. From this moment I was able to be more open and honest with my parents and actually believe what they told me.

Neurologically, when we affirm what we believe, we get a little hit of dopamine. The release of dopamine is a form of information, a message that tells the organism "Do that again." In the past, we thought that dopamine was the pleasure neurotransmitter. We now know that dopamine serves the role of motivation rather than pleasure; our opioid system looks after pleasure. It is a subtle but important distinction. UCLA neuroscientist Russel Poldrack illustrated this through clever experiments with rodents. He states, "You can block the dopamine system in rats and they will still enjoy rewards, but they just won't work to get them."[6]

Innate processes, such as approach-avoid, combine with our experiences to create our beliefs. These beliefs then exert an automatic, nonconscious influence. Pursuing a goal activates relevant situational features; they then operate outside of conscious awareness and guidance. For example, when Christina encounters problems in the future, she is more likely to approach her father, not because she consciously thinks, "I now feel comfortable approaching my father"; rather, the seminal episode with the car accident changed the valence to approach. She does it instinctively.

Ryan told me he spent his early years as timid, with few friends, and that it all changed for him when he joined a karate studio at age six. He reported how he then became a new person, outgoing and confident, with success at school and abundant friendships. At age ten that suddenly turned upside down, but then he recovered the next day, all because of a surprise comment from his coach. For the first time, he failed a belt test. Feeling devastated, he remembers crying all night as he came to the decision to quit. After all, he thought, school and friendships were strong now. Who needed karate? That carefully deliberated decision reversed instantly when he went to tell his instructor. In Ryan's words:

> He told me, "Son, you are one of the hardest working kids that I know. I believe that you will bounce back from this, and I know that one day you are going to be a fantastic instructor." At the time, it didn't seem like much, but his words got me to come back. I'm so glad that I did. I passed my red belt test the very next time and went on to get my black belt a couple of years later. After receiving my black belt, I went on to become an assistant instructor and then a head instructor for six years. When I think about this story today, I can't help but get emotional. What if my sensei had let me quit? How different would my life be?

> For several years during his early karate training, martial arts had a positive valence for Ryan. It changed dramatically when he failed his red-belt test, and he decided to give it up. The astute coach's comment not only recaptured his love for karate (positive valence), but it also instilled a vastly superior and more generalized mindset: Hard work and resilience will overcome obstacles. The coach achieved this by surprising him with an unanticipated comment, describing Ryan's behavior as industrious, "the hardest working kid I know" and his character as resilient, "You will bounce back from this." Ryan commented that the coach's words got him to come back. Learning about ourselves often develops serendipitously through comments by others.

Creating Meaning from Behavior

As we go about our lives, events unfold, and we automatically respond. We produce an extraordinary amount of behavior every day. Much of our lives is routine. Fully aware, continuous conscious considerations is not how we evolved. Spending considerable conscious effort imbuing our behavior with meaning would immensely tax our valuable mental resources. Our beliefs evolve from patterns developed from prior behavior. Imagine that someone sees a portion of your behavior and infuses it with meaning. During an idle conversation, an associate asks what new goal you've set for yourself. You pause to ponder the question. The associate says, "Your ability to think clearly helps you make thoughtful decisions." Prior to that comment, you weren't necessarily aware of your pondering as thinking clearly, but now it's named.

You'll probably accept the comment because it flatters you. Everyone likes to believe they think clearly. You also instinctively accept the implied link that *clear thinking* leads to *thoughtful decisions*. If you're like most people, you don't critically examine the casual remark to assess if you were indeed thinking clearly nor whether clear thinking inevitably leads to thoughtful decisions. You simply accept the complimentary comment and respond, "Thank you."

There's a lot going on here. Let's unpack it. 1) Behavior takes place: You pause to ponder. 2) It gets labeled: clear thinking. 3) Meaning-making follows: Your ability to think clearly helps you make thoughtful decisions. 4) Now that some wise observer labeled the meaning of your behavior, you either accept it or reject it. Recall from prior chapters that our default is to accept incoming information. Since you've accepted the link between "clear thinking" and "thoughtful decisions," it becomes part of your personal mental architecture; you own it. You not only agree with that conceptual link, you actually embody it. Your colleague merely described it. This cognitive adjustment takes place instantly, automatically, and usually outside our awareness.

Neurologically, because it names a positive personal feature, the behavior named also sparks a positive valence—approach—and is more likely to be exhibited. Since you have acted in a way that seems consistent with a particular belief, you respond with an inclination to endorse that belief by triggering a tendency to look for affirming evidence. Statements such as these work this way because they are phrased in the positive and drive the subject to find supporting evidence. I call them Cause-Effect-Resource Statements (CERSs). These statements link a cause, "clear thinking" to the effect, "thoughtful decisions," thereby creating a personal resource for the recipient: The comment infuses the recipient with the ability to use clear thinking to make thoughtful decisions. A CERS is not manipulating as much as it is asserting that the person is already the person they want to be, because the evidence, the

C in CERS, indicates so. I explain the powerful linguistic importance of CERSs in more detail in chapter 8.

Not every comment someone makes influences the recipient to form a belief or even accept the comment as meaningful. But we can raise the likelihood of productive results by triggering a surprise or using one if it occurs naturally. Recall the story of award-winning singer-songwriter Carly Simon mentioned in the introduction. As a teenager, a surprising comment by her boyfriend made a momentous impact on her. Now we can examine it in more detail.

Carly grew up with a stammer and chronic anxiety. At school, she dreaded the thought of fellow students making fun of her. She learned that singing helped her communicate smoothly. She learned to reach out to other students and became popular in her own right. By eleventh grade her stuttering reduced, but she still had a minor stammer. Still embarrassed, she tried to keep her stammer a secret. By then, she had a boyfriend. Sitting in his car with him, overlooking the reservoir, he commented, "My mother thinks you have a stammer." Devastated, she wept uncontrollably. In response, he surprised her with, "But I find it so charming." She writes, "After that, I realized, I didn't have to hide my stammer anymore. Nick had given me a new name for it. It was *charming*." Neurologically, the dopamine valence associated with her stammer noticeably shifted from negative (*devastating*) toward positive (*charming*).[7]

When something happens out of the ordinary, we instinctively try to make sense of it. Psychologists often call this meaning-making, the process of how people construe, understand, or make sense of life events, relationships, and the self. Through meaning-making, we reaffirm, revise, or replace elements of our belief system to develop a more useful system. As I've shown in earlier chapters, surprise reaches the pinnacle of novelty, and we typically accept the first explanation we receive.

Not all messages carry weight. Communication ranges in persuasiveness from minuscule to profound. A vast body of research shows us what works, what doesn't, and how to maximize the degree of influence in a statement. In the next chapter, we'll explore this fascinating topic thoroughly. I'll introduce the *Elaboration-Likelihood Model*. It remains the gold standard for examining and parsing out the critical elements of persuasiveness. I'll include the powerful *Cognitive Response Model* to reveal a simple formula for constructing powerful messages that stick.

Summary

This chapter introduced the idea of using surprise strategically to influence others. I started with illustrated stories of harmful events and asked you to construct a more beneficial intervention. Learning how to intervene is the first step in becoming a powerful influence agent, one that uses surprise as a catalyst. You learned how to recognize the signs of opportunity for influence and to use whatever current behavior is present as a tool for change. You then learned to look for the underlying functional elements of all behavior, to use these as potential personal resources, to trigger nonconscious goals. To conclude this chapter, I showed how the meaning we make from our behavior is often determined by comments from others. Now that we know how to use surprise strategically, the next chapter teaches us how to intentionally trigger surprise events.

CHAPTER EIGHT

~

Activating Surprise

This chapter teaches you how to activate transformative moments. Armed with the ability to trigger surprises or recognize surprise opportunities, you will want to maximize your positive influence. I examine the current literature on persuasion and formulate a linguistic structure to maximize the effect of your comments.

Some readers might think I'm offering them a method to instantly change someone's belief. It can happen, and it does happen, but it's not a magical tool. A screwdriver is a valuable tool that works effectively in the right conditions if that's what's called for. In the same way, a surprise can change someone's beliefs under the right conditions.

It's important to note that no strategic intervention is going to work with certainty whenever you apply it. Yet these approaches consistently heighten the probability of success. Often, that is enough to gain a decisive advantage. A second advantage for success also exists: These methods clear the way to positive growth by bypassing conscious resistance.

Not Magic, But Magic-ish

A magician throws a ball into the air three times with his left hand. On the fourth throw, he secretly puts the ball in his right hand and no ball flies. We *expected* the ball to fly; the surprise delights us. In the classic shell game, a magician places three shells on a napkin, and one of them has a pea hidden underneath. He moves the shells around and lets the observer correctly guess where he hid the pea. The observer builds confidence and *expects* to guess correctly each time. Then the magician does it one more time, but this time the guess is wrong. Surprise! Magicians know that inducing expectations, then violating them, heightens surprise.

Sometimes a comment itself triggers a surprise. To the scatterbrained worker: "Your ability to see what others miss makes you a valued member of the team." That comment might surprise the worker. Can we intensify that surprise, possibly triggering phasic dopamine? Imagine this scenario. Keith works at CanTelUs. He knows he has a reputation for scatterbrained behavior that frequently prompts scorn from coworkers. The supervisor calls him into her office. She looks down at some papers on her desk, scowls at the work, then suddenly lifts her head, smiles, and announces to Keith, "Your ability to see what others miss makes you a valued member of the team. I just thought I'd tell you." She picks up her phone and starts dialing, waving him out of the office. Keith, feeling a little stunned and somewhat excited, turns and leaves. The supervisor strategically set up Keith's expectations, then violated them. The result: enhanced surprise.

Acting Surprised Creates a Surprise

Parents often act surprised as they try to encourage their young children, "Wow! I can't believe you did that puzzle in only five minutes." Seeing someone surprised raises our emotional arousal too. In our evolutionary past, when a companion appeared surprised by sudden danger or opportunity, those circumstances triggered surprise in us as well. Vicariously experiencing another person's surprise similarly alerted us to fleeting danger or opportunity. When someone possesses knowledge that we don't, it also triggers our curiosity, a receptive state. Humans have mirror neurons. These fire when we witness an action or emotion in others; we experience a complementary version of it ourselves as if we are having the observed experience. This is why we shiver when we see a spider on someone else's neck or cringe when we witness a needle puncture a person's arm as they receive an injection. It explains contagious laughter. It's also how we understand emotions and intentions, by vicariously experiencing them ourselves when we observe them in others.

The example below illustrates the elevated emotions of a student worried about making a good impression. Her surroundings intimidated her, prompting moods of vulnerability and nervousness. This emotional posture positioned her for influence. The teacher's surprise reaction nudged her into a state of soaring susceptibility.

I attended a more advanced school for my freshman year, and I was afraid of not being able to compete academically. Nevertheless, English was a favorite subject and the one that I put in most of my effort. One fateful day, we were all to compose a thesis statement and write it on the board to be critiqued. Although I had written essays and topic sentences before, this one would be seen and judged by the class as well as the teacher. As I brought it to life on the whiteboard using my neatest penmanship, I remember thinking that I would have to deny that this was my sentence. I was certain that those around me had written an incredible, higher-level thesis statement. Instead, this happened: After reading and revising a few sentences, Mrs. R read mine. While I cannot recall what I wrote, I do remember what my teacher had to say. She read my sentence aloud, and she paused. I braced myself. Finally, she said, sounding as surprised as her words made me feel, "This is actually really good. Who wrote this?" I raised my hand, and she continued to congratulate me on my composition skills. It was in that moment when I vowed to continue to work hard in her class and my future English classes because my skill was validated. It was then that I felt most driven and excited to do something with this newfound passion.

Note that it could have gone horribly with a decidedly negative surprise comment such as, "Oh my goodness! Who wrote this nonsense?" Luckily for her, she received an encouraging remark. The surprise comment worked to embed a desire for writing. While not a life-changing experience, the emotions triggered by the unexpected response boosted her pride and enhanced a "favorite" subject to a "newfound passion."

I recently coached a novice hockey player in power-skating. During his practice strides, I acted surprised and stated, "Wow! You seem to take to this skill incredibly quickly. There must be something in your past that helps you pick this up so fast." He looked surprised, thought for a moment, then answered, "Well I play football and I know how to get power from my legs." When someone is surprised, they need to make sense of it. By driving him to make meaning of my surprise comment, he formed his new belief: I can learn this quickly and thoroughly. That motivates him to develop that skill more intentionally. My observation worked because it surprised him. Whether he actually learned more swiftly than most is not relevant. He now sees himself as a studious and skilled apprentice in power-skating with the inevitable ability to improve rapidly.

Acting surprised can create a surprise, but sometimes the reverse works too. If you act indifferently when someone expects an elated response, as if someone's outstanding accomplishment was simply expected, your response may produce a surprise. Not acting impressed when it is expected will also trigger a surprise. The statement that follows then boosts conviction by showing inordinate faith in that person.

Graduate student Aden described a class he took with an extremely strict teacher who always demanded a best effort. This teacher enrolled the entire class in a local speech competition and required all the students to meet with her individually to rehearse. Aden worked hard, memorizing and preparing for his presentation. When the time arrived, he proudly delivered his speech, expecting an enthusiastic response.

> She looked unamused. She just stared at me and said, "You have the ability to light up any place you go. Use it." Something switched in my head when she said that, and it has stuck with me since then.

That switch in his head was the formation of a new belief: "I have the ability to light up a room." Expecting excited enthusiasm but receiving tedium is surprising, making the recipient instinctively respond cognitively with *What happened? Why such a response? What does this mean?* The explanation, given as a matter-of-fact remark, packs the weight of conviction, especially during an expected moment. You can trigger a surprise intentionally by using this strategy, responding matter-of-factly when the other person expects excitement.

If you use this strategy, be sure to acknowledge the results and note the exemplary work. Be sure to credit positive results to effort.

Your children—and for that matter your coworkers and employees—especially thrive on the approval of doing well and that hard work produces results. Your reaction should denote sincere faith, not indifference.

Use this strategy thoughtfully. This differs considerably from having a dismal reaction because you don't care or think something is not noteworthy. A spiteful response, done this way, during a surprise can cause harm. Surprise still arises, but the emotional tone will drive a negative mindset.

For example, Robert recalls a time in school when he loved art but hated his art class because of the grouchy teacher. Accordingly, his performance declined considerably, as he did the bare minimum to avoid the teacher's wrath. Somehow this token effort produced a win at a local contest. His interest piqued as a result, that is, until his teacher surprised him by scowling at his success. Robert said, "That day, I honestly think my subconscious was ingrained with the realization that I could do well while maintaining the smallest effort possible."

This pivotal moment triggered a negative mindset. What if Ms. F. had said something productive like, "Your ability to make simple images so charming shows true artistic talent"? A comment such as that may have embedded a belief in, and pursuit of, an artistic capacity. Without an interpretation for the surprise, the emotional mood will create one. In this case, the student developed a destructive one: Do the least possible. Any time you expect one response, but receive a dramatically different one, surprise results. To trigger surprise in others, consider the deliberate strategy of doing the opposite.

Doing the Opposite

I frequently get asked, "I can see how surprises trigger a moment of soaring suggestibility, but how do you generate surprises?" One of the best ways to do this strategically is by doing the opposite of what someone expects. The best examples are when someone expects scorn, ridicule, or scolding. These opportunities generate moments of positive influence for doing the opposite.

In the following story of surprise, a young child named Susan felt insecure about her ability to succeed. The comment by her teacher surprised her because she expected one reaction but got a different one. Susan accepted the teacher's comment and instantly formed a new mindset that continues to last into her adult years.

Although she liked school, she found math confusing. Accordingly, she sometimes cried when she didn't understand a new concept. Before the new school year began, she found herself with an opportunity to meet the new teacher. She thought she should warn her.

> I cleared my throat and quietly let her know that I sometimes did not understand math. Instead of looking surprised or disappointed, Mrs. G just nodded at me and assured me that we were all there to learn, and not understanding was a part of learning. I thought that maybe the reason that she was being so accepting was that she had misunderstood me, so I told her that I sometimes cried, too. When I said that, Mrs. G gave me the most caring smile, and said, "Crying isn't a bad thing. It means that you feel frustrated. And we can work with that." With that, she made me feel like a heavy weight lifted off of my chest. No longer did I feel stupid when I felt like crying, I knew that I was just frustrated, and that was something I could work with. I have carried that feeling with me since then; frustration is a doorway to learning.

Note how she expected disappointment from her teacher and when she didn't get it, she tried again: "I thought that maybe the reason that she was being so accepting was that she had misunderstood me, so I told her that I sometimes cried, too." Even at this young age, she was trying to make her teacher's perception match her own—confirmation bias. She expected disappointment, and when she didn't get it, she tried again to get the anticipated response. Her clever teacher saw what was taking place and surprised her with a shift in perception: "Crying isn't a bad thing. It means that you feel frustrated. And we can work with that." That comment surprised Susan, creating the impetus to instantly change her mindset. This new mindset became a fundamental belief that generalized to all learning—"frustration is the doorway to learning"–and not just math.

Imagine that your salesperson worries that he loses sales because he thinks he sounds phony with customers. Wait. Did he tell you something authentic and genuine? Use it. Surprise him by stating, "Your instinctive ability to know how others perceive your messages will help you form genuine relationships." If you surprised him, he now has a new focus with a different and more productive belief.

Unexpected Laughter Is a Two-Edged Sword

Unexpected laughter can carve out a beneficial mindset or cut a devastating wound. It's a delicate tool to wield effectively. Recall the story of Carly Simon's youth from chapter 7. Carly dreaded that her stammer would become an item of ridicule among her peers. During a tender moment, her boyfriend laughed and referred to her stammer as "charming." She credited this rebranding of her stammer as a turning point in her life. Laughter triggered that moment of belief revision.[1]

If you are a teacher and your student feels flustered because she fears she isn't working fast enough, walk up and give an insightful laugh. The student will expect ridicule or condemnation. Surprise her with, "Your eagerness to focus on the details and learn carefully is the sign of a strong learner." Then walk away. Say it like it's an obvious fact. If you surprised her, now working slowly links neurologically with being methodical while focusing on details and learning carefully. At the very least, the comment diminishes the anxiety that inhibited her learning. This same comment also works with employees and your children. Yes, you can use the exact expression. Why reinvent the wheel?

Let's recast this last example into an office scenario. Replace teacher/student with supervisor/worker. If you prefer, you can do parent/child or coach/player.

If you are a supervisor and your worker feels flustered because she fears she isn't working fast enough, walk up and give an insightful laugh. The worker will expect ridicule or condemnation. Surprise her with, "Your eagerness to focus on the details and learn carefully is the sign of a strong learner." Then walk away. Say it like it's an obvious fact. If you surprised her, now working slowly links neurologically with being methodical while focusing on details and learning carefully. At the very least, the comment diminishes the anxiety that inhibited her learning.

Laughter, when unexpected, sparks a surprise response because laughter is such a strong and typically spontaneous emotional reaction. Spontaneity usually signifies an authentic and genuine response, one without social graces or considered political correctness. We almost always remember what follows a laugh because the laughter itself hijacks our attention.

Laughter can wound or engage. Carly Simon's boyfriend didn't laugh because she stammered; he laughed because she had totally misjudged how he perceived it. Inappropriate laughter can be downright abusive when it's used to injure, bully, or exclude. Imagine how Carly would have responded if her boyfriend had laughed *at* her stammer to be mean. In Carly's case, he explained why he laughed. If you don't explain why you laughed, the target of the laughter will assume it is *at* them.

In the following story, when Angela gave an answer in class, her teacher laughed. When he didn't explain why he laughed, Angela immediately assumed that it was *her* that he was laughing at, and she immediately felt anger and embarrassment. As a result, she changed her confident-with-math mindset to one of doubt.

Angela entered senior AP statistics full of confidence and excitement. The teacher had a great reputation but also liked to tease his students. She recalls one fateful day that changed her outlook instantly. She'd worked hard on her calculations and confidently offered her results in class. His response surprised her.

> He laughed. He laughed for a good ten seconds, said nothing about my answer, and then moved on to the next student's answer. I felt humiliated, absolutely mortified. In the span of ten seconds, and with something as simple as a laugh, Mr. H. stole all my confidence. For the rest of the school year, I did not raise my hand once. I never participated unless he directly asked me. My math grade began to drop lower and lower, and I dreaded going to math. Prior to that event, I looked forward to this class, and this teacher, and had a lot of confidence in my mathematical abilities. But Mr. H took all of that away.

Sadly, that moment of unexpected laughter could have easily produced fulfilling and productive results. The laughter surprised her, readying her for instant influence. Imagine how it could have played out differently if, after his ten seconds of laughter, he had stated eloquently, "Wow! I didn't expect that. Your ability to think outside the box shows clever insight." Her confidence and subsequent motivation would most certainly have increased.

I use laughter regularly as a catalyst to trigger the high-suggestibility window of a surprise state. It might be the fastest way to grab someone's attention with a chance to influence that person in a positive way. Imagine that your colleague Carl comes to you, anxious about speaking at an upcoming presentation. You listen to his concerns and then laugh. He looks at you stunned, as he probably expected sympathy, and you say, "Are you kidding me? Your ability to captivate an audience with your detailed delivery keeps everyone engaged." Now he's cued to think about engaging the audience with a detailed delivery. Imagine that you coach a young basketball player who believes he's not good enough to crack the starting lineup. You could comment, "Ha! Your focus on slow and steady improvement shows commendable progress." Now he is cued to think of slow and steady improvement as a gateway to success.

Making a Presumed Deficit an Asset

In a recent workshop for teachers, one participant noted fellow teacher Rafael's ability to multitask. Later in the class, I walked over to Rafael and remarked, "Your ability to multitask will help you create a responsive learning environment." This surprised him. He smiled and gave me a quizzical look, then responded with, "I've always thought of my multitasking as a shortfall. I'd never really thought of it as a strength." Chapter 7 showed how finding the underlying assets of a behavior can produce personal resources. Rafael now thinks he has a valuable tool in his teaching toolbox: the ability to multitask. Rather than avoid it, or feel guilty when catching himself multitasking (negative valence), he will intentionally use it constructively when teaching (positive valence). In Rafael's case, his quizzical look showed the meaning-making process. It is not always visible.

In an anecdote from chapter 7, teenage Samantha was unexpectedly named captain of her swim team. She wondered why she was picked, because she was quiet and reserved; she assessed these qualities as incongruent with leadership. The coach surprised her by naming *the ability to speak with thoughtful reflection* as an essential aspect of leadership.

When she looked back at that pivotal moment, she marveled at how he made these qualities "an asset rather than a negative thing." When you are convinced that an attribute you exhibit produces one set of results, you'll be surprised when someone else, particularly an authority figure with conviction, points out the opposite.

Danna used to believe she was hopeless at math. She even considered that she might have a math phobia. With a history of math failures in the early grades, she subsequently failed several math classes in high school. She laughs when recalling how many of her math teachers became friends because she spent so much time in their rooms after hours, trying to improve and pass. Despite her self-assessed dire ability with math, she still wanted to become an elementary school teacher. She worried though because that would require passing math classes. But most disconcerting for her was the belief that she might pass on her feelings of math anxiety to her future students.

This all changed in a flash while sitting with her math professor during a tutoring appointment. She expressed her concerns to the professor.

> My instructor told me, "The people who struggle the most with math often make the best teachers because they have had to look at the numbers in so many different ways that they end up with all those tools up their sleeve." Since then, math is now one of my favorite subjects to teach. I love that moment when a student finally gets it. When they have been struggling, and my heart struggles right with them, then all of the sudden all the pieces fall into place and it makes sense. It didn't happen overnight, and I am still timid with new math at first, but I now accept the challenge instead of shy away from it.

Her mindset changed because the valence of math changed for her. She now *approaches* math as a growth opportunity that will make her a better teacher rather than *avoiding* math because she struggles. She now feels confident with her ability to help struggling learners. The struggle with math itself, while still ongoing, now signifies success.

Danna's comment, "It didn't happen overnight," reminds us that while mindsets may change instantly at an unconscious level, awareness of the change may evolve slowly, or not at all. Some recognize the change immediately and may refer to it as an epiphany or sudden realization. Others may not notice the mindset shift and subsequent behavior change for a long period of time. This is illustrated quite nicely in Harvard researcher Amy Cuddy's famous TED talk on "Power Posing." As a student, Amy wanted to quit graduate school because she felt she didn't belong. Her advisor vehemently disagreed and told her to "fake it until you make it." In other words, act like you belong. She didn't realize that she actually had "become it" until she experienced an epiphany five years later; she finally recognized that she was no longer *acting* like she belonged.[2]

Your fundamental role as a supervisor, parent, coach, teacher, or healer is to enrich the lives of those with whom you work. We all grow more productive when someone notices our strengths. We also grow when someone notices an inherent strength in what we presumed was a personal weakness. Think of your presumed weaknesses. Your efforts to compensate for them developed into signature strengths. I grew up with a reading disorder. As a result, I have to read slowly, deliberately, and often reread passages. My compensation for a reading disorder generated superior comprehension. What about you?

Sometimes the resource named isn't so much a deficit as a previously undiscovered asset. This, too, may trigger a surprise response and mindset revision. Your child tidies up without being asked, and you note her ability to act responsibly. Your employee asks a lot of questions, and you note his eagerness to thrive in competitive environments. Your athlete laughs at a mistake she made, and you note her eagerness to thrive in tough circumstances. If your comments are surprises, they will trigger dopamine and increased motivation. If they are merely affirmative statements, they still serve to underscore personal strengths.

As a student, Thomas already knew he was skilled in finding and making humor. He rarely took things seriously and often made fun of those who did. One momentous day, his teacher asked him to stay after class. Thomas expected the usual scolding, but she surprised him by telling him he was a natural leader who others looked up to. She then asked him, "Which way are you going to lead people? To bigger and brighter futures or down the wrong path? That's a decision that you'll have to make." From then on, he was much more careful and positive, always trying to make the right decisions, to be a good role model.

Did his teacher create leadership qualities in Thomas or merely underscore them with a comment that changed his mindset? Clearly, his mindset changed, and he began to focus on this *new* tool. His focus, and subsequent determined development, evolved from the teacher's comment. Mrs. O's intentional confrontation surprised Thomas and raised his curiosity. He now linked his skill with humor to an aptitude for leadership.

Similarly, multi-Grammy-winning musician Dave Matthews experienced a mindset shift in his youth. While his perception and belief changed immediately, it was only upon reflection as an adult that he recognized it as a pivotal moment that changed his mindset.

At eight years of age, Dave Matthews felt obsessed with music and sang all the time. A seemingly innocuous comment by his father triggered an idea that he might be able to *do* music rather than just appreciate it. He was sitting at the dining table with his family. He deliberately disrupted the meal by annoying everyone with singing. His father turned to his mother and commented, "Look, he sings so well he can sing off-key." He expected admonishment, but this comment surprised him, filling him with pride. He stopped singing off-key and dinner proceeded, but since then, he thought, "Everything was different: I could sing." In his own words, he started thinking, "Maybe music isn't just something I like. Maybe it's what I am."[3]

Dave was eight at the time of this event. He vividly remembers how that story unfolded. However, cognitive research now shows us that memories are flawed. While the details of the story may not be *exact*, the meaning to Dave remains fixed.

Details of Stories Are Not Important

I think of Erik Vance's book, *Suggestible You: The Curious Science of Your Brain's Ability to Deceive, Transform, and Heal,* when I recall a memorable incident I shared with my wife. One quote, in particular, comes to mind: "The stories we are told—and those we tell ourselves— shape our vision of the world."[4] I should note that my spouse's version is somewhat different, but since I'm the one writing this book, I'll tell you the *real* version. You may have smirked at my description in italics as *real*. Instinctively you know that while people experience similar events, they remember them differently.

Here's what happened. My version: My spouse Laura breaks her wrist while ice skating with our family in Vancouver, British Columbia. We go to the hospital emergency room for repairs. After X-rays, we meet with the physician. I rub Laura's feet gently while she lies on the gurney, grimacing in pain. The doctor confirms that her wrist broke in two places. He asks how it happened. She tells him she was ice skating. He tilts his head toward me and asks her, "Was your son with you when you fell?" I smile. She replies sternly, "That's not my son. That's my husband!" He turns his gaze to me for an appraisal and asks me, "Oh, who cuts your hair?" I smile and my wife angrily replies, "He's too cheap. He cuts his own hair." We all laugh lightly.

It now occurs to me that this might be Laura's first cast. (As a hockey player, I've had many.) I inquire, "Laura, is this your first cast?" She scoffs indignantly, "Yes." The doctor replies, "Me too." Now we're all giggling. He assures us he's formed hundreds in the past. A male nurse arrives to help. He attempts to take off Laura's sweater to get at her wrist. She says, "It's just an old sweater. Cut it off." The male nurse replies, "That's okay. I'm really good at taking people's clothes off without them noticing." Now it's full-on laughter by all of us. This is exactly how I remember it. I believe my version is more accurate because, after all, I was more lucid, unaffected by pain and anxiety.

Laura's version is recognizable as similar to mine, the gist is the same, and she swears hers is the *true* version. We merely disagree about small details. She lets me tell my version at social gatherings because it's funny. The point is this: While we may experience the same event, the versions of it usually differ. Essentially though, in this case, the essence is the same; only the minor details are embellished or hazy.

Some of my colleagues ask about the accuracy of the stories I collect for illustrations in this text. They ask, "Is that anecdote true?" My response is "I don't know, and it doesn't matter." The stories I collect reflect a belief that a person holds, an evolved memory, a perception. What my associates are trying to find out is if the details are precise. Our recollections and memories are complex and dynamic. The form our stories take reflects how we remember events, their meaning to us, and how we express our beliefs. In that sense, they are true; they represent the teller. Are the details accurate? Do they precisely depict, exactly, what the story indicates? Maybe not, because memories are fallible that way. And when it comes to the day of the week, who said what, and the exact string of words, it doesn't matter. What matters is the meaning it holds, the belief it portrays, and the message it conveys.

We think in narrative and explain ourselves to others in story. This is partly why placebos and hypnosis work as well as they do. They tell a story, and if it resonates as true for us, we accept it, along with the accompanying suggestion.

Words and Syntax Matter

I stood in a circle of female acquaintances as they chatted about some topic de jour. At some point, I made a comment. I don't even know what it was, except that one stopped and looked at me intently, drawing the others' attention to me. She looked perplexed, and I wondered if I had said something deemed offensive or stupid. She said, "You're not like other men; you actually listen." The others nodded and then went on immediately with their conversation. That was three decades ago, and I didn't think of that moment until deep into writing this book. That moment bears all the hallmarks of surprise as a formative moment: Her intent look, amid mundane conversation, captivated me, piquing my curiosity, readying me for a powerful pronouncement. The comment surprised me because it was out of context (we weren't talking about listening skills). Since then, I believe I have extraordinary listening skills. (My spouse might disagree.) I don't know if they reach the extraordinary level, but I believe they do and therefore practice them intentionally and paraphrase often. While her comment was not a textbook delivery, it had an effect. This chapter and the next is about the textbook delivery.

Some words and syntax work better than others. Constructing meaningful and powerful linguistic structures requires some scientific knowledge combined with artistic prowess. Over the last three decades, I've composed and honed a powerful language construction, Cause-Effect-Resource Statements (CERSs), described in chapter 7. This organization works well because it ratifies a compelling story, gives an explanation of events, and enlists a potent personal resource. This next section examines the composition and delivery of a CERS in greater depth.

At first blush, the structured comments I propose may seem like simple affirmative remarks. And without a surprise, they would prob-ably be just that. Praise produces feelings of comfort, satisfaction, and excitement; it feels nice. To be clear, encouraging statements on their own have merit, but that is not the point of this book. Delivered as a surprise, or during a surprise, they become game changers. Neuro-logically, declarations delivered during a surprise come with phasic dopamine, a motivation to keep doing whatever was noted, and the potential to spark a new belief.

Persuasion

Before I jump into the construction of a CERS, let's examine the cur-rent literature on persuasion. After World War II, people began asking, "How could people participate in genocide?" Research on *persuasion* evolved as the central focus of psychology. By the early seventies, this collective body of investigations was a mess. Much of this research caused confusion and often showed conflicting results. In one situation a study might show one effect, while in another, it might indicate no effect or even an opposite effect. It was all just a jumble of findings with no conceptual coherence or underlying principles.

The assumption at the time came from the idea that the effective-ness of a persuasive message hinged on how well the target of the message, the receiver, learned what that message said. But as we now recognize, learning the message has little to do with being persuaded by it. We enjoy a wealth of nutrition information but still suffer from an obesity crisis. We can quote the importance of exercise or the danger of sweets, but simply *knowing* doesn't change our behavior. Persuasion is not just knowing.

In 1986, Richard Petty and John Cacioppo developed what remains one of psychology's most robust theories for explaining how and why some messages change people's minds and some don't. What makes some stick, while others fade in influence over time. It's called the *Elaboration Likelihood Model*. It changed the course of how psychologists understand persuasion.[5]

We now know that more effective persuasion includes an *elaboration* component. Elaboration means that the message triggers a high degree of cognition by the receiver. More simply stated, the message makes the receiver think. Anthony Greenwald first proposed this idea in 1968, calling it the Cognitive Response Model.[6] He claimed that the persuasiveness of the communication lies in the *self-talk* of a communication, rather than the content itself. Think of self-talk as analogous to the *thinking* feature of cognitive elaboration. In essence, if a communication makes us think, we are more apt to accept it. Why?

When thinking, we engage in the meaning of a communication. This engagement differs markedly from arguing. Arguments look like thinking, but they are mostly automatic responses. In arguments, we already have a point of view, a vested position to defend and express. Arguments focus on winning, not learning. The thinking that drives persuasion is the pondering kind: What can I learn from this? When triggered effectively, elaboration prompts pondering, not defensive posturing.

A teacher I worked with wrote about an incident that occurred when she was in high school. As you read this illustration, note how the teacher's comment triggered elaborative thinking.

> I had a teacher my freshman year of high school who made a point of getting to know her students very well. At the end of the first term, she led a ceremony where she addressed each student and told them one quality that she really admired about them. Each quality was unique and not applied to more than one person. As she went through the class and said each person's quality, I found myself agreeing with her. She had identified the best qualities in everyone. When she came to me, she told me she admired my compassion. What? I had never seen myself this way before. I was actually a little disappointed that she chose compassion. It felt like she had made an effort to get to know everyone but me. For the next few days, I thought about that word a lot. I began to see ways it applied to me, and I began to look for it in other people. I will always remember this teacher because she changed the way I see myself and the way I see those around me. Compassion is now a quality that I look for in people and try to recognize in my students.

An unexpected comment, a surprise, instinctively triggers the elaboration process and increases the persuasiveness of a comment. The results of Elaboration Likelihood research show that messages received this way tend to be relatively enduring, resistant, and predictive of behavior. Add the surprise factor, and you exponentially increase the likelihood of creating a formative moment.

Note: Not all formative moments trigger cognitive elaboration. Some occur with no conscious thought at all. In these cases, the formative event happens so fast that it doesn't register. I discuss the research on persuasion for two reasons. First, to illustrate how and why I created the CERS: to maximize the effect of a persuasive comment. The second reason is to illustrate the cognitive process that takes place during a CERS whether consciously or unconsciously.

Because humans are *cognitive misers*, looking to reduce mental effort, messages are most persuasive when they are short, precise, and relevant. A CERS meets these important criteria. They are one-sentence long (short), link one cause to one effect (precise), and proclaim the receiver's resourcefulness (relevant). The Elaboration Likelihood model also stresses the importance of *motivation* and *ability* as the most influential factors.

Think of motivation as the desire to process the message. This relates directly to relevance. Does this information affect me? For example, a statement directed to an avid hunter that links a vegan lifestyle to healthy living will likely lack motivation. Conversely, a comment directed to a budding writer that links attention to detail with higher readability is prone to yield greater motivation. We are all drawn to comments that bear applicability to our lives.

Ability refers to the availability of cognitive resources and the capacity to focus without distraction. That pretty much describes what a surprise initiates. During an intense surprise, the brain rallies our cognitive resources to focus exclusively on the cause of the surprise, make meaning of it, then construct an appropriate new belief.

Summary

I started this chapter by stressing that not all strategic interventions yield productive results, but the use of the methods discussed in this chapter improve the likelihood of beneficial effects exponentially. Generally, doing the opposite of what someone expects often triggers a surprise. This chapter then noted some specific strategies. Acting surprised and its inverse, not being impressed when it is expected, both trigger a surprise response. The unexpected laugh also triggers a surprise response. Laughter indicates an authentically charged emotional response. When it is unexpected, or expected and not present, the result bewilders the recipient, begging for an answer to this surprising incident. The most effective and instantly workable method to trigger a positive surprise moment takes place when you reframe what someone views as a weakness is actually an asset. I finished the chapter with a review of the literature on persuasion.

In the next chapter, you'll see how the CERS method embeds each of the essential elements of persuasion.

CHAPTER NINE

~

Shaping Understanding

While writing on my computer the other day, music suddenly started to play somewhere. The abrupt melody surprised me, diverted my attention, and triggered my curiosity, *Where is that coming from? I need to stop it to get back to work undisturbed.* The shift in attention and triggered curiosity happened automatically, without any volition, and I couldn't have stopped it. I needed to make meaning of this disruptive event. Here's what happened cognitively. I focused intently on listening for the origin of the sound. *Is it a neighbor's loud music, my spouse playing piano in another room? Why is she doing that? She knows I'm writing. Or is the radio in front of me broken, and it inadvertently turned itself on? Where is that coming from?* Within a few seconds, I figured out that I'd left open a tab in my browser where an advertisement had started to play. I closed the tab, wrote these thoughts, and got back to my other work.

This unexpected event captured my attention instantly and triggered an instinctive eagerness to solve the mystery. The next time I hear unexpected music while writing, what do you think I'll examine first? You're right; my mind is now predisposed to check my browser. Once we form a conclusion (the opened tab caused the music), subsequent mysterious music will instinctively prompt me to check my tabs first. My music computer story illustrates an example of something that occurs regularly but rarely makes it to conscious processing: A success predisposes us to instinctively attempt the same solution in subsequent trials. It's easy to see how this dynamic plays out in the world of objective and concrete cause-effect circumstances such as mysterious music and open tabs on a computer. The same dynamic also plays out in the subjective realm, but it's not so visible, and the links may not be detectible.

You step into an empty room and a chime rings. *Hmm?* You step outside and reenter to see if it was a coincidence or a motion detector. It happened again . . . then again. Aha. It must be some detector. In the concrete world that we experience with our senses, we can check our hypothesis and then form a belief. That's our instinctive positive test strategy at work: We make a hypothesis (there is a motion detector present) then attempt to affirm it. In our subjective world, the positive test strategy is confirmation bias. When someone surprises you with a comment about your self-concept (e.g., your unique way of seeing things helps you come up with creative ideas), you can't immediately test it. Here's what happens instead. Your mind instinctively searches your memory bank for evidence and undoubtedly finds several examples. Comment affirmed.

You tell your friend, "The way you play music so effortlessly means you have an ear for learning languages." This unexpected observation surprises her, elicits her attention, and she instinctively tries to make meaning of it. Since the link between abstract concepts such as an *ear for music* and *learning languages* is not nearly as easy to confirm or dispute as those in the concrete world of mysterious music sounds, she accepts the remark because it seems genuine, praises her, and she has no reason to dismiss it. Just as my mind is now oriented to look for mysterious music erupting from my computer, her mind instinctively looks for evidence that her natural proficiency with languages is also true. Now when she hears a foreign expression, her mind orients toward listening receptively. After all, she has *an ear for learning languages*.

The instinctive cognitive processes described above happen all day long, and we rarely take notice unless one stirs a strong emotional response or generates a prolonged search for the answer (or in my case, because I'm writing about it). Once we have an explanation (belief), that explanation drives similar events in the future. This is what happens with a CERS. Let's spend a moment reviewing this important concept.

Cause-Effect-Resource Statements: Crafting Experience

Imagine that your director of software design tells you, "Your willingness to fail with such gusto makes you a productive employee." Your willingness to fail with such gusto (the cause) makes you a productive employee (the effect), which is resourceful. This comment surprises you because you were unaware you were *failing with such gusto.* You don't question the link between *failing with gusto* leading to *working productively* because you have no basis to dispute it. The cognitive act of making sense of this abstract statement induces a tacit acceptance of its meaning. Once a behavior is labeled, it now has value. You'll also accept it because it was stated as an observation with objective truth, similar to "You are wearing a blue shirt."

Important point: Your goal is to state a declarative statement, not praise. Praise can sound phony or manipulative: "My, but you're such a hard worker." Declarative statements give the feel of conviction; just the cold, hard facts. I developed and refined these structures through two decades of practical application.

With Cause-Effect-Resource Statements, you literally construct experience. This example of a CERS attempts to move the valence of failure from avoid at all costs, to accept and learn. If it does, you now get a little rush of dopamine, the motivator neurotransmitter, every time you fail. This makes you more determined shortly after a failure. Last, the remark compliments you by noting a strength. So, you accept the obvious truth and say, "Thank you." (I understand that failure is vastly more complicated than I portray in this illustration. Failing to stop at a red light differs significantly from failing while preparing a new dish. It's the latter I'm referring to here.)

It's also important to note in the prior example that I could have replaced "a productive worker" with "an innovative thinker" or "a powerful optimist." Like Google searches, you can link almost anything. Sadly, negative links may produce grave effects. What if someone had said, "Your willingness to fail so energetically makes you slow to understand complex ideas"? If you accept such a statement, you'll feel discouraged when you inevitably face complex ideas. Juxtapose that with "Your willingness to fail so energetically makes you *quick* to understand complex ideas." Now you'll feel encouraged (positive valence) when facing those complex ideas.

Would such a comment surprise you? It doesn't matter. While we may witness some typical stereotyped signals of surprise—eyes widened, mouth agape, wrinkled forehead—we may not. It's also important to note that these cultural signals of surprise vary dramatically or may not even be present. CERSs work because of their linguistic structure, but they work much more emphatically during a surprise. Just as I'm now prone to check my computer tabs when I hear sudden music erupt while working, you may also find yourself predisposed to link failure to learning. All this takes place automatically and typically outside your awareness, until now. Now that you know how these kinds of statements influence cognition and behavior, you are empowered to deliberately accept the ones you like and reject the ones you don't.

Constructing CERSs

Some readers may wonder, "What ethical or moral right do we have to influence each other intentionally in this manner?" We should always question our moral and ethical intentions. My intention for triggering surprise and using CERSs strategically is to enlist a person's strengths and resourcefulness so that they may build a personal toolbox to challenge their struggles and build a path to success and happiness. My goal is the broad development of growth and human potential for all.

Are CERSs important or can any simple affirmative comment work? Consider the following illustration. Employee Mitch sends a memo to his supervisor, Serge. It offers a time-saving suggestion. Supervisor Serge responds to Mitch, "Wow! Great idea." Mitch gets a surge of dopamine from this pleasant response, but we don't know the meaning he makes. Does it mean, *The boss likes me*, or *I have good ideas*, or *The boss is lazy and an easy way to get on his good side is to appeal to his slothfulness*, or some other notion? Instead, imagine that Supervisor Serge had made a more targeted reply, "Wow! Your ability to simplify complex issues into workable solutions shows creative intelligence." Now we know what meaning Mitch will make from this exchange. He has creative intelligence and an ability to simplify complex issues. The first comment feels nice. The second, more targeted comment fosters growth and a productive mindset. Yes, language matters.

The literal construction of a CERS is straightforward. You observe a behavior and link it to a probable effect that underscores a resourceful strength for the receiver. For instance, you see a colleague working hard (cause) on a proposal. You decide that this hard work links nicely to a thorough (effect) proposal. That's it. You've linked hard work to thorough results. This is scarcely groundbreaking. But what if you see your colleague sitting and thinking, and you know the upcoming proposal lingers? This time you creatively name the cause, "focusing on details," and link this to an effect, "creative approach." You state with conviction, "Your thoughtful focus on the details helps you produce a creative approach." You've identified your colleague as a detail-oriented and imaginative worker; that's a nice resource. Now your colleague is prone to focus on detail and think imaginatively. Fruitfully determining what to name as the cause, and then the effect, requires some artistry. Here are the three steps:

1. Identify a skill, ability, or potential that lies inherent in the information you gathered (e.g., sitting quietly means "focusing on details").
2. Determine a positive outcome (e.g., "imaginative worker").
3. Link them together with a strong verb (e.g., "Your thoughtful focus on the details *helps* you produce a creative approach").

Let's reverse the cause and effect segments of that statement: "Your imaginative approach helps you focus on the important details." This assertion also works for the same reasons: Making sense of it invests you in accepting it, it's hard to refute, and it seems genuinely complimentary. At this point, you may be wondering if you can say almost anything regarding a person's perceived behavior. The answer is yes, as long as the statement is relevant to the receiver, you phrase the statement in the CERS form, and you don't claim anything obviously refutable. Let's revert to the concrete realm for an example.

If you comment on someone's red shirt, that person will notice the red shirt. If you comment on the blue pants, that person will notice the blue pants. If you comment on how the red shirt makes the blue pants appear more vibrant, that person will look for evidence of that too. The point of a CERS is to get the receiver to notice a personal resource that actively works toward an imminent goal while emphasizing that the receiver is already performing it successfully. If your CERS creates a surprise, or takes hold during a surprise, it contains all the cognitive and neurological machinery to make an indelible mark, a blossoming self-affirming belief. That's a formative moment.

When creating a CERS, make sure to frame the statements as positive constructions—what to do, rather than what not to do. It's easier to understand and respond to the comment "Clear your mind" rather than "Don't think." To which are you more receptive: "listen carefully" or "stop interrupting"?

Your belief system determines what you look for and notice. What one sees as a stumbling block, another sees as a developmental opportunity. What one experiences as an insurmountable obstacle, another might experience as a definitive challenge. One person may perceive a high degree of difficulty as discouraging, while another person may perceive a high degree of difficulty as challenging. What you believe about your world, how you fit into it, and your abilities determine your approach.

Consider the humorous story of the little boy overheard talking to himself as he practiced his baseball swing. "I am the greatest batter in the world," he would say proudly while throwing the ball in the air. Time after time he swung and missed with the bat, all the time repeating his claim, "I'm the greatest batter in the world." After countless missed swings he appeared frustrated, paused, then smiled as he proclaimed, "Wow! What a great pitcher!" He found a way to constructively name a personal resource to build upon.

This cute example illustrates the inventiveness of seeing potential strengths and resourcefulness. If you expect to see emerging potential in others, a belief, you'll always find it because you instinctively look for it and feel rewarded when you notice it. All behavior, whether for good or for bad, contains functional elements. Even the dastardly criminal has a resourceful skill set. Elements of that particular skill set, like crafty planning, are what may help lead that person to eventually produce beneficial behavior too.

When you deliver a CERS, you make a presumptive leap. The statement, "Your careful attention to detail makes you an effective leader" only states what is plausible and that, if used that way, it can be resourceful. Presumptions (beliefs that are accepted as true based on probability) such as this elicit a degree of faith and often pass unchallenged because of their irrefutable nature and complimentary tone. The notion to consciously challenge a presumptive statement diminishes because the underlying assumption is never really stated directly. The same content, stated declaratively, such as "Effective leaders pay careful attention to detail" may elicit debate.

Presumptive comments generate responses because of their implicit meanings. They elicit expectations that orient the person's mental framework and behavior toward fulfilling those very expectations. One of my graduate teachers relayed the following story that illustrates an unintentional emphasis from a Cause-Effect-Resource Statement given to a thirteen-year-old boy. Young Terence works very hard but only receives average grades and then feels discouraged. The teacher thought she'd give him a CERS:

> Upon receiving a grade on a recent paper, Terence showed a sad look on his face, put his head on his desk, and let out a sigh. I walked over to him and said, "Your ability to stay in control when upset will help you when you're facing difficult times in college." He responded with, "You think I'm going to college?" Which, by the way, was not what I was thinking he'd pick up on, and I said, "Why wouldn't you? That's where all the hard workers go." He has been much more upbeat lately, and he doesn't sigh anymore when I return his assignments.

This teacher effectively changed the valence of Terence's efforts. Now, Terence's assignment results indicate progress along a rocky road toward college, rather than a reminder that he faces insurmountable challenges.

We make presumptive judgments all the time, yet they remain mostly unspoken. When you see a fellow worker show up late repeatedly, you might think to yourself that this person is careless: presumption. This person might be a single parent juggling the driving of children to school or dropping them off at daycare. If your supervisor shows frustration when you ask him to repeat an explanation, you might *presume* he thinks you're not very intelligent. He might feel frustrated at himself for a *presumed* inability to explain ideas clearly. Since we make presumptions instinctively, why not use them as opportunities to foster strengths?

Before you continue to read this next section, let me remind you that while my lab for teaching and examining CERSs is practicing teachers, the strategies noted in these examples also work outside the classroom. I focus on teachers because they have an immense opportunity to deliver CERSs. They work with the same people on a regular basis, are interested in creating and noticing resources in their population, are trained observers of behavior, and show a willingness to discuss their results.

CERS Samples

I remember shopping for a new belt when I was in my late twenties. I had a waist size of thirty-one inches. I thought I should buy a belt with a range of thirty-one to thirty-four because I was nearing middle age and middle-aged men usually put on weight. On my way to the cashier, I thought, *This is crazy. I don't have to surrender to the middle-age bulge.* I returned that belt, purchased one my current size, began regular exercise, and several decades later, I still have the same waist size. I didn't show any telltale signs of a belief change, or mindset shift, but it still occurred instantly. While this wasn't a CERS, the story illustrates the difficulty of noticing a belief change. I'm sure that those who knew me at the time in my life noticed nothing different. I didn't notice much different about myself either, but for that one small belief change. It is only upon reflection, many years later, that I recognize that moment as pivotal.

The examples I use to illustrate various aspects of CERSs all show visible results. I chose them for that reason. I designed CERS to maximize their effects; however, like any approach, they are not always effective. Another reason you may not see immediate effects with your attempts is that although the belief change occurs instantly, subsequent results may emerge slowly, and the outcomes may occur years later. If a person's belief in their ability shifts from "I'll never amount to anything" to "I can do anything if I work hard enough," it may not become apparent for several years, or maybe at all. The person who holds the belief "I'll never amount to anything" will feel devastated with failure and avoid trying new challenges. The person who holds the belief "I can do anything if I work hard enough" still finds failure disappointing but will recover faster and move forward more ambitiously. Beliefs shift perception, and with the corresponding shift in perception, the experience changes. Beliefs evolve out of our experiences, and a shift in beliefs may not always come with telltale signs.

Brian, a student in my graduate counseling class, taught a body mechanics class in a massage program at a local college. He told me about one student who constantly talked during the class, pulling other students' attention from the lessons and generally disrupting the process. He wanted to intervene but was unsure of how to proceed. I asked him what he wanted from this student. He said, "I'd like her to engage and fully participate in class." I suggested linking her engagement to group participation. I recommended further that he deliver the comment in an offhand, matter-of-fact manner and in front of the entire group. He crafted a CERS, and during the next session, he found an opportunity during a group activity. Brian explains,

> I said, "The way you engage the class really draws in the participation of the entire group." I dropped it off in a completely matter-of-fact tone and immediately went on with the rest of the lesson. Immediately, this student deepened her class participation. Subsequently, she has been one of the most attentive students and seems almost upset when other classmates joke or otherwise attempt to derail the lesson. I've had a couple of chances to reinforce this student's behavior, and, so far, things are going great.

Brian's story illustrates the planning he undertook to compose a Cause-Effect-Resource Statement that felt natural to him. While CERSs may sound natural to the listener, most of us don't usually deliver comments in this fashion. They may seem awkward at first, as it did with Brian, but the more times you deliver such statements, the more naturally they flow like a regular conversation. Note also the importance of commenting in a matter-of-fact tone. Describing something as if it is an obvious truth makes it sound more convincing. Noting something in someone that others have missed also makes you appear astute. Comments from astute observers prompt curiosity, which in turn increases receptivity. An astute observer, noticing something complimentary, also boosts rapport, which increases receptivity even further.

The Pygmalion effect, whereby higher expectations lead to increased results, also arises when you deliver a CERS. Once conveyed, the deliverer invests in seeing the expected results and then reinforcing them through acknowledgment. We all succumb to confirmation bias. If we believe our CERS is effective, we instinctively look for evidence to support our beliefs. As discussed in the early chapters, we tend to look for and find that which confirms our beliefs. Psychologists call this the "Positive Test Strategy," an instinctive preference to search for verification rather than negation. In deciding whether a possibility is correct, we typically look for hits rather than misses, for confirmation of the idea rather than disconfirmation.

In Brian's case, he is now vested in seeing positive results from his CERS so that he can reinforce them. He is prone to see what he expects to see: confirmation bias. Reinforcing them cements them. From the student's perspective, she now behaves as *if her engagement draws others in to participate.* She, too, is prone to see the results of her new perspective through confirmation bias.

We see this form of confirmation bias play out clearly in the following example provided by a different teacher in an elementary classroom:

> A young girl asked me to check one of her answers on a worksheet. Her answer was good, but I wanted her to use a few more details. I then said, "Your ability to pay close attention to detail makes you a great writer." She didn't respond to what I said, but I noticed that for the rest of her answers on her worksheet she used a few more details than usual.

The teacher didn't request more details. If she had, the increased amount of detail would indicate a simple response to a simple request. The clever teacher merely noted a link between the student's *apparent* attention to detail and the student being a great writer. *Important note:* Recall that the initial reason for the teacher's comment was a lack of detail in the student's writing. Here, the increased amount of detail— that wasn't present at the outset—likely appeared because she accepted the comment that she was *a good writer* and that's what good writers do.

Upon analysis, the Cause-Effect-Resource Statement appears to have worked. When you label a behavior, it becomes evident. Now that it's evident, it is noticed and reinforced. Labeling a distinctive behavior as a signifier of growth orients the person toward that goal.

In his absorbing new book, *The Catalyst: How to Change Anyone's Mind*, Jonah Berger examines persuasion from a new angle. He itemizes the natural resistances we have to persuasion and suggests that we are more effective when we diminish these resistances rather than try to overcome them. He writes, "Rather than using more energy, it's easier to reduce barriers. That's a catalyst." He listed these natural resistances in a clever acronym: REDUCE.

- Reactance: When you push someone, they push back.
- Endowment: Folks feel attached to what they already have.
- Distance: There's only so far people are willing to travel from their comfort zone.
- Uncertainty: If people have doubts, it's hard to get them to accept something new.
- Corroborating Evidence: People need to hear it from more than one source.[1]

My CERS model stacks up quite well with Berger's findings. Let's examine the example from the previous anecdote: "Your ability to pay close attention to detail makes you a great writer."

This CERS implied that the receiver already exhibited the attribute in question or already exhibited the personal resources to demonstrate it. The student was not paying close attention to detail at the time, but the Cause in the CERS implied she was. Stating something is already present bypasses Reactance (no pushback) and indicates Endowment (I already have this). This CERS also removed the Distance needed to change. No distance exists; it's already present. Uncertainty disappears because it's not new; it's already present. And of course, the Corroborating Evidence is our old friend confirmation bias. The instinct for finding evidence in your memory bank that this statement is true confirms its accuracy. Who among us could argue effectively against the statement, "Your ability to pay close attention to detail makes you a great writer."

The Future Is Present

Behavioral scientists tell us that the best way to make a person's response persist is to arrange for the individual to commit to that behavior. Effective commitments reach into the future by incorporating behaviors that affect one's identity. A powerful aspect of a CERS is that it implicitly suggests that the commitment is already actively being undertaken. The Cause in the CERS indicates just that. This manipulated self-perception makes it appear like the future is already present.

Creative influencers use noticeable behaviors to find something beneficial in what they observe and then link them to personal resources. Laura observed a student crying about an impending failure and turned it into a potential benefit. When she announced that it was time to take the weekly quiz, one student put his head down and started crying. She quietly asked if it was about the quiz, and the boy replied that it was.

> I told him, "I see you really care about your education. *Someone who cares about their education as much as you do will end up being a very successful businessman.*" He almost immediately stopped crying and worked diligently on his quiz.

She saw sadness, labeled it as a zest for learning, then linked it creatively to imminent success in business. The student's sudden and unexpected response showed that the statement made an impression on him. Now, rather than feeling defeated with math, he sees business success in his future and feels a zest for learning. Regardless of the test results, he is now predisposed to perceive them as a struggle on the path to success rather than an insurmountable challenge. When you surprise someone with a pleasant CERS, that comment becomes encoded with a burst of dopamine that signals, "Do that again!"

Common Oversights When Delivering a CERS

In this section, I presented artful examples for delivering a CERS. While it may look deceptively easy, the nuances are critically important. Accordingly, I've added this segment to illustrate common oversights: simply praising without a surprise, waiting to *catch* someone exhibiting behavior you wish to reinforce, explaining the meaning of your comment, or trying to *sell* the comment. While I refer to these as oversights, it's important to note that they are only slips in that they don't deliver the maximum effect. These missteps, although not as effective as they can be, are still, at the very minimum, positive.

Commenting about someone thinking creatively, while that person is thinking creatively, may be praiseworthy, but it won't be surprising. But if you see your colleague or student showing signs of concentration, you might say, "Your ability to think deeply helps you come up with creative solutions." That comment might be surprising and may even spur a confident approach to divergent thinking.

Waiting to catch someone exhibiting some form of leadership skill so that you can reinforce it may keep you waiting a long time. Even if it happens in some form, your comment will be simple praise, not a surprise. It's better to select an already present aspect of that person's behavior and then artfully relate it to leadership skills *as if* those skills are already present: "Your ability to work thoroughly makes you a strong leader." Now you can give a leadership task. "Please help me get us started with this next project."

While explaining the meaning of your CERS may sound instinctively appropriate, a critical part of the CERS effectiveness is that it requires receivers to make their own meaning. Their own *meaning-making* is an implicit cognitive act of affirming the statement, *making their own truth*.

You want the receiver of a CERS to use the process of elaboration to entrench the statement. Imagine that you're sitting in an auditorium, listening to an interesting TED talk. As the engaging speaker presents new information and novel insights, you digest the information like you devour a chocolate chip cookie. You fulfill your role as a passive receiver of information. Later that day, a friend asks you to talk about your experience. Now, even though you report about the same information you heard, you're not a passive receiver anymore. An important nuance takes place. When asked to describe our understanding, we move from passive receivers to active producers of information.

As active producers, we construct what influenced us. What influenced us is based upon our personal history, preferences, reasons for attending, and availability bias (what is top of mind). We remember what was significant to us and ignore or miss that which is irrelevant. In essence, we construct our version of the message with our built-in embellishments, interpretations, and emphasis of those parts we found engaging. We synthesized our experience. This process of active production invests us in our blend of ideas. We construct a personal meaning. We believe what we report, even if it's not what the TED talk presented.

Asking someone to explain, examine, or give an example is literally a request for elaboration. After you give a CERS, ask the receiver for an illustration. If they can't, say, "I don't know how you do it either." Let them figure it out. Then they own it. This underscores the importance of asking a pointed question after delivering a CERS. The question stimulates the cognitive response of elaboration, entrenching the thought into a belief. For example, you see someone who generally lacks confidence, pausing in a conversation. You say, "Your ability to let your mind make connections helps you form interesting responses. How do you do it?" or "When else do you do it?" If the receiver can't explain or come up with examples, it's best to give a shrug and say. "It's something you do well," or "I don't know how you do it. You just do it." It's hard to dispute such a display of pronounced confidence. You've left them with a mystery, and their instinctive positive test mechanism will eventually affirm it.

Here's how Melissa's high-school Spanish teacher avoided explaining while implicitly encouraging elaboration.

> Melissa is a student with a fairly low language level. She experiences difficulty in Spanish class because she understands so little of it. One day, while helping her with some deskwork, she said she couldn't do it because she was stupid. I briefly mentioned that she wasn't supposed to be getting it all because it is a Spanish 1 class. I wanted to give her a little more of a push so I added, "I can tell you're very courageous by the way you show up and try every day. That's really going to help you." She was a little surprised and tried to explain how I was wrong, but I just redirected her back to her work and walked away.

We can see that the message makes its mark. It surprised Melissa to the point that she instantly disputed it. The teacher's conviction—it's the obvious truth—with an unwillingness to explain it triggers elaboration. Now Melissa has to make sense of the remark on her own. She may not accept it. Only time will tell if the comment spurred a perseverance mindset. We don't always get to see the fruits of our work.

Attention Matters, a Lot

While you're reading this book, take a moment and notice the sounds around you, the smell of the room, the type of font you see on this page, the feel of the clothes on your skin, the ambient temperature around you. That's just your immediate surroundings. Our brain is a highly efficient organ, but there is simply far too much going on in the environment to process, even when merely reading a book. Evolution solved this overload problem by developing an attention system so we wouldn't get overwhelmed by all the sensory data around us.

Attention allows us to notice, select, and direct the brain's resources. Attention researcher and neuroscientist Amishi Jha puts it like this, "Attention is the leader of the brain. Wherever attention goes, the brain follows."[2] CERSs work smoothly because the factor most likely to capture a person's attention in any given situation is not the one that offers the most accurate or useful guidance; instead, it is the one that is elevated in attention at the moment. A CERS seizes attention in the moment.

For some, this CERS mechanism may appear somewhat overstated. Do such links and attention to detailed language make much of a difference? Yes! A study done in a U.S. hospital by Adam Grant and David Hofmann noted that even though handwashing is strongly recommended before each patient examination, most physicians wash their hands less than half as often as the guidelines prescribe. Not only that, various interventions aimed at reducing the problem proved ineffective. This puts both doctors and patients at greater risk of infection. Grant and Hofmann applied two different approaches to solve the problem. One approach focused on *concern for the patients* while the other emphasized *concern for the physicians themselves*.[3]

The researchers placed signs above the examination room gel dispensers. For the *concern for themselves* application the sign read, "Hand hygiene protects you from catching diseases." For the *concern for their patients* application the sign read, "Hand hygiene protects patients from catching diseases." The sign that reminded the doctors to protect themselves had no effect on soap and gel use. But the sign reminding them to protect their patients increased handwashing by 45 percent. The researchers concluded that the intervention worked because the sign unconsciously connected their behavior to a deep concern for patient welfare. I review this study here to illustrate that *links* are powerful tools that connect ideas below conscious awareness. This is one reason that a CERS works so effectively.

Life After CERS

Seeing someone flourish as the result of a well-placed CERS feels immensely gratifying. Hopefully, the strategic use of CERSs initiates a self-fulfilling cycle of belief: belief change—notice affirming evidence—strengthen belief—further notice of more affirmations. When possible, the CERS agent should also acknowledge the positive results. A key to acknowledging positive results is to take whatever you see as evidence of success. I once treated a young boy who regularly wet his bed. After nearly two weeks of dry sleeps he woke up to a small bedwetting event. He sadly described the disappointing news to me, worried that his bedwetting would return. I cheered. My response surprised him. He expected sympathy, but I enthusiastically told him that the occasional setback signifies success. He smiled broadly. Now, he ignores the occasional wet episode. He learned that success is viewing slipups as information, not failure. (See "Working with What You Get" in chapter 7.)

If your employee feels inefficient, you can point out the inefficiencies, and you'll both focus on them, and they will likely increase due to your now-shared hypervigilance. Or you can look for, and creatively find, episodes of efficiency upon which to build. You both want the same thing, and you can be the creator of a more productive attentiveness. Now you're both productive.

We don't always get to witness only positive and productive comments delivered to our coworkers, students, children, or others. While we may now understand how CERSs and surprise work to strategically create positive moments of growth and empowerment, what do you do if you observe a destructive CERS? As we now know, beliefs take hold instantly, often without any agency, and negative ones need to be corrected immediately. This next chapter teaches the reader effective methods to counter negative influence events and diminish the effects they have on the receiver.

Summary

This chapter illustrated the linguistic construction of powerful influence statements named Cause-Effect-Resource Statements (CERS). We learned how they work and then how to construct them. While they are powerful tools, they may not always yield immediate results. I also provided several examples to illustrate how a CERS shifts perception, triggers the Pygmalion effect, and builds rapport.

We looked at several common mistakes for delivering a CERS that dilute its effectiveness. I emphasized the most common mistake is to explain the meaning of a CERS because this interferes with the elaboration process. This chapter finished by noting that while delivering a CERS feels empowering, we don't always get to see the fruits of our efforts.

CHAPTER TEN

~

Preventing Negative Events

We know how to trigger surprise events and linguistically structure our comments to produce powerfully beneficial effects. This chapter focuses on effective methods to undo negative events once they've already unfolded. You will also learn how you can recognize potentially negative events and deal with them immediately before negative mindsets evolve and confirm themselves.

Shifting the Valence

The conventional treatment for exam anxiety or a fear of public speaking is relaxation management. Harvard researcher Alison Wood Brooks took a more novel approach. She sees both anxiety and excitement as high-arousal emotions, but anxiety is negative, and excitement is positive. In her research, she put participants into stressful situations, such as singing competitions, public math exams, and debates. She instructed them to say either, "I am anxious," or "I am excited." When they said, "I am excited," and they relabeled the high emotional arousal from negative to positive, they overcame it and performed significantly better. They harnessed the high-arousal part and got rid of the negative valence. Brooks discovered that it was easier to change the valence from negative (avoid) to positive (approach) than it was to change their level of arousal.[1]

Numerous similar studies looked at performance on math tests such as the GRE and found that students achieve higher scores when they recategorize anxiety as merely a sign that the body is coping. The U.S. Marine Corps has a motto that embodies this principle: "Pain is weakness leaving your body." In the following story, Kristen notes how her intense fear of speaking transformed after surprising comments from professors. She still feels the arousal, but she now labels it as excitement. She credits the surprising comments from her professors as valence-changers.

> Public speaking had been a big fear of mine growing up. I barely made it through Speech class in high school and hated to get in front of the class. In my sophomore year of college, I had three classes that required oral presentations, and all the presentations fell in the same week. I was extremely nervous and anxious about the entire week. All three of my presentations went well, and I remember that one professor told me I appeared poised as I presented. I received similar feedback from another professor. This feedback was very surprising to me because this was not how I saw myself at all. Since then, I developed a love for public speaking. It is one of my favorite things to do. I have a completely different view of myself in this way, and that has made me more confident.

In *How Emotions Are Made*, groundbreaking researcher Lisa Feldman Barrett shows how emotions are felt, but not understood until they are labeled and described. She describes an emotion as the brain's creation of what your bodily sensations mean in relation to what is going on around you in the world. Your brain makes meaning of a sensation. In other words, if someone identifies and labels your response during a surprise, it may determine the valence. To illustrate this phenomenon, she describes a humorous experience she had while dating. A fellow researcher in a lab where she worked wanted to date her, but she didn't feel attracted to him. Eventually, she agreed to go for coffee. During the coffee date, she experienced stirrings and found herself wondering if she indeed felt attracted to him. Accordingly, she agreed to date him again. She then went home and vomited with the flu and remained in bed for three days. She says she had misattributed her jittery feeling as attraction, when in fact she had been experiencing the early symptoms of a flu virus.[2]

We can leverage our brain's meaning-making disposition to effectively transform potentially negative events right as they unfold. In chapter 1, I described a scenario whereby first-grade student Samuel experienced frustration while working on math problems. I described two possible comments typical teachers might make. Comment A: "Goodness, Samuel. You sure struggle with math." Comment B: "Goodness, Samuel. Your willingness to stick with tough problems makes you a strong student." The first comment identifies his experience and labels his frustration as "weak at math." The second also identifies his emotional state but labels it as signifying a "strong learner." As Lisa Feldman Barrett shows, *how we experience an emotion is not understood until it is labeled and described.* With the second statement, Samuel will now experience a little boost of the motivator neurotransmitter dopamine whenever he struggles with math. Here's how. As a reward-predictor neurotransmitter, dopamine now prompts Samuel to keep working after a struggle to maintain the proud attribute "strong learner." Statements such as these spark belief formations.

What to Do When You Witness a Negative Event

Once we form a belief, our entire arsenal of belief-protection armament jumps on that bandwagon. Prior chapters explained that once we form a new belief, we see the world through this new belief filter, instinctively look fervently for evidence to support it, dismiss or diminish evidence that contradicts it, and operate as if this belief were present all along.

The example below illustrates how beliefs become robust after they form.

I play drop-in hockey in a small hockey market. Attendance at matches is irregular. Reggie, the organizer, nags players to get them to attend more regularly. He *believes* his nagging helps. Most players find his nagging annoying and wish he would stop. Here is how his nagging affirms itself. If he nags and attendance increases, he sees evidence that nagging works. If he nags and attendance is low, he believes he should double down on nagging. If he doesn't nag and attendance increases, he then believes that the day of increased attendance was an anomaly and that with a little more nagging, he can make this a regular event. If he doesn't nag and attendance is low, he believes he is vindicated, "I should have nagged." No matter what happens, nagging or not nagging, his belief that nagging works, gets affirmed. I believe he is trapped in a negative self-fulfilling pattern. No amount of evidence would likely change his belief. The best way to avoid developing a mistaken belief is to avoid making it in the first place.

In chapter 7, I illustrated stories of negative events and asked, "What would you do?" Similarly, in the story that follows, you'll see a story whereby a child receives a destructive comment that generates a negative mindset about her math ability. In this section, ask yourself what you would do if you witnessed a harmful event. What could you do to negate the destructive mindset or even use it to produce a more productive one?

> In first grade, my teacher was an old lady who despised children. She smelled of old cheap perfume and always had such a disappointed look on her face. One day when we were doing a math worksheet that had to do with adding and subtracting fractions, she began to walk around the room and critique us on our math abilities. I had no idea what I was doing; I couldn't understand how to find a common denominator. I already felt terrified of her, so the thought of her staring down at my confused scribbles had my heart racing. When she reached my desk, I slowly moved my arm out of the way to show her what little I had gotten done. After a long sigh, she took the paper out from under my hands, threw it in the recycling, and gave me a new blank piece of paper with no problems on it. She said, "If you can't do math then use your time doing something you know how to do." She then continued the math lesson with the rest of the class while I sat at my desk staring down at the empty blue-lined paper. I eventually transferred to a different school, and she was fired weeks later. Ever since, math has been my least favorite subject and something I struggle with all the time. Over the years I've come to accept that math doesn't come to me naturally, and to this day I get easily discouraged and insecure with math.

Here is a terrified student who is expecting a disparaging comment. A supportive comment would have surprised her. Her already elevated arousal is ready for labeling. Your goal is to instill a growth mindset, one that encourages effort as a means to success and mistakes as learning opportunities. The teacher might have triggered such a positive mindset by surprising her with, "Your serious effort to tackle these hard problems shows a growing math mind." A Cause-Effect-Resource Statement such as that would label her emotional arousal as *serious effort* and the comment would brand her as a developing math mind. Sadly, this didn't take place. Unfortunately, the teacher's negative comment instilled a mindset of "struggles with math."

Ideally, when you witness the evolution of a destructive mindset, you would immediately counter it, while the emotional arousal is still high and receptivity remains peaked. It's most effective if you can also generate a surprise event on the same theme. A two-pronged approach works best, whereby you dismiss the prior negative mindset and insert the new positive mindset. Either alone may be sufficient, but they are synergistically more effective when done together.

In the following story (previously discussed in chapter 3), an astute teacher witnessed a budding negative mindset. Sensing a window of opportunity, the teacher quickly used the child's emotional arousal as a tool to discredit the negative comment and replace it with a positive and productive one.

Mrs. G, my third-grade teacher, was a big proponent of including parents as helpers to assist with activity centers. One day, a mom came in to help with activity centers, and my table's activity was math patterns. The patterns started simple and I succeeded easily with them. The parent praised us all for doing a good job. Near the end of the activity, I started struggling with a pattern sequence. The other kids were almost done, and I hadn't even begun with it yet. I sat there and stared at my paper, trying to figure out the pattern. The parent noticed I was falling behind and halted the rest of the group so I could catch up. I felt an incredible amount of pressure at that point and frantically tried to scribble down the numbers. She rounded the table and pointed out that the pattern was wrong, "really wrong," and that I needed some help. She squatted down next to me and told me to try again, but I was so nervous my mind just went blank. After a moment or two, she grew very frustrated, snatched my pencil out of my hand, and wrote the first number in the sequence for me. I looked at the number she had written on the paper, still unsure how the number was the next in the pattern or how it connected to the number following it. "Do you get it?" she asked me, and when I shook my head no, she got up and walked away.

She told Mrs. G that she couldn't help me and that I needed to be in a different group. I felt so embarrassed that I cried. Mrs. G took me into the hallway so I could get myself together. She told me she didn't agree with what the volunteer mom had done, that she believed in me, and that I could accomplish whatever I wanted to, even a "silly old math problem" like the one I had gotten stuck on. We returned to the classroom, I got my piece of paper, and within a few minutes had the rest of the pattern figured out and the worksheet finished. Mrs. G was so proud that she put a big fat star on it and loudly told me what a good job I had done. All the uncertainty and shame I had had before melted away as I proudly looked at my star on the sheet of paper that signified my triumph. I still may not like math, but thanks to Mrs. G, I know that if I work hard enough that I can do it, and that I can accomplish what others or even I think I can't do.

In this situation, the knowing teacher masterfully seized the malleable moment before the student formed a belief of *inadequate at math*. Mrs. G dismissed the prior negative comment from the parent and replaced it by confidently asserting that the student had enough ability and could challenge any struggle with effort (stated as a matter of fact). She then consolidated this assertion with an affirmative star to signify success.

Witnessing a negative comment and intervening quickly is qualitatively different from debriefing it later. During the initial comment, you can still use the arousal as a window to counteract the destructive influence. If you can't correct a negative influence event immediately, the next most important consideration is that you intervene before sleep. Most researchers believe that dreaming consolidates memories and mindsets. If you suffer a physical injury, icing it while it's still acute decreases soreness and speeds healing. Similarly, treating emotional trauma in the form of a harmful mindset works best when done during the acute stage.

Current sleep research confirms that the sleeping brain rehashes waking experiences to create long-term memories.[3] Your current perception of events strengthens during sleep. If you can manipulate the perception of events with a positive CERS before sleep, these beneficial connections are the ones that get strengthened. Think of the brain's firing of connections during dreaming like you would of yourself forging a path in the bushes. Tramping over the path several times cements it further. It now becomes the go-to path whenever you approach those bushes. It's much easier to deal with a negative event before a corresponding negative mindset path fortifies.

If you don't witness the negative event itself, or if you witness it but can't deal with it immediately, you still have an opportunity to counteract the influence before sleep. Research by prominent Yale researcher John Bargh informs us that influence effects can disappear when the subject is led to make external attributions.[4] For instance, instead of thinking "I'm bad at math" (internal attribution), think "She's just a frustrated parent" (external attribution). A teacher, parent, or even another student might counter the consolidation of a negative mindset by commenting later that day, "That parent was sure frustrated. You're really good at math when you're not harassed like that." Such a comment could externalize the volunteer's negative assertion while reasserting the student's ability.

After the passage of significant time, attempts to correct or manage an ingrained dysfunctional belief pattern can be effective, but now you face the potentially immense task of countering a belief with all its accompanying instinctive confirmation bias dispositions. Here we see the dichotomy of belief formation: incremental versus spontaneous. Challenging a firmly held belief may take an enormous amount of countering evidence over a long time. On the other hand, a more functional mindset may form instantly during a surprise event. Since this book is about the latter, let's refer to a few examples that I previously discussed.

Recall graduate student Danna, who used to believe she was hopeless at math and even considered that she might have a math phobia. Math became her favorite subject in college after an instructor surprised her by saying, "The people who struggle the most with math often make the best teachers because they have had to look at the numbers in so many different ways that they end up with all those tools up their sleeve." Similarly, graduate student Michael believed he was hopeless at math. A clever college professor reversed this belief when he linked *mathematical competence* to Michael's *ability to proficiently explain ideas*.

The most effective approach when witnessing the formation of a negative mindset is to redirect the focus of an internal attribution to an external one, then quickly insert a positive perspective. First, you acknowledge the feeling, "I see you're upset." Next, you diminish the message by externalizing the threat, "She's just angry and frustrated." Then, you change the meaning to one of growth, "Being upset means you care about your math and can overcome difficulties with continued effort."

Adult comments to children carry more weight because of the imbalance of authority and life experience. Still, though, comments from peers often generate indelible mindsets. If you work with children, it's prudent to be watchful of their peers' comments. Counter negative comments by disqualifying them immediately and replacing them with something more productive. In the following story, ten-year-old Holly received a discouraging comment from a classmate. Her teacher intervened by capitalizing on Holly's elevated emotion and then presenting a growth-mindset comment.

> All of my childhood I knew I was going to be a veterinarian. I was so passionate about animals that I spent much of my free time studying up on the most recent discoveries related to biology. I even owned leopard geckos and an incubator for their eggs. I knew everything that went into reptile husbandry and even how their genetics work.
>
> One day, a peer of mine told me I could never be a vet because I was not very good at math. Although he was wrong, I was still so hurt and so deeply affected by his comment. I began to think that I was not capable of being a herpetologist or a vet. What happened next is what completely changed my life. My fourth-grade teacher had overheard the entire conversation and calmly made her way over to us. With a genuine smile on her face, she said, "Holly, you can be whatever you want. I mean that." From that moment, I knew I wasn't going to be a vet; I was going to be a teacher. I was so deeply touched by her kind and genuine words that I felt the need to do the very same thing for another child someday.

It seems comical that Holly decided to become a teacher at the very moment she was surprised by the teacher's mundane comment, "You can be whatever you want." We've all heard that well-worn expression many times, but it takes on a deeper meaning during the highly recep-tive moment following a surprise. In the end, Holly combined her love of animals with a career in teaching. She currently teaches high school biology.

Confusion, a Revision State

Since a surprise causes confusion, it's easy to see how both can produce the same revision effect. Similar to surprise, confusion regarding some aspect of your identity creates the same qualitative state: soaring recep-tiveness because of this existential uneasiness.

The state of confusion triggers a desire to solve: Uncertainty prompts curiosity. When scientists receive unexpected results in an experiment, they are not surprised regarding their self-concept, only surprised at the external results of the data. This creates a state of curiosity. Confu-sion regarding your model of the worldview or yourself, is qualitatively different from confusion about why an experiment produced unantici-pated results, or which box to fill while doing a tax return. Confusion about your identity triggers disorientation, a psychological discomfort that generates a drive to quell this cognitive distress. If the confusion is extreme, mental chaos erupts because your model of the world doesn't work anymore. Like surprise, we eagerly accept any information if it restores a sense of equilibrium, a psychological all-systems-okay.

The example that follows illustrates how identity confusion can momentarily disorient a person's sense of self and the world.

Upon reflection, I can see how a moment in twelfth-grade influenced my subsequent life choice. Sitting on the metro on our way back to school from a field trip, my classmates and teacher discussed what was going on for us outside school. I found that time of my life challeng-ing. I had recently moved out of my parent's home and spent most of my time with school and part-time employment. I remember feeling overwhelmed with life in those days. I shared a few of my struggles, looking for support and understanding, but instead of being empathic about my situation, my teacher said, "You know, Gesa, I just don't worry about you. You will go your way." This comment confused me. I asked myself, "Why doesn't he worry about me? Can't he feel my struggle?" At the same time, I felt his care for me. I couldn't completely process the moment mentally; however, the statement and tone stuck with me. Reflecting back, I feel the support of my teacher's statement. What he said didn't address me in that moment, struggling with the content of my life, but he saw my capacity for succeeding and he tried to reflect that to me. This moment helped me develop confidence and trust in my choices, despite my challenges and struggles. My teacher saw a strength in me I hadn't fully discovered for myself yet, and his statement helped me develop it.

In Gesa's case, the teacher's comment confused her because it didn't match her current mindset: Life is overwhelming and a struggle. This state of personal confusion created a malleable moment. During her suggestible state, she processed the tone of the message because the verbal comment seemed elusive. She understood the message as, "You are competent with life's decisions during its inevitable struggles." Our mind interprets messages according to the perceived context. Gesa was lucky to perceive a positive tone and interpret it accordingly. If you use such a strategy yourself, it's safer to issue clarity rather than hope the tone produces a constructive result. It's sounder to say, "Your ability to make responsible decisions during stressful times will help you successfully navigate through life's challenges."

Summary

This chapter showed how to effectively treat moments of destructive influence. I demonstrated how it's easier to change the valence of an event from negative to positive than to change the level of arousal once it is triggered. We also learned how profound confusion about your identity parallels the soaring susceptibility characteristic of moments of surprise.

Throughout this text, I regularly referred to the growth mindset, a belief that we can develop our intelligence and abilities through dedication and hard work. In the next chapter, I examine this empirically proven approach to a greater extent. This well-documented field delivers the foundation for productive outlooks to success and happiness.

SECTION V

~

BENEFICIAL BELIEFS

CHAPTER ELEVEN

~

Constructive Living

Genius is 1% inspiration and 99% perspiration.

Thomas Edison

I began my teaching career in a small junior high school in Canada. I taught several grades of science and physical education. Ron, a student in my seventh-grade science class, struggled to succeed. He gave up regularly, failed often, usually sat quietly, and appeared dejected about school success. I also coached the school track team. Ron showed promise as a runner. He made the track team as a sprinter and finished second in a regional meet. He qualified for the city championship and finished seventh as his schoolmates cheered him on. With my urging, Ron joined a track club. In eighth grade, he finished first in the city and second in the province. In ninth grade, he set a city record in the 400-meter race and finished first in the province.

His hard work and devotion to training in track produced similar results in his schoolwork. Now, instead of giving up, he worked through his obstacles and ended up graduating in ninth grade with a solid B-average. That was unthinkable when I first started teaching him three years prior.

Fellow teachers noted Ron's development, crediting the rise in his self-esteem as a precursor to his successes. I didn't buy it. The relationship between self-esteem and school success is complex. We all know people with low self-esteem (*I'm fat, I'm ugly, I'm a loser*) who do very well in school. We also know people with high self-esteem (*I'm cool, I'm pretty, I'm great*) who struggle with academics. In my opinion, Ron learned that hard work and strategic effort is the key to success. He developed a growth mindset. His self-esteem grew, but that was a by-product. He also showed a lot of grit (passion with perseverance). I discuss both in this chapter.

The Growth Mindset

We can attribute the common use of the term growth mindset to Stanford researcher Dr. Carol Dweck. In her remarkably insightful *Mindset: The New Psychology of Success*, she examined the power of our beliefs, both conscious and unconscious, and how changing even the simplest of them can have a profound impact on nearly every aspect of our lives.[1]

As a young researcher, something happened that changed her life. She obsessed about understanding how people cope with failures and studied it by watching how students grapple with difficult problems. She gave children puzzles to solve and watched their reactions. The first ones were fairly easy, then progressed to be much harder. She probed their thinking and feeling. Some felt crushed by failure and gave up easily, while others rebounded. She found something surprising that changed her research agenda for the next two decades: Some thrived on the challenge of hard puzzles. She writes, "What's wrong with them? I always thought you coped with failure or you didn't cope with failure. I never thought anyone loved failure. Not only weren't they discouraged by failure, they didn't even think they were failing. Were these alien children or were they on to something?"

After decades of research, she found that people tend to fall into one of two mindsets, fixed or growth.

> In a fixed mindset, students believe their basic abilities, their intelligence, their talents, are just fixed traits. They have a certain amount and that's that, and then their goal becomes to look smart all the time

and never to look dumb. In a growth mindset, students understand that they can develop their talents and abilities through effort, good teaching, and persistence. They don't necessarily think everyone's the same or anyone can be Einstein, but they believe everyone can get smarter if they work at it.

At first glance, this may seem rather mundane and even inconsequential. That is, until you see it play out. Here are some typical results from her research. Researchers praised some students for their ability. They were told: "Wow, you got eight right. That's a really good score. You must be *smart* at this." They praised other students for their effort: "Wow you got eight right. That's a really good score. You must have *worked really hard*." Researchers praised the first group for innate ability. They praised the second group for being industrious.

Both groups were exactly equal, to begin with. But right after the praise, they began to differ. Dweck notes, "As we feared, the ability praise pushed students right into the fixed mindset, and they showed all the signs of it, too: When we gave them a choice, they rejected a challenging new task that they could learn from." Kids labeled smart don't want to do anything that could expose their flaws and call their talent into question. These "smart" kids become averse to making mistakes, which they can avoid by steering clear of challenges where they might fail. They prefer to hide failures rather than learn from them.

In contrast, 90 percent of the students praised for their effort wanted the challenging new task so that they could learn from it. People who hold a growth mindset understand that their intelligences and capabilities are always growing, changing, and developing. These people know that they can learn and grow and become better at things. They understand that they accomplish this by trying new things, taking risks, and focusing on growth and development.

We all have a mixed bag of growth and fixed mindsets. You might have a fixed mindset with athletics ("I'm a natural" or "I'm hopeless with sports") while holding a growth mindset with writing ("I'm excited to see progress after working hard").

The way we praise kids drives the mindsets they develop. Dweck worries that parents, teachers, supervisors, and coaches can inadvertently send the wrong message. She writes, "In fact, every word and action can send a message. It tells children—or students, or athletes—how to think about themselves. It can be a fixed-mindset message that says: 'You have permanent traits and I'm judging them.' Or it can be a growth-mindset message that says: 'You are a developing person, and I am interested in your development.'" This is where a CERS works its magic, especially if it surprises the receiver.

Cognitive behavior therapy (CBT) teaches people to rein in their extreme judgments and make them more reasonable. For example, suppose Alana does poorly on a test and draws the conclusion, "I'm stupid." That's a fixed mindset. CBT teaches her to look more closely at the facts by asking: What is the evidence for and against your conclusion? With prodding, Alana compiles a list of ways in which she showed competence in the past, and may then profess, "I guess I'm not as incompetent as I thought."

She is also encouraged to think of reasons she did poorly on the test other than stupidity, and these may further temper her negative judgment. With CBT, Alana learns how to do this for herself, so that when she judges herself negatively in the future, she can refute the judgment and feel better. If Alana had a growth mindset, she wouldn't need this form of therapy. She would already embody it.

CBT is a long, methodical, and rational process. It tries to build a positive mindset by constantly battling negative thoughts (low dopamine) with positive counterparts (higher dopamine). In essence, CBT tries to change the valance of dopamine from negative ("I'm stupid") to positive ("I can get this with strategic effort").

I strongly endorse CBT and use it myself to counteract irrational thoughts and self-defeating beliefs. But, when I work with others, I use a strategic surprise when I can. A well-timed, surprise CERS bypasses the focused deliberate efforts by instantly establishing a self-affirming growth mindset. You can get the same result as CBT because of the phasic dopamine. Now, instead of looking for evidence that she is stupid, then disputing it, she instinctively looks for and finds affirmative evidence that she is improving ("I can get this with strategic effort"). This new instinct outperforms conscious efforts because it takes place naturally.

Caveat: I'm not saying that you can create a growth mindset with one surprise comment. If that were the case, we could all do that, and watch people flourish. That said, the growth mindset, or critical elements of it, often emerge spontaneously during a surprise. This book examines these special conditions scientifically, then extolls a plan to maximize them in order to produce powerful results.

The more confidence people have in their abilities to master a given task, the better they perform. Since we already know that one of the most important and consistent predictors of people's performance is their perceived self-efficacy, we should target that with a CERS. When you deliver a CERS, you trigger intrinsic motivation, a belief that that person can control outcomes. *Motivation in general seems to rely on believing we're in control.*

If you are a teacher and your student is frozen with a fear of making mistakes, catch that student making a mistake. Then give that perceptive laugh or go, "Wow!" The student will expect ridicule or condemnation. Surprise him with, "Your eagerness to take risks and make mistakes boldly is the sign of a strong learner." Then walk away. Say it like it's an obvious fact. If you surprised him, now mistakes are linked neurologically to being a *strong learner.* This works with employees, athletes, and your children, too. If the comment surprises him, it changes the valence of failure, even if only a little. It adds dopamine to taking risks because it's now linked to strong learning.

Tennis star Maria Sharapova describes a focus on outcomes as the worst mistake that beginning tennis players make. Watch the ball as long as you can, Sharapova cautions, and zero in on the process. The outcome will eventually follow.[2]

While Dweck initially researched students, she found applications in business, parenting, and athletics. A CERS such as "Your ability to identify your obstacles helps you plan strategies to overcome them" works with any group by eliciting a growth mindset. Multiply its effectiveness with a surprise. Celebrate the struggle of learning, whether in school, at home, in the gym, or at work. Would this surprise you if someone said this right after you floundered at work? "Wow! You fail like a pro. Your willingness to fail shows a thriving drive for success."

Grit: Passion with Perseverance

Smooth seas do not make skillful sailors.

African Proverb

Grit is a key personality trait that predicts success. But some core features of grit prove more amendable to acknowledgment. Conscientiousness (focusing on the task at hand) and perseverance (buckling down and staying with it) are key aspects of grit. We may not always be passionate about our task, but conscientiousness and perseverance will get it done. These aspects of grit are generalizable; you can show perseverance in many areas. Passion is specific. Passion for music doesn't necessarily transfer to cooking.

Andrea struggled with math throughout her years in school. At thirteen she already felt discouraged about math impeding her ability to attend college. She wrote, "I took twice as long to complete homework and tests. Teacher after teacher became tired of having to re-explain concepts to me." She felt frustrated and exasperated. At the end of grade seven, her teacher placed her in a remedial class to repeat seventh-grade math. At the end of that remedial year, her teacher handed out some awards.

> I was secretly hoping to get one, despite how much I hated math and dreaded my future. I crossed my fingers, hoping to get "most improved." It proves to our peers that we have what it takes to achieve something. Some kid who spoke Spanish got it. I felt crushed. Then, the teacher announced, "Last and definitely not the least, a very special award. This award is for the most enthusiasm for math." My heart sank. I hated math. I complained every day. She continued, "I am proud to present this award to a student who is not afraid to ask questions, who always speaks up when they need help, whose energy is infectious, and whose determination and dedication to math guarantees her success through high school." Then she said my name. I was shocked. I immediately thought, "You know what, yeah! I am the most enthusiastic. Everyone might be better at math than me, but no one is as determined and passionate to succeed than me." Suddenly, I felt motivated. All these years later (now a teacher), I realize that my teacher gave me a gift. She recognized how much I struggled, and publicly gave it an alternative name:

enthusiasm. From then on, I continued my enthusiasm to conquer math, and I did.

While not a classic CERS, it followed the same formula: See something, label it, and endorse it as a resource. Andrea states it this way, "She recognized how much I struggled, and publicly gave it an alternative name: enthusiasm." You see the cognitive elaboration, the meaning-making, takes place when she acknowledges, "You know what, yeah! I am the most enthusiastic." You see, her dopamine level boost considerably, from almost giving up to becoming a signature strength: "I felt motivated." The lifelong impact from this moment emerged because it surprised her. It became a signature attribute. If you get what you expect, there's no surprise, and no phasic dopamine.

Where is your grit? In the opening story, Ron developed a growth mindset in track that generalized to academics. You probably also noticed that he showed grit. People with grit show a strong passion to pursue a long-term goal and the ability to persevere and persist in overcoming obstacles to achieve that goal. The research suggests that having the quality of grit can predict future academic performance in students. Not only that, it plays a key role in every achievement-related outcome for all ages. Eminent grit researcher Angela Duckworth states, "But when you look at grit scores and measures of life satisfaction, we get this straight-line relationship; even at the very tippy-top of the grit scale, the more grit you have, the more happiness you report. What I don't know is whether the people who live with the super-gritty people are happy. Ha!"

Summary

This chapter described the growth mindset and grit. It illustrated how the growth mindset is the foundation of grit and that while the growth mindset is often generalizable, grit applies to one field. I showed how Cognitive Behavior Therapy, CBT, parallels the process of a CERS, but that the CERS may take place instantly with a built-in self-affirmation process.

CHAPTER TWELVE

∼

Final Word

Georgia, a characteristically timid teacher candidate, stood up in front of her grad-school classmates and sang an original song. After class, several students commended her for her courage. She described their response as a formative moment:

> They told me how brave I was. That surprised me. People usually consider me a shy person. When I heard someone saying I was brave, it made me think about how far I have come in my ability to share, communicate, and put myself out there. After I got over my initial feeling of surprise, I found myself owning that quality. I thought, "Yes, I am brave, and yes, I have come a long way, even if I still have far to go." This thought motivated me because I deal with self-doubt. But if I've come this far, there is not much stopping me from growing even more as a person and an educator.

I finish this book with this story because of its simple elegance. To a fly on the wall, this event looks inconsequential, but it changed Georgia dramatically. It bears all the hallmarks of a surprise-triggered formative event.

Grace believed she was shy. That belief generated a timid mindset: Be wary of standing out, for you may be ridiculed. While feeling apprehensive after her uncharacteristic performance, fellow students surprised her by noting her courage: "They told me how brave I was." She describes her cognitive elaboration process (meaning-making), with her comment, "Then after I got over my initial feeling of surprise, I found myself owning that quality. I thought, 'Yes, I am brave, and yes, I have come a long way, even if I still have far to go.'" Her next comment reflects increased dopamine: "This thought motivated me because I deal with self-doubt." Her dopamine burst, triggered by the surprise comment, reflects a belief shift that we see reflected in her new mindset: "But if I've come this far, there is not much stopping me from growing even more as a person and an educator." Dopamine tells the brain what to pay attention to. Her new mindset instinctively pursues evidence for courageous behavior. Confirmation bias now becomes an ally. Her prior mindset hunted for evidence to confirm her self-doubt.

It's unlikely that her fellow students would notice any difference in Georgia. While this moment proved memorable for Georgia, it likely passed as unremarkable for them. For her, the surprise created an instant belief shift, but visible results may take time to emerge. A surprise germinates fruitful seeds for future growth.

Effective and Meaningful

How hard will you work at something you perceive you are not good at? Effectiveness is a mindset. Comments that foster self-efficacy or cultivate a sense of meaning appeal to all of us. The more confidence people have in their abilities, the better they perform. In Dan Ariely's best-selling book, *The Payoff: The Hidden Logic That Shapes Our Motivation*, his research emphasizes that "people are always drawn toward feeling that they matter, they are effective." Next to existing abilities and skills, one of the most important and consistent predictors of people's performance is their perceived self-efficacy.[1]

Growing up with a reading disorder made me read slowly by paying attention to detail. This compensation to overcome my reading problems fostered what I now see as a strength: reading carefully. But I didn't know it was a strength until someone pointed it out to me. Then my valence for reading shifted from avoid to approach. Sometimes a signature strength develops from how we overcome a presumed weakness. When you point that out to someone for the first time, it triggers a surprise. We all produce an enormous variety of behaviors throughout the day. Point out how underlying skills serve a purpose for others. Channel their assets to serve productive ends. We don't always create a big moment, but we can still employ linguistic mechanisms to maximize our probabilities. Practice the CERS structure so that it becomes automatic.

You can explain to someone that failure is how we learn, and that person gains knowledge. You can surprise someone who thinks they just messed up by saying, "Wow! Your willingness to learn from your mistakes shows great leadership potential." A surprise ignites a lightning strike of new awareness. Whatever you learned, you learned more deeply if you were surprised.

The most important role you can play in life is to positively influence someone and watch them flourish. The element of surprise exponentially increases the effect of a comment. Put this tool in your toolbox, and use it regularly to make lives richer. This book showed you how surprise can trigger formative moments. You now have the wherewithal to strategically do what Georgia's classmates did for her: Make others' lives richer. The next time you find yourself with an opportunity to inspire someone, to trigger a new belief that releases their potential, ask yourself, "How can I surprise this person so that they see themselves anew?"

Notes

Introduction

1. Marlo Thomas, *The Right Words at the Right Time* (New York: Simon and Schuster, 2004).

2. A fictious name. He is deceased.

Chapter One

1. Michel Bitbol, "Neurophenomenology of Surprise," *Surprise at the Intersection of Phenomenology and Linguistics* 11 (2019): 9.

2. Andy Clark, "Whatever Next? Predictive Brains, Situated Agents, and the Future of Cognitive Science," *Behavioral and Brain Sciences* 36, no. 3 (2013): 181–204.

3. Anil Seth, "Your Brain Hallucinates Your Conscious Reality," TED.com, 2017, https://www.ted.com/talks/anil_seth_how_your_brain_hallucinates _your_conscious_reality.

4. Lisa Feldman Barrett, *How Emotions Are Made: The Secret Life of the Brain* (New York: Houghton Mifflin Harcourt, 2017).

5. Dale Purves and R. Beau Lotto, *Why We See What We Do: An Empirical Theory of Vision* (Oxford, UK: Sinauer Associates, 2003).

6. Jerome S. Bruner and Cecile C. Goodman, "Value and Need as Organizing Factors in Perception," *The Journal of Abnormal and Social Psychology* 42, no. 1 (1947): 33.

7. M. Gazzaniga, *Who's in Charge?: Free Will and the Science of the Brain* (London: Hachette UK, 2012).

8. Ap. Dijksterhuis and Loran F. Nordgren, "A Theory of Unconscious Thought," *Perspectives on Psychological Science* 1, no. 2 (2006): 95–109.

Chapter Two

1. Andrew Newberg and Mark Robert Waldman, *Why We Believe What We Believe: Uncovering Our Biological Need for Meaning, Spirituality, and Truth* (New York: Simon and Schuster, 2006).

2. Michael Shermer, *The Believing Brain: From Ghosts and Gods to Politics and Conspiracies: How We Construct Beliefs and Reinforce Them As Truths* (New York: Macmillan, 2011).

3. Sam Harris, Sameer A. Sheth, and Mark S. Cohen, "Functional Neuroimaging of Belief, Disbelief, and Uncertainty," *Annals of Neurology* 63, no. 2 (2008): 141–47.

4. Daniel Kahneman, *Thinking, Fast and Slow* (New York: Macmillan, 2011).

5. Shai Davidai, and Thomas Gilovich, "The Headwinds/Tailwinds Asymmetry: An Availability Bias in Assessments of Barriers and Blessings," *Journal of Personality and Social Psychology* 111, no. 6 (2016): 835.

Chapter Three

1. Andrew Newberg and Mark Robert Waldman, *Why We Believe What We Believe: Uncovering Our Biological Need for Meaning, Spirituality, and Truth* (New York: Simon and Schuster, 2006).

2. Albert Bandura, "Self-efficacy: Toward a Unifying Theory of Behavioral Change," *Psychological Review* 84, no. 2 (1977): 191.

3. Hugo Mercier and Dan Sperber, *The Enigma of Reason* (Cambridge, MA: Harvard University Press, 2017).

4. Hugo Mercier and Dan Sperber, *The Enigma of Reason* (Cambridge, MA: Harvard University Press, 2017).

5. Scott O. Lilienfeld, Steven Jay Lynn, John Ruscio, and Barry L. Beyerstein, *50 Great Myths of Popular Psychology: Shattering Widespread Misconceptions About Human Behavior* (Hoboken, NJ: John Wiley & Sons, 2011).

6. Mark Humphries, "The Crimes Against Dopamine," *The Spike: Medium*, March 13, 2017, https://medium.com/the-spike/the-crimes-against-dopamine -b82b082d5f3d.

7. Joseph E. Dunsmoor, Marijn C. W. Kroes, Jian Li, Nathaniel D. Daw, Helen B. Simpson, and Elizabeth A. Phelps, "Role of Human Ventromedial Prefrontal Cortex in Learning and Recall of Enhanced Extinction," *Journal of Neuroscience* 39, no. 17 (2019): 3264–276.

8. *Inside Out*, directed by Pete Docter and Ronnie Del Carmen (2015; Burbank, CA: Walt Disney Movie Studios.)

9. Ulric Neisser and Nicole Harsch, "Phantom Flashbulbs: False Recollections of Hearing the News about Challenger," in *Emory Symposium on Cognition*, ed. E. Winograd and U. Neisser, 9–31 (Cambridge, UK: Caambridge University Press, 1992).

10. Nassim Nicholas Taleb, *The Black Swan: The Impact of the Highly Improbable*, Vol. 2. (New York: Random House, 2007).

Chapter Four

1. Sara E. Gorman and Jack M. Gorman, *Denying to the Grave: Why We Ignore the Facts That Will Save Us* (Oxford, UK: Oxford University Press), 2016.

2. Keith E. Stanovich, Richard F. West, and Maggie E. Toplak. "Myside Bias, Rational Thinking, and Intelligence," *Current Directions in Psychological Science* 22, no. 4 (2013): 259–64.

3. Keith E. Stanovich, Richard F. West, and Maggie E. Toplak. "Myside Bias, Rational Thinking, and Intelligence," *Current Directions in Psychological Science* 22, no. 4 (2013): 259–64.

4. Sam Harris, Sameer A. Sheth, and Mark S. Cohen, "Functional Neuroimaging of Belief, Disbelief, and Uncertainty," *Annals of Neurology* 63, no. 2 (2008): 141–47.

5. Russell Golman, David Hagmann, and George Loewenstein, "Information Avoidance," *Journal of Economic Literature* 55, no. 1 (2017): 96–135.

6. The Nobel Assembly at the Karolinska Institute in Stockholm, Sweden awarded the 2005 Nobel Prize for Physiology or Medicine to Dr. Barry J. Marshall, 54, and Dr. J. Robin Warren, 68, for their discovery of the Helicobacter pylori (H. pylori) bacterium and its role in gastritis and peptic ulcer disease.

7. *Freakonomics Radio*, episode 286, "How Big Is My Penis (And Other Things We Ask Google)?" Stephen J. Dubner, May 10, 2017, NPR, http:// freakonomics.com/podcast/big-penis-things-ask-google/.

8. Fictitious study.

9. Fictitious study.

10. Fictitious study.

11. Erik Vance, *Suggestible You: The Curious Science of Your Brain's Ability to Deceive, Transform, and Heal* (Washington, DC: National Geographic Books, 2016).

12. Hugo Mercier and Dan Sperber. "Why Do Humans Reason? Arguments for an Argumentative Theory," *Behavioral and Brain Sciences* 34, no. 2 (2011): 57–74.

13. "Feelings vs Fact—Newt Gingrich—RNC Topic on Violent Crime—Feelings Trump FBI Stats!" YouTube, July 27, 2016, https://www.youtube.com/watch?v=xnhJWusyj4I.

14. Paul H. Thibodeau and Lera Boroditsky, "Metaphors We Think With: The Role of Metaphor in Reasoning," *PloS one* 6, no. 2 (2011): e16782.

15. "Live Talks Business Forum: Dr. Zak interviews Nobel Laureate Daniel Kahneman," YouTube, Dec. 17, 2011, https://www.youtube.com/watch?v=HaTrJV9rvCc.

16. Andrew Newberg and Mark Robert Waldman, *Why We Believe What We Believe: Uncovering Our Biological Need for Meaning, Spirituality, and Truth* (New York: Simon and Schuster, 2006).

17. *Schitt's Creek*, created by Eugene Levy and Dan Levy, Canadian Broadcasting Corporation, 2015.

Chapter Five

1. *Candid Camera*, created by Allen Funt (1960; Allen Funt Productions, CBS Studio 50, 1960).

2. Marret K. Noordewier and Seger M. Breugelmans, "On the Valence of Surprise," *Cognition & Emotion* 27, no. 7 (2013): 1326–34.

3. Marret K. Noordewier, Sascha Topolinski, and Eric Van Dijk, "The Temporal Dynamics of Surprise," *Social and Personality Psychology Compass* 10, no. 3 (2016): 136–49.

4. Mark Humphries, "The Crimes Against Dopamine," *The Spike: Medium*, March 13, 2017, https://medium.com/the-spike/the-crimes-against-dopamine-b82b082d5f3d.

5. Wolfram Schultz, "Dopamine Reward Prediction-Error Signalling: A Two-Component Response," *Nature Reviews Neuroscience* 17, no. 3 (2016): 183.

6. Donald G. Dutton and Arthur P. Aron, "Some Evidence for Heightened Sexual Attraction Under Conditions of High Anxiety," *Journal of Personality and Social Psychology* 30, no. 4 (1974): 510.

7. Daniel Gilbert, *Stumbling on Happiness* (Toronto: Vintage Canada, 2009).

8. Thomas Gilovich and Lee Ross, *The Wisest One in the Room: How You Can Benefit from Social Psychology's Most Powerful Insights* (New York: Simon and Schuster, 2016).

9. Leon Festinger, Hiroshi Ono, and Clarke A. Burnham. "Efference and the Conscious Experience of Perception," *Journal of Experimental Psychology* 74, no. 4, p. 2 (1967): 1.

10. Erik Vance, *Suggestible You: The Curious Science of Your Brain's Ability to Deceive, Transform, and Heal* (Washington, DC: National Geographic Books, 2016).

11. Thomas N. Robinson, Dina L. G. Borzekowski, Donna M. Matheson, and Helena C. Kraemer, "Effects of Fast Food Branding on Young Children's Taste Preferences," *Archives of Pediatrics & Adolescent Medicine* 161, no. 8 (2007): 792–97.

12. Christian Rudder, "We Experiment on Human Beings," *OK Trends: Dating Research from OKCupid (Blog)*, 2014, http://blog.okcupid.com/index.php/we-experiment-on-human-beings.

13. Robert Rosenthal and Lenore Jacobson, "Pygmalion in the Classroom," *The Urban Review* 3, no. 1 (1968): 16–20.

14. Jean Piaget, Howard E. Gruber, and J. Voneche, "Jacques: The Essential Piaget." 1977.

15. Sang Wan Lee, John P. O'Doherty, and Shinsuke Shimojo, "Neural Computations Mediating One-Shot Learning in the Human Brain," *PLoS Biol* 13, no. 4 (2015): e1002137.

16. Marieke Jepma, Rinus G. Verdonschot, Henk Van Steenbergen, Serge A. R. Rombouts, and Sander Nieuwenhuis, "Neural Mechanisms Underlying the Induction and Relief of Perceptual Curiosity," *Frontiers in Behavioral Neuroscience* 6 (2012): 5.

17. Vincent D. Costa, Valery L. Tran, Janita Turchi, and Bruno B. Averbeck, "Dopamine Modulates Novelty Seeking Behavior During Decision Making," *Behavioral Neuroscience* 128, no. 5 (2014): 556.

18. Amy Rankin, Rogier Woltjer, and Joris Field, "Sensemaking Following Surprise in the Cockpit—A Re-framing Problem," *Cognition, Technology & Work* 18, no. 4 (2016): 623–42.

19. Judith Schomaker and Martijn Meeter, "Short- and Long-lasting Consequences of Novelty, Deviance and Surprise on Brain and Cognition," *Neuroscience & Biobehavioral Reviews* 55 (2015): 268–79.

20. Abraham S. Luchins, "Mechanization in Problem Solving: The Effect of Einstellung," *Psychological Monographs* 54, no. 6 (1942): i.

21. Merim Bilalić and Peter McLeod, "Why Good Thoughts Block Better Ones," *Scientific American* 310, no. 3 (2014): 74–79.

Chapter Six

1. Jeffrey Ely, Alexander Frankel, and Emir Kamenica, "Suspense and Surprise," *Journal of Political Economy* 123, no. 1 (2015): 215–60.

2. Lisa Cron, *Wired for Story: The Writer's Guide to Using Brain Science to Hook Readers from the Very First Sentence* (Berkeley, CA: Ten Speed Press, 2012).

3. Morgan Spurlock in an interview with Manoush Zomorodi, "Brand Over Brain," *Ted Radio Hour*, March 9, 2014, http://www.npr.org/programs/ted-radio-hour/308752278/brand-over-brain.

4. Michael Rousell, "Surprise: How Your Brain Secretly Changes Your Beliefs," TEDxSalem, March 18, 2019, https://www.youtube.com/watch?v=K5O6mFWpgZo&feature=youtu.be.

5. Nick Marson, *Leading by Coaching: How to Deliver Impactful Change One Conversation at a Time* (New York: Springer, 2019).

Chapter Seven

1. *Freakonomics Radio*, episode 243, "How to Be More Productive," Stephen J. Dubner, April 20, 2016, NPR, https://freakonomics.com/podcast/how-to-be-more-productive/.

2. Lisa Feldman Barrett, *How Emotions Are Made: The Secret Life of the Brain* (New York: Houghton Mifflin Harcourt, 2017).

3. *Field of Dreams*, directed by Phil Alden Robinson (1989; Universal City, CA: Universal Pictures, 1989).

4. Marlo Thomas, *The Right Words at the Right Time* (New York: Simon and Schuster, 2004).

5. J. Hawkings and S. Blakeslee, "On Intelligence: How a New Understanding of the Brain will Lead to the Creation of Truly Intelligent Machines," *An Owl Book* (New York: Henry Holt and Company, 2004).

6. Adam R. Aron and Russell A. Poldrack, "Cortical and Subcortical Contributions to Stop Signal Response Inhibition: Role of the Subthalamic Nucleus," *Journal of Neuroscience* 26, no. 9 (2006): 2424–33.

7. Marlo Thomas, *The Right Words at the Right Time* (New York: Simon and Schuster, 2004).

Chapter Eight

1. Marlo Thomas, *The Right Words at the Right Time* (New York: Simon and Schuster, 2004).
2. Amy Cuddy, "Your Body Language May Shape Who You Are," TED, June 2012, https://www.ted.com/talks/amy_cuddy_your_body_language_may _shape_who_you_are?language=en.
3. Marlo Thomas, *The Right Words at the Right Time* (New York: Simon and Schuster, 2004).
4. Erik Vance, *Suggestible You: The Curious Science of Your Brain's Ability to Deceive, Transform, and Heal* (Washington, DC: National Geographic Books, 2016).
5. Richard E. Petty and John T. Cacioppo, "The Elaboration Likelihood Model of Persuasion," In *Communication and Persuasion* (New York: Springer, 1986), 1–24.
6. Anthony G. Greenwald, "Cognitive Learning, Cognitive Response to Persuasion, and Attitude Change," *Psychological Foundations of Attitudes* (1968): 147–70.

Chapter Nine

1. Jonah Berger, *The Catalyst: How to Change Anyone's Mind* (New York: Simon and Schuster, 2020).
2. Amishi P. Jha, Elizabeth A. Stanley, Anastasia Kiyonaga, Ling Wong, and Lois Gelfand, "Examining the Protective Effects of Mindfulness Training on Working Memory Capacity and Affective Experience," *Emotion* 10, no. 1 (2010): 54.
3. Adam M. Grant and David A. Hofmann, "It's Not All About Me: Motivating Hand Hygiene Among Health Care Professionals by Focusing on Patients," *Psychological Science* 22, no. 12 (2011): 1494–99.

Chapter Ten

1. Alison Wood Brooks, "Get Excited: Reappraising Pre-performance Anxiety as Excitement," *Journal of Experimental Psychology: General* 143, no. 3 (2014): 1144.
2. Lisa Feldman Barrett, *How Emotions Are Made: The Secret Life of the Brain* (New York: Houghton Mifflin Harcourt, 2017).

3. Krisitn E. G. Sanders, Samuel Osburn, Ken A. Paller, and Mark Beeman, "Targeted Memory Reactivation During Sleep Improves Next-Day Problem Solving," *Psychological science* 30, no. 11 (2019): 1616–24.

4. John A. Bargh, Kay L. Schwader, Sarah E. Hailey, Rebecca L. Dyer, and Erica J. Boothby, "Automaticity in Social-Cognitive Processes," *Trends in Cognitive Sciences* 16, no. 12 (2012): 593–605.

Chapter Eleven

1. Carol S. Dweck, *Mindset: The New Psychology of Success* (New York: Random House Digital, Inc., 2008).

2. Ozan Varol, *Think Like a Rocket Scientist* (New York: PublicAffairs, 2020).

Chapter Twelve

1. Dan Ariely, *Payoff: The Hidden Logic That Shapes Our Motivations* (New York: Simon and Schuster, 2016).

Bibliography

Abolafia, Mitchel Y. "Narrative Construction as Sensemaking: How a Central Bank Thinks." *Organization Studies* 31, no. 3 (2010): 349–67.

Achor, Shawn. *The Happiness Advantage: The Seven Principles of Positive Psychology that Fuel Success and Performance at Work.* New York: Random House, 2011.

Adler, Jonathan E. "Surprise." *Educational Theory* 58, no. 2 (2008): 149–73.

Aguiar, Henrique. "The Inner Workings of the Human Mind." Medium.com. August 2, 2018. https://medium.com/@henriquereisaguiar/the-mysterious -mechanisms-of-the-mind-e2c2340b5e4b.

Alaa, Ahmed M., and Mihaela Van Der Schaar. "Balancing Suspense and Surprise: Timely Decision Making With Endogenous Information Acquisition." *Advances in Neural Information Processing Systems* (2016): 2910–18.

Alban, Deanne. "How to Increase Dopamine Naturally." Be Brain Fit. 2012. https://bebrainfit.com/increase-dopamine/.

Allen, James B., Douglas T. Kenrick, Darwyn E. Linder, and Michael A. McCall. "Arousal and Attraction: A Response-Facilitation Alternative to Misattribution and Negative-Reinforcement Models." *Journal of Personality and Social Psychology* 57, no. 2 (1989): 261.

Almenberg, Johan, and Anna Dreber. "When Does the Price Affect the Taste? Results from a Wine Experiment." *SSE/EFI Working Paper Series in Economics and Finance* no. 717 (2010).

Ambady, Nalini, and Robert Rosenthal. "Thin Slices of Expressive Behavior as Predictors of Interpersonal Consequences: A Meta-analysis." *Psychological Bulletin* 111, no. 2 (1992): 256.

Anderson, Eric, Erika H. Siegel, Eliza Bliss-Moreau, and Lisa Feldman Barrett. "The Visual Impact of Gossip." *Science* 332, no. 6036 (2011): 1446–48.

Angela, J. Yu, and Peter Dayan. "Uncertainty, Neuromodulation, and Attention." *Neuron* 46, no. 4 (2005): 681–92.

Ariely, Dan. *Payoff: The Hidden Logic That Shapes Our Motivations*. New York: Simon and Schuster, 2016.

Aron, Adam R., and Russell A. Poldrack. "Cortical and Subcortical Contributions to Stop Signal Response Inhibition: Role of the Subthalamic Nucleus." *Journal of Neuroscience* 26, no. 9 (2006): 2424–33.

Arriaga, Moises, and Edward B. Han. "Structured Inhibitory Activity Dynamics During Learning." bioRxiv (2019): 566257.

Badgaiyan, Rajendra. *Neuroscience of the Nonconscious Mind*. Cambridge, MA: Academic Press, 2019.

Baldassarre, Gianluca, Tom Stafford, Marco Mirolli, Peter Redgrave, Richard M. Ryan, and Andrew Barto. "Intrinsic Motivations and Open-Ended Development in Animals, Humans, and Robots: An Overview." *Frontiers in Psychology* 5 (2014): 985.

Bækgaard, Per, Michael Kai Petersen, and Jakob Eg Larsen. "Separating Components of Attention and Surprise." *arXiv preprint arXiv:1608.08492* (2016).

Bandura, Albert. "Self-efficacy: Toward a Unifying Theory of Behavioral Change." *Psychological Review* 84, no. 2 (1977): 191.

Bargh, John A., Peter M. Gollwitzer, Annette Lee-Chai, Kimberly Barndollar, and Roman Trötschel. "The Automated Will: Nonconscious Activation and Pursuit of Behavioral Goals." *Journal of Personality and Social Psychology* 81, no. 6 (2001): 1014.

Bargh, John A., Kay L. Schwader, Sarah E. Hailey, Rebecca L. Dyer, and Erica J. Boothby. "Automaticity in Social-Cognitive Processes." *Trends in Cognitive Sciences* 16, no. 12 (2012): 593–605.

Barrett, Lisa Feldman. *How Emotions Are Made: The Secret Life of the Brain*. New York: Houghton Mifflin Harcourt, 2017.

Barrett, L. F., R. Adolphs, S. Marsella, A. Martinez, and S. D. Pollak. "Emotional Expressions Reconsidered: Challenges to Inferring Emotion from Human Facial Movements." *Psychological Science in the Public Interest* 20, no. 1 (2018).

Barto, Andrew, Marco Mirolli, and Gianluca Baldassarre. "Novelty or Surprise?" *Frontiers in Psychology* 4 (2013): 907.

Bellet, Clement, Jan-Emmanuel De Neve, and George Ward. "Does Employee Happiness Have an Impact on Productivity?" *Saïd Business School WP* 13 (2019).

Bellucci, Gabriele. "Psychological and Neural Dynamics of Trust." PhD diss., 2020.

Belova, Marina A., Joseph J. Paton, Sara E. Morrison, and C. Daniel Salzman. "Expectation Modulates Neural Responses to Pleasant and Aversive Stimuli in Primate Amygdala." *Neuron* 55, no. 6 (2007): 970–84.

Benchenane, Karim, Adrien Peyrache, Mehdi Khamassi, Patrick L. Tierney, Yves Gioanni, Francesco P. Battaglia, and Sidney I. Wiener. "Coherent Theta Oscillations and Reorganization of Spike Timing in the Hippocampal-Prefrontal Network Upon Learning." *Neuron* 66, no. 6 (2010): 921–36.

Berger, Jonah. *The Catalyst: How to Change Anyone's Mind.* New York: Simon and Schuster, 2020.

Berger, Jonah. *Invisible Influence: The Hidden Forces That Shape Behavior.* New York: Simon and Schuster, 2016.

Bilalic', Merim, and Peter McLeod. "Why Good Thoughts Block Better Ones." *Scientific American* 310, no. 3 (2014): 74–79.

Bitbol, Michel. "Neurophenomenology of Surprise." *Surprise at the Intersection of Phenomenology and Linguistics* 11 (2019): 9.

Bloom, Paul. *How Pleasure Works: The New Science of Why We Like What We Like.* New York: Random House, 2010.

Boll, Sabrina, Matthias Gamer, Sebastian Gluth, Jürgen Finsterbusch, and Christian Büchel. "Separate Amygdala Subregions Signal Surprise and Predictiveness During Associative Fear Learning in Humans." *European Journal of Neuroscience* 37, no. 5 (2013): 758–67.

Borwein, David, Jonathan M. Borwein, and Pierre Marechal. "Surprise Maximization." *The American Mathematical Monthly* 107, no. 6 (2000): 517–27.

Brooks, Alison Wood. "Get Excited: Reappraising Pre-performance Anxiety as Excitement." *Journal of Experimental Psychology: General* 143, no. 3 (2014): 1144.

Brophy, Sean. "Humanizing Healthcare." In *The Wiley Handbook of Personal Construct Psychology.* Oxford, UK: Wiley & Sons, 2015.

Brouwers, Melissa C., and Richard M. Sorrentino. "Uncertainty Orientation and Protection Motivation Theory: The Role of Individual Differences in Health Compliance." *Journal of Personality and Social Psychology* 65, no. 1 (1993): 102.

Brown, Andrew D. "Making Sense of the Collapse of Barings Bank." *Human Relations* 58, no. 12 (2005): 1579–604.

Brown, Andrew D., Patrick Stacey, and Joe Nandhakumar. "Making Sense of Sensemaking Narratives." *Human Relations* 61, no. 8 (2008): 1035–62.

Bruner, Jerome S., and Cecile C. Goodman. "Value and Need as Organizing Factors in Perception." *The Journal of Abnormal and Social Psychology* 42, no. 1 (1947): 33.

Burklund, Lisa Jane, J. David Creswell, Michael Irwin, and Matthew Lieberman. "The Common and Distinct Neural Bases of Affect Labeling and Reappraisal in Healthy Adults." *Frontiers in Psychology* 5 (2014): 221.

Candid Camera, created by Allen Funt. Allen Funt Productions, CBS Studio 50, 1960.

Caplin, Andrew, and John Leahy. "Psychological Expected Utility Theory and Anticipatory Feelings." *The Quarterly Journal of Economics* 116, no. 1 (2001): 55–79.

Carr, Margaret F., Shantanu P. Jadhav, and Loren M. Frank. "Hippocampal Replay in the Awake State: A Potential Substrate for Memory Consolidation and Retrieval." *Nature Neuroscience* 14, no. 2 (2011): 147.

Chakravarty, Sucheta, Esther Fujiwara, Christopher R. Madan, Sara E. Tomlinson, Isha Ober, and Jeremy B. Caplan. "Value Bias of Verbal Memory." *Journal of Memory and Language* 107 (2019): 25–39.

Chamberland, Justin, Annie Roy-Charland, Melanie Perron, and Joël Dickinson. "Distinction Between Fear and Surprise: An Interpretation-Independent Test of the Perceptual-Attentional Limitation Hypothesis." *Social Neuroscience* 12, no. 6 (2017): 751–68.

Chamorro-Premuzic, Tomas. "Stop Focusing on Your Strengths, *Harvard Business Review*, Ep. 506, January 21, 2016. https://hbr.org/ideacast/2016/01/stop-focusing-on-your-strengths.html.

Churchill, Andrew, Jamie A. Taylor, and Royston Parkes. "The Creation of a Superstitious Belief Regarding Putters in a Laboratory-Based Golfing Task." *International Journal of Sport and Exercise Psychology* 13, no. 4 (2015): 335–43.

Cialdini, Robert. *Pre-suasion: A Revolutionary Way to Influence and Persuade.* New York: Simon and Schuster, 2016.

Clark, Andy. *Surfing Uncertainty: Prediction, action, and the Embodied Mind.* Oxford UK: Oxford University Press, 2015.

Clark, Andy. "Whatever Next? Predictive Brains, Situated Agents, and the Future of Cognitive Science." *Behavioral and Brain Sciences* 36, no. 3 (2013): 181–204.

Collins, Anne G. E., and Michael J. Frank. "Surprise! Dopamine Signals Mix Action, Value and Error." *Nature Neuroscience* 19, no. 1 (2016): 3.

Costa, Vincent D., Valery L. Tran, Janita Turchi, and Bruno B. Averbeck. "Dopamine Modulates Novelty Seeking Behavior During Decision Making." *Behavioral Neuroscience* 128, no. 5 (2014): 556.

Crocker, Jennifer. "A Schematic Approach to Changing Consumers' Beliefs." *Advances in Consumer Research* 11, no. 1 (1984).

Cron, Lisa. *Wired for Story: The Writer's Guide to Using Brain Science to Hook Readers from the Very First Sentence*. Berkeley, CA: Ten Speed Press, 2012.

Cuddy, Amy. "Your Body Language May Shape Who You Are." TED, June 2012. https://www.ted.com/talks/amy_cuddy_your_body_language_may _shape_who_you_are?language=en.

Davidai, Shai, and Thomas Gilovich. "The Headwinds/Tailwinds Asymmetry: An Availability Bias in Assessments of Barriers and Blessings." *Journal of Personality and Social Psychology* 111, no. 6 (2016): 835.

de Jong, Johannes W., Seyedeh Atiyeh Afjei, Iskra Pollak Dorocic, James R. Peck, Christine Liu, Christina K. Kim, Lin Tian, Karl Deisseroth, and Stephan Lammel. "A Neural Circuit Mechanism for Encoding Aversive Stimuli in the Mesolimbic Dopamine System." *Neuron* 101, no. 1 (2019): 133–51.

De Vivo, Luisa, Michele Bellesi, William Marshall, Eric A. Bushong, Mark H. Ellisman, Giulio Tononi, and Chiara Cirelli. "Ultrastructural Evidence for Synaptic Scaling Across the Wake/Sleep Cycle." *Science* 355, no. 6324 (2017): 507–10.

Diederen, Kelly M. J., and Paul C. Fletcher. "Dopamine, Prediction Error and Beyond." *The Neuroscientist* (2020): 1073858420907591.

Dijksterhuis, Ap, and Loran F. Nordgren. "A Theory of Unconscious Thought." *Perspectives on Psychological Science* 1, no. 2 (2006): 95–109.

Docter, Pete, and Ronnie del Carmen, dir. *Inside Out*. 2015; Burbank, CA: Walt Disney Movie Studios.

Dubner, Stephen, J. *Freakonomics Radio*, episode 243, "How to Be More Productive," April 20, 2016, NPR. https://freakonomics.com/podcast/how-to -be-more-productive/.

Dubner, Stephen, J. *Freakonomics Radio*, episode 286, "How Big Is My Penis (And Other Things We Ask Google)?" May 10, 2017, NPR. http://freako nomics.com/podcast/big-penis-things-ask-google/.

Duckworth, Angela. *Grit: The Power of Passion and Perseverance*. New York: Scribner, 2016.

Dunsmoor, Joseph E., Marijn C. W. Kroes, Jian Li, Nathaniel D. Daw, Helen B. Simpson, and Elizabeth A. Phelps. "Role of Human Ventromedial Prefrontal Cortex in Learning and Recall of Enhanced Extinction." *Journal of Neuroscience* 39, no. 17 (2019): 3264–276.

Dunsmoor, Joseph E., Vishnu P. Murty, Lila Davachi, and Elizabeth A. Phelps. "Emotional Learning Selectively and Retroactively Strengthens Memories for Related Events." *Nature* 520, no. 7547 (2015): 345–48.

Dutton, Donald G., and Arthur P. Aron. "Some Evidence for Heightened Sexual Attraction Under Conditions of High Anxiety." *Journal of Personality and Social Psychology* 30, no. 4 (1974): 510.

Dweck, Carol S. *Mindset: The New Psychology of Success.* New York: Random House Digital, Inc., 2008.

Dweck, Carol S. *Self-theories: Their Role in Motivation, Personality, and Development.* East Sussex, UK: Psychology Press, 2000.

Ely, Jeffrey, Alexander Frankel, and Emir Kamenica. "Suspense and Surprise." *Journal of Political Economy* 123, no. 1 (2015): 215–60.

Faraji, Mohammadjavad, Kerstin Preuschoff, and Wulfram Gerstner. "A Novel Information Theoretic Measure of Surprise." In *International Conference on Mathematical Neuroscience* (ICMNS), 2016.

Faraji, Mohammad Javad, Kerstin Preuschoff and Wulfram Gerstner. "Balancing New Against Old Information: The Role of Surprise." *ArXiv* abs/1606.05642 (2016).

"Feelings vs Fact—Newt Gingrich—RNC Topic on Violent Crime—Feelings trump FBI Stats!," *YouTube*, July 27, 2016. https://www.youtube .com/watch?v=xnhJWusyj4I.

Fenker, Daniela B., Julietta U. Frey, Hartmut Schuetze, Dorothee Heipertz, Hans-Jochen Heinze, and Emrah Duzel. "Novel Scenes Improve Recollection and Recall of Words." *Journal of Cognitive Neuroscience* 20, no. 7 (2008): 1250–65.

Fenker, Daniela, and Hartmut Schütze. "Learning by Surprise." *Scientific American Mind* 19, no. 6 (2008): 47.

Festinger, Leon, Hiroshi Ono, and Clarke A. Burnham. "Efference and the Conscious Experience of Perception." *Journal of Experimental Psychology* 74, no. 4p2 (1967): 1.

Field of Dreams, directed by Phil Alden Robinson. Universal City, CA: Universal Pictures, 1989.

Fiorillo, Christopher D., Philippe N. Tobler, and Wolfram Schultz. "Discrete Coding of Reward Probability and Uncertainty by Dopamine Neurons." *Science* 299, no. 5614 (2003): 1898–1902.

Forgas, Joseph P. "Happy Believers and Sad Skeptics? Affective Influences on Gullibility." *Current Directions in Psychological Science* (2019): 0963721419834543.

Foster, Meadhbh, and Mark T. Keane. "Surprise: You've Got Some Explaining to Do." arXiv preprint arXiv:1308.2236 (2013).

Garrido, Marta Isabel, Chee Leong James Teng, Jeremy Alexander Taylor, Elise Genevieve Rowe, and Jason Brett Mattingley. "SurpriseR in the Human Brain Demonstrate Statistical Learning Under High Concurrent Cognitive Demand." *npj Science of Learning* 1 (2016): 16006.

Gazzaniga, M. *Who's in Charge?: Free Will and the Science of the Brain.* London: Hachette UK, 2012.

Gershman, Samuel J., and Naoshige Uchida. "Believing in Dopamine." *Nature Reviews Neuroscience* 20, no. 11 (2019): 703–14.

Gilbert, Daniel. *Stumbling on Happiness.* Toronto: Vintage Canada, 2009.

Gilovich, Thomas, and Lee Ross. *The Wisest One in the Room: How You Can Benefit from Social Psychology's Most Powerful Insights.* New York: Simon and Schuster, 2016.

Gladwell, M. *Blink: The Power of Thinking without Thinking.* New York: Little Brown, 2005.

Golman, Russell, David Hagmann, and George Loewenstein. "Information Avoidance." *Journal of Economic Literature* 55, no. 1 (2017): 96–135.

Gordan, Jeremy. "An Illustrated Overview of How Our Brains (Might) Think: The Fascinating Intuition of the Generative Predictive Model," Medium, The Spike: The Brain Explained. June 12, 2017. https://medium.com/the -spike/generative-predictive-models-f39eb8f10584.

Gorman, Sara E., and Jack M. Gorman. *Denying to the Grave: Why We Ignore the Facts That Will Save Us.* Oxford, UK: Oxford University Press, 2016.

Grant, Adam M., and David A. Hofmann. "It's Not All About Me: Motivating Hand Hygiene Among Health Care Professionals by Focusing on Patients." *Psychological Science* 22, no. 12 (2011): 1494–99.

Grassi, Pablo R., and Andreas Bartels. "Magic, Bayes and Wows: A Bayesian Account of Magic Tricks." *PsyArXiv.* October 12, 2020. doi:10.31234/osf .io/m4ux2.

Greenwald, Anthony G. "Cognitive Learning, Cognitive Response to Persuasion, and Attitude Change." *Psychological Foundations of Attitudes*, New York: Academic Press (1968): 147–70.

Grupe, Dan W., and Jack B. Nitschke. "Uncertainty and Anticipation in Anxiety: An Integrated Neurobiological and Psychological Perspective." *Nature Reviews Neuroscience* 14, no. 7 (2013): 488–501.

Gurney, Kevin N., Mark D. Humphries, and Peter Redgrave. "A New Framework for Cortico-striatal Plasticity: Behavioural Theory Meets in Vitro Data at the Reinforcement-Action Interface." *PLoS biology* 13, no. 1 (2015): e1002034.

Harris, Sam, Sameer A. Sheth, and Mark S. Cohen. "Functional Neuroimaging of Belief, Disbelief, and Uncertainty." *Annals of Neurology* 63, no. 2 (2008): 141–47.

Hass-Cohen, Noah, and Joanna M. A. Clyde Findlay. "The Art Therapy Relational Neuroscience Memory Reconsolidation Protocol." *The Arts in Psychotherapy* 63 (2019): 51–59.

Harmon-Jones, Eddie, Jack W. Brehm, Jeff Greenberg, Linda Simon, and David E. Nelson. "Evidence that the Production of Aversive Consequences Is Not Necessary to Create Cognitive Dissonance." *Journal of Personality and Social Psychology* 70, no. 1 (1996): 5.

Hawkings, J., and S. Blakeslee. *On Intelligence: How a New Understanding of the Brain Will Lead to the Creation of Truly Intelligent Machines.* New York: Macmillan, 2004.

Hayden, Benjamin Y., Sarah R. Heilbronner, John M. Pearson, and Michael L. Platt. "Surprise Signals in Anterior Cingulate Cortex: Neuronal Encoding of Unsigned Reward Prediction Errors Driving Adjustment in Behavior." *Journal of Neuroscience* 31, no. 11 (2011): 4178–87.

Horstmann, Gernot. "The Surprise-Attention Link: A Review." *Annals of the New York Academy of Sciences* 1339, no. 1 (2015): 106–15.

Horstmann, Gernot, and Ulrich Ansorge. "Surprise Capture and Inattentional Blindness." *Cognition* 157 (2016): 237–49.

Hsia, Yen-Teh. "Belief and Surprise - A Belief-Function Formulation." In *Uncertainty Proceedings,* edited by Bruce D. D'Ambrosio, Philippe Smets, and Piero P. Bonissone, 165–73. Burlington, MA: Morgan Kaufmann, 1991.

Humphries, Mark. "The Crimes Against Dopamine." Medium: The Spike. March 13, 2017. https://medium.com/the-spike/the-crimes-against-dopamine-b82b082d5f3d.

Humphries, Mark. "Did I Do That: How the Brain Learns Causality." Medium: The Spike: Theories of Mind. June 29, 2017. https://medium.com/s/theories-of-mind.

Humphries, Mark D., Mehdi Khamassi, and Kevin Gurney. "Dopaminergic Control of the Exploration-Exploitation Trade-off Via the Basal Ganglia." *Frontiers in Neuroscience* 6 (2012): 9.

Humphries, Mark D., Ric Wood, and Kevin Gurney. "Dopamine-Modulated Dynamic Cell Assemblies Generated by the GABAergic Striatal Microcircuit." *Neural Networks* 22, no. 8 (2009): 1174–88.

Iigaya, Kiyohito. "Adaptive Learning and Decision-making Under Uncertainty by Metaplastic Synapses Guided by a Surprise Detection System." *Elife* 5 (2016): e18073.

Itti, Laurent, and Pierre Baldi. "Bayesian Surprise Attracts Human Attention." *Elsevier* 49, no. 10 (2009): 1295–306.

Jang, Anthony I., Matthew R. Nassar, Daniel G. Dillon, and Michael J. Frank. "Positive Reward Prediction Errors During Decision-making Strengthen Memory Encoding." *Nature Human Behaviour* 3 (2019): 719–32.

Jepma, Marieke, Rinus G. Verdonschot, Henk Van Steenbergen, Serge A. R. Rombouts, and Sander Nieuwenhuis. "Neural Mechanisms Underlying the Induction and Relief of Perceptual Curiosity." *Frontiers in Behavioral Neuroscience* 6 (2012): 5.

Jha, Amishi P., Elizabeth A. Stanley, Anastasia Kiyonaga, Ling Wong, and Lois Gelfand. "Examining the Protective Effects of Mindfulness Training on Working Memory Capacity and Affective Experience." *Emotion* 10, no. 1 (2010): 54.

Johnson, Steven. *Wonderland: How Play Made the Modern World.* London: Pan Macmillan, 2016.

Johnson, Samuel G. B., Amanda Royka, Peter McNally, and Frank Keil. "The False Promise of Sexiness: Are Counterintuitive Findings More Scientifically Important?" *PsyArXiv* (2019). doi:10.31234/osf.io/45rth.

Jones, Edward E. "Constrained Behavior and Self-Concept Change." In *Self-Inference Processes: The Ontario Symposium, Volume 6*, edited by James M. Olson, Mark P. Zanna, and C. Peter Herman, 69–86. Hillsdale, NJ: Erlbaum Associates, 1990.

Kahneman, Daniel. *Thinking, Fast and Slow.* New York: Macmillan, 2011.

Kamins, Melissa L., and Carol S. Dweck. "Person Versus Process Praise and Criticism: Implications for Contingent Self-worth and Coping." *Developmental Psychology* 35, no. 3 (1999): 835.

Kang, Min Jeong, Ming Hsu, Ian M. Krajbich, George Loewenstein, Samuel M. McClure, Joseph Tao-yi Wang, and Colin F. Camerer. "The Wick in the Candle of Learning: Epistemic Curiosity Activates Reward Circuitry and Enhances Memory." *Psychological Science* 20, no. 8 (2009): 963–73.

Kaptchuk, Ted J., William B. Stason, Roger B. Davis, Anna R. T. Legedza, Rosa N. Schnyer, Catherine E. Kerr, David A. Stone, Bong Hyun Nam, Irving Kirsch, and Rose H. Goldman. "Sham Device v Inert Pill: Randomised Controlled Trial of Two Placebo Treatments." *Bmj* 332, no. 7538 (2006): 391–97.

Kay, Aaron C., Jennifer A. Whitson, Danielle Gaucher, and Adam D. Galinsky. "Compensatory Control: Achieving Order Through the Mind, Our Institutions, and the Heavens." *Current Directions in Psychological Science* 18, no. 5 (2009): 264–68.

Kelly, George Alexander. *The Psychology of Personal Constructs. Volume 1: A Theory of Personality.* New York: W. W. Norton and Company, 1955.

Kenrick, Douglas T., Steven L. Neuberg, Robert B. Cialdini, and Robert B. Cialdini. *Social Psychology: Goals in Interaction.* Boston, MA: Pearson, 2010.

Kieling, Ana Paula, Vinicius Brei, and Valter Afonso Vieira. "The Influence of Negative Surprise on Hedonic Adaptation." *Brazilian Business Review* 13, no. 3 (2016): 111–32.

Klayman, Joshua, and Young-Won Ha. "Confirmation, Disconfirmation, and Information in Hypothesis Testing." *Psychological Review* 94, no. 2 (1987): 211.

Kleck, Robert E., and Angelo Strenta. "Perceptions of the Impact of Negatively Valued Physical Characteristics on Social Interaction." *Journal of Personality and Social Psychology* 39, no. 5 (1980): 861.

Knox, Robert E., and James A. Inkster. "Postdecision Dissonance at Post Time." *Journal of Personality and Social Psychology* 8, no. 4, p. 1 (1968): 319.

Kolbert, Elizabeth. "Why Facts Don't Change Our Minds." *The New Yorker* 27, no. 2017 (2017): 47.

Kreps, David M., and Evan L. Porteus. *Temporal Resolution of Uncertainty and Dynamic Choice Theory.* Standford, CA: Graduate School of Business, Stanford University, 1976.

Kruger, Justin, and Matt Evans. "The Paradox of Alypius and the Pursuit of Unwanted Information." *Journal of Experimental Social Psychology* 45, no. 6 (2009): 1173–79.

Kruglanski, Arie W., Katarzyna Jasko, and Karl Friston. "All Thinking is 'Wishful' Thinking." *Trends in Cognitive Sciences* 24, no. 6 (2020).

Kuhn, Thomas S. *The Structure of Scientific Revolutions.* Chicago: University of Chicago Press, 2012.

Lapish, Christopher C., Sven Kroener, Daniel Durstewitz, Antonieta Lavin, and Jeremy K. Seamans. "The Ability of the Mesocortical Dopamine System to Operate in Distinct Temporal Modes." *Psychopharmacology* 191, no. 3 (2007): 609–25.

Lee, Hongjoo J., Jina M. Youn, Michela Gallagher, and Peter C. Holland. "Role of Substantia Nigra–Amygdala Connections in Surprise-Induced Enhancement of Attention." *Journal of Neuroscience* 26, no. 22 (2006): 6077–81.

Lee, H. J., J. M. Youn, Michela Gallagher, and Peter C. Holland. "Temporally Limited Role of Substantia Nigra–Central Amygdala Connections in Surprise-Induced Enhancement of Learning." *European Journal of Neuroscience* 27, no. 11 (2008): 3043–49.

Lee, Sang Wan, John P. O'Doherty, and Shinsuke Shimojo. "Neural Computations Mediating One-Shot Learning in the Human Brain." *PLoS Biol* 13, no. 4 (2015): e1002137.

Lerner, Jennifer S., Ye Li, Piercarlo Valdesolo, and Karim S. Kassam. "Emotion and Decision Making." *Annual Review of Psychology* 66 (2015): 799–823.

Li, Shaomin, William K. Cullen, Roger Anwyl, and Michael J. Rowan. "Dopamine-Dependent Facilitation of LTP Induction in Hippocampal CA1 by Exposure to Spatial Novelty." *Nature Neuroscience* 6, no. 5 (2003): 526–31.

Lilienfeld, Scott O., Steven Jay Lynn, John Ruscio, and Barry L. Beyerstein. *50 Great Myths of Popular Psychology: Shattering Widespread Misconceptions about Human Behavior*. Hoboken, NJ: John Wiley & Sons, 2011.

Lisman, John E., and Anthony A. Grace. "The Hippocampal-VTA Loop: Controlling the Entry of Information into Long-term Memory." *Neuron* 46, no. 5 (2005): 703–13.

"Live Talks Business Forum: Dr. Zak interviews Nobel Laureate Daniel Kahneman." YouTube, December 17, 2011. https://www.youtube.com/watch?v=HaTrJV9rvCc.

Lohani, Sweyta, Adria K. Martig, Suzanne M. Underhill, Alicia DeFrancesco, Melanie J. Roberts, Linda Rinaman, Susan Amara, and Bita Moghaddam. "Burst Activation of Dopamine Neurons Produces Prolonged Post-burst Availability of Actively Released Dopamine." *Neuropsychopharmacology* 43, no. 10 (2018): 2083–92.

Lorini, Emiliano, and Cristiano Castelfranchi. "The Cognitive Structure of Surprise: Looking for Basic Principles." *Topoi* 26, no. 1 (2007): 133–49.

Loewenstein, George. "The Psychology of Curiosity: A Review and Reinterpretation." *Psychological Bulletin* 116, no. 1 (1994): 75.

Luchins, Abraham S. "Mechanization in Problem Solving: The Effect of Einstellung." *Psychological Monographs* 54, no. 6 (1942): i.

Malecek, Nicholas J., and Russell A. Poldrack. "Beyond Dopamine: The Noradrenergic System and Mental Effort." *Behavioral and Brain Sciences* 36, no. 6 (2013): 698.

Manjaly, Z., and Sandra Iglesias. "A Computational Theory of Mindfulness Based Cognitive Therapy from the 'Bayesian Brain' Perspective." *Frontiers in Psychology* 11 (2019): 404.

Marson, Nick. *Leading by Coaching: How to Deliver Impactful Change One Conversation at a Time*. New York: Springer, 2019.

McClure, S. M., J. Li, D. Tomlin, K. S. Cypert, L. M. Montague, and P. R. Montague. (2004). "Neural Correlates of Behavioral Preference for Culturally Familiar Drinks." *Neuron* 44, no. 2, 379–87.

McGuire, Michael. *Believing: The Neuroscience of Fantasies, Fears, and Convictions*. Amherst, NY: Prometheus Books, 2013.

Meier, Beat, Nicolas Rothen, and Stefan Walter. "Developmental Aspects of Synaesthesia Across the Adult Lifespan." *Frontiers in Human Neuroscience* 8 (2014): 129.

Mellers, Barbara, Katrina Fincher, Caitlin Drummond, and Michelle Bigony. "Surprise: A Belief or an Emotion?" *Progress in Brain Research* 202 (2013): 3–19.

Mercier, Hugo, and Dan Sperber. "Why Do Humans Reason? Arguments for an Argumentative Theory." *Behavioral and Brain Sciences* 34, no. 2 (2011): 57–74.

Mercier, Hugo, and Dan Sperber. *The Enigma of Reason*. Cambridge, MA: Harvard University Press, 2017.

Meyer, Wulf-Uwe, Rainer Reisenzein, and Achim Schützwohl. "Toward a Process Analysis of Emotions: The Case of Surprise." *Motivation and Emotion* 21, no. 3 (1997): 251–74.

Mischel, Walter. "Processes in Delay of Gratification." *Advances in Experimental Social Psychology* 7 (1974): 249–92.

Molden, Daniel C., and Carol S. Dweck. "'Finding Meaning' in Psychology: A Lay Theories Approach to Self-regulation, Social Perception, and Social Development." *American Psychologist* 61, no. 3 (2006): 192.

Monosov, Ilya E. "How Outcome Uncertainty Mediates Attention, Learning, and Decision-Making." *Trends in Neurosciences* 43, no. 10 (2020): 795–809.

Montgomery, Guy H., and Irving Kirsch. "Classical Conditioning and the Placebo Effect." *Pain* 72, no. 1–2 (1997): 107–13.

Morgan III, Charles A., Steven Southwick, George Steffian, Gary A. Hazlett, and Elizabeth F. Loftus. "Misinformation Can Influence Memory for Recently Experienced, Highly Stressful Events." *International Journal of Law and Psychiatry* 36, no. 1 (2013): 11–17.

Müller, Patrick A., and Dagmar Stahlberg. "The Role of Surprise in Hindsight Bias: A Metacognitive Model of Reduced and Reversed Hindsight Bias." *Social Cognition* 25, no. 1 (2007): 165–84.

Murty, Vishnu P., Kevin S. LaBar, and R. Alison Adcock. "Distinct Medial Temporal Networks Encode Surprise During Motivation by Reward Versus Punishment." *Neurobiology of Learning and Memory* 134 (2016): 55–64.

Myers, Chelsea A., Cheng Wang, Jessica M. Black, Nicolle Bugescu, and Fumiko Hoeft. "The Matter of Motivation: Striatal Resting-State Connectivity Is Dissociable Between Grit and Growth Mindset." *Social Cognitive and Affective Neuroscience* 11, no. 10 (2016): 1521–27.

Neisser, Ulric, and Nicole Harsch. "Phantom Flashbulbs: False Recollections of Hearing the News about Challenger." In *Emory Symposium on Cognition*, edited by E. Winograd and U. Neisser, 4. *Affect and Accuracy in Recall: Studies of "Flashbulb" Memories*, 9–31. Cambridge, UK: Cambridge University Press, 1992.

Newberg, Andrew, and Mark Robert Waldman. *Why We Believe What We Believe: Uncovering Our Biological Need for Meaning, Spirituality, and Truth.* New York: Simon and Schuster, 2006.

Ng, Betsy. "The Neuroscience of Growth Mindset and Intrinsic Motivation." *Brain Sciences* 8, no. 2 (2018): 20.

Noordewier, Marret K. "The Dynamics of Surprise and Curiosity." PhD diss., Leiden, Netherlands: Leiden University, 2016.

Noordewier, Marret K., and Eric van Dijk. "Curiosity and Time: From Not Knowing to Almost Knowing." *Cognition and Emotion* 31, no. 3 (2017): 411–21.

Noordewier, Marret K., and Eric van Dijk. "Surprise: Unfolding of Facial Expressions." *Cognition and Emotion* 33, no. 5 (2019): 915–30.

Noordewier, Marret K., and Seger M. Breugelmans. "On the Valence of Surprise." *Cognition & Emotion* 27, no. 7 (2013): 1326–34.

Noordewier, Marret K., Sascha Topolinski, and Eric Van Dijk. "The Temporal Dynamics of Surprise." *Social and Personality Psychology Compass* 10, no. 3 (2016): 136–49.

Nour, Matthew M., Tarik Dahoun, Philipp Schwartenbeck, Rick A. Adams, Thomas H. B. FitzGerald, Christopher Coello, Matthew B. Wall, Raymond J. Dolan, and Oliver D. Howes. "Dopaminergic Basis for Signaling Belief Updates, but Not Surprise, and the Link to Paranoia." *Proceedings of the National Academy of Sciences* 115, no. 43 (2018): E10167–E10176.

O'Connor, Joseph, and Andrea Lages. *Coaching the Brain: Practical Applications of Neuroscience to Coaching.* New York: Routledge, 2019.

O'Doherty, John, Sangwan Lee, Reza Tadayonnejad, Jeffrey Cockburn, Kiyohito Iigaya, and Caroline J. Charpentier. "Why and How the Brain Weights Contributions from a Mixture of Experts." *PsyArXiv* (2020). doi:10.31234/osf.io/ns6kq.

Olson, James M., Mark P. Zanna, and C. Peter Herman, eds. *Self-inference Processes.* Vol. 6. East Sussex, UK: Psychology Press, 1990.

Papalini, Silvia, Tom Beckers, and Bram Vervliet. "Dopamine: From Prediction Error to Psychotherapy." *Translational Psychiatry* 10, no. 164 (2020).

Petty, Richard E., and John T. Cacioppo. "The Elaboration Likelihood Model of Persuasion." *Communication and Persuasion.* New York: Springer, 1986. 1–24.

Piaget, Jean, Howard E. Gruber, and J. Voneche. "Jacques: The Essential Piaget." New York: Basic Books, 1977.

Pink, Daniel H. *Drive: The Surprising Truth About What Motivates Us.* New York: Penguin, 2011.

Plaks, Jason E., Sheri R. Levy, and Carol S. Dweck. "Lay Theories of Personality: Cornerstones of Meaning in Social Cognition." *Social and Personality Psychology Compass* 3, no. 6 (2009): 1069–81.

Preuschoff, Kerstin, Bernard Marius Hart, and Wolfgang Einhauser. "Pupil Dilation Signals Surprise: Evidence for Noradrenaline's Role in Decision Making." *Frontiers in Neuroscience* 5 (2011): 115.

Price, Donald D., Leonard S. Milling, Irving Kirsch, Ann Duff, Guy H. Montgomery, and Sarah S. Nicholls. "An Analysis of Factors That Contribute to the Magnitude of Placebo Analgesia in an Experimental Paradigm." *Pain* 83, no. 2 (1999): 147–56.

Proulx, Travis, Michael Inzlicht, and Eddie Harmon-Jones. "Understanding All Inconsistency Compensation as a Palliative Response to Violated Expectations." *Trends in Cognitive Sciences* 16, no. 5 (2012): 285–91.

Purves, Dale, and R. Beau Lotto. *Why We See What We Do: An Empirical Theory of Vision.* Oxford, UK: Sinauer Associates, 2003.

Qiu, Jiang, Hong Li, Jerwen Jou, Jia Liu, Yuejia Luo, Tingyong Feng, Zhenzhen Wu, and Qinglin Zhang. "Neural Correlates of the 'Aha' Experiences: Evidence from an fMRI Study of Insight Problem Solving." *Cortex* 46, no. 3 (2010): 397–403.

Ranasinghe, Nadeesha, and Wei-Min Shen. "The Surprise-Based Learning Algorithm." Technical Report for University of Southern California, Information Sciences Institute – 11th April 2008. Internal document.

Rankin, Amy, Rogier Woltjer, and Joris Field. "Sensemaking Following Surprise in the Cockpit—A Re-framing Problem." *Cognition, Technology & Work* 18, no. 4 (2016): 623–42.

Rao, T. S. Sathyanarayana, M. R. Asha, K. S. Jagannatha Rao, and P. Vasudevaraju. "The Biochemistry of Belief." *Indian Journal of Psychiatry* 51, no. 4 (2009): 239.

Real, Leslie A. "Animal Choice Behavior and the Evolution of Cognitive Architecture." *Science* 253, no. 5023 (1991): 980–86.

Redick, Scott. "Surprise Is Still the Most Powerful Marketing Tool." *Harvard Business Review.* 2013. https://hbr.org/2013/05/surprise-is-still-the-most-powerful.

Regan, Dennis T., and Martin Kilduff. "Optimism About Elections: Dissonance Reduction at the Ballot Box." *Political Psychology* (1988): 101–7.

Reisenzein, Rainer, Gernot Horstmann, and Achim Schützwohl. "The Cognitive-Evolutionary Model of Surprise: A Review of the Evidence." *Topics in Cognitive Science* 11, no. 1 (2019): 50–74.

Robinson, Thomas N., Dina L. G. Borzekowski, Donna M. Matheson, and Helena C. Kraemer. "Effects of Fast Food Branding on Young Children's Taste Preferences." *Archives of Pediatrics & Adolescent Medicine* 161, no. 8 (2007): 792–97.

Robson, David. *The Intelligence Trap: Revolutionise Your Thinking and Make Wiser Decisions.* London: Hachette UK, 2019.

Rosenthal, Robert, and Lenore Jacobson. "Pygmalion in the Classroom." *The Urban Review* 3, no. 1 (1968): 16–20.

Rousell, Michael A. *Sudden Influence: How Spontaneous Events Shape Our Lives.* Westport, CT: Greenwood Publishing Group, 2007.

Rousell, Michael. "Surprise: How Your Brain Secretly Changes Your Beliefs." TEDxSalem, March 18, 2019. https://www.youtube.com/watch?v=K5O6mF WpgZo&feature=youtu.be

Rudder, Christian. "We Experiment on Human Beings." *OK Trends: Dating Research from OKCupid* (Blog), 2014. http://blog. okcupid.com/index.php /we-experiment-on-human-beings.

Sanders, Kristin E. G., Samuel Osburn, Ken A. Paller, and Mark Beeman. "Targeted Memory Reactivation During Sleep Improves Next-Day Problem Solving." *Psychological Science* 30, no. 11 (2019): 1616–24.

Schacter, Daniel L. *Searching for Memory: The Brain, the Mind, and the Past.* New York: Basic Books, 2008.

Scherer, Klaus R., Marcel R. Zentner, and Daniel Stern. "Beyond Surprise: The Puzzle of Infants' Expressive Reactions to Expectancy Violation." *Emotion* 4, no. 4 (2004): 389.

Schitt's Creek, created by Eugene Levy and Dan Levy. Canadian Broadcasting Corporation, 2015.

Schomaker, Judith, and Martijn Meeter. "Short- and Long-lasting Consequences of Novelty, Deviance and Surprise on Brain and Cognition." *Neuroscience & Biobehavioral Reviews* 55 (2015): 268–79.

Schultz, Wolfram. "Dopamine Reward Prediction-Error Signalling: A Two-Component Response." *Nature Reviews Neuroscience* 17, no. 3 (2016): 183.

Schultz, Wolfram. "Neuronal Reward and Decision Signals: From Theories to Data." *Physiological Reviews* 95, no. 3 (2015): 853–951.

Schultz, Wolfram. "Recent Advances in Understanding the Role of Phasic Dopamine Activity." *F1000Research* 8, no. 1680 (2019): 1680.

Schultz, Wolfram. "Updating Dopamine Reward Signals." *Current Opinion in Neurobiology* 23, no. 2 (2013): 229–38.

Schützwohl, Achim, and Rainer Reisenzein. "Children's and Adults' Reactions to a Schema-Discrepant Event: A Developmental Analysis of Surprise." *International Journal of Behavioral Development* 23, no. 1 (1999): 37–62.

Schutzwohl, A., R. Reisenzein, and G. Horstmann. "The Cognitive-Evolutionary Model of Surprise: A Review of the Evidence." *Topics in Cognitive Science* 11, no. 1 (2017): 50–74.

Schwarze, Ulrike, Ulrike Bingel, and Tobias Sommer. "Event-related Nociceptive Arousal Enhances Memory Consolidation for Neutral Scenes." *Journal of Neuroscience* 32, no. 4 (2012): 1481–87.

Seitz, Rüdiger J., and Hans-Ferdinand Angel. "Belief Formation—A Driving Force for Brain Evolution." *Brain and Cognition* 140 (2020): 105548.

Sekoguchi, Takahiro, Yuki Sakai, and Hideyoshi Yanagisawa. "Mathematical Model of Emotional Habituation to Novelty: Modeling with Bayesian Update and Information Theory." *2019 IEEE International Conference on Systems, Man and Cybernetics (SMC)*, Bari, Italy, 2019, pp. 1115-1120, doi: 10.1109/SMC.2019.8914626.

Seth, Anil. "Your Brain Hallucinates Your Conscious Reality." TED.com. 2017. https://www.ted.com/talks/anil_seth_how_your_brain_hallucinates _your_conscious_reality.

Sharot, Tali, Tamara Shiner, Annemarie C. Brown, Judy Fan, and Raymond J. Dolan. "Dopamine Enhances Expectation of Pleasure in Humans." *Current Biology* 19, no. 24 (2009): 2077–80.

Shermer, Michael. *The Believing Brain: From Ghosts and Gods to Politics and Conspiracies: How We Construct Beliefs and Reinforce Them As Truths.* New York: Macmillan, 2011.

Shogenji, Tomoji. "Probability and Proximity in Surprise." *Synthese* (2020): 1–19.

Silvia, Papalini, Tom Beckers, and Vervliet Bram. "Dopamine: From Prediction Error to Psychotherapy." *Translational Psychiatry* 10, no. 1 (2020).

Singh, Laura, Laurent Schüpbach, Dominik A. Moser, Roland Wiest, Erno J. Hermans, and Tatjana Aue. "The Effect of Optimistic Expectancies on Attention Bias: Neural and Behavioral Correlates." *Scientific Reports* 10, no. 1 (2020): 1–13.

Soltani, Alireza, and Alicia Izquierdo. "Adaptive Learning Under Expected and Unexpected Uncertainty." *Nature Reviews Neuroscience* (2019): 1.

Spurlock, Morgan. "Brand Over Brain." *Ted Radio Hour*, March 9, 2014. http:// www.npr.org/programs/ted-radio-hour/308752278/brand-over-brain.

Stahl, Aimee E., and Lisa Feigenson. "Observing the Unexpected Enhances Infants' Learning and Exploration." *Science* 348, no. 6230 (2015): 91–94.

Stanovich, Keith E., Richard F. West, and Maggie E. Toplak. "Myside Bias, Rational Thinking, and Intelligence." *Current Directions in Psychological Science* 22, no. 4 (2013): 259–64.

Stojic, Hrvoje, Jacob L. Orquin, Peter Dayan, Raymond J. Dolan, and Maarten Speekenbrink. "Uncertainty in Learning, Choice and Visual Fixation." *Proceedings of the National Academy of Sciences* 117, no. 6 (2020): 3291–300.

Susperreguy Jorquera, María Inés, Pamela E. Davis-Kean, Kathryb Duckworth, and Meichu Chen. "Self-concept Predicts Academic Achievement Across Levels of the Achievement Distribution: Domain Specificity for Math and Reading." *Child Dev.* 89, no. 6 (2017): 2196–214.

Sutton, Richard S., and Andrew G. Barto. *Reinforcement Learning: An Introduction.* Cambridge, MA: MIT Press, 2018.

Taleb, Nassim Nicholas. *The Black Swan: The Impact of the Highly Improbable.* Vol. 2. New York: Random House, 2007.

Thibodeau, Paul H., and Lera Boroditsky. "Metaphors We Think With: The Role of Metaphor in Reasoning." *PloS one* 6, no. 2 (2011): e16782.

Thomas, Cyril, and André Didierjean. "Magicians Fix Your Mind: How Unlikely Solutions Block Obvious Ones." *Cognition* 154 (2016): 169–73.

Thomas, Marlo. *The Right Words at the Right Time.* New York: Simon and Schuster, 2004.

Tobin, Vera. "Cognitive Bias and the Poetics of Surprise." *Language and Literature* 18, no. 2 (2009): 155–72.

Tobin, Vera. "Where Do Cognitive Biases Fit Into Cognitive Linguistics? An Example from the 'Curse of Knowledge.'" *Language and the Creative Mind* (2014): 347–63.

Tononi, Giulio, and Chiara Cirelli. "Sleep and the Price of Plasticity: From Synaptic and Cellular Homeostasis to Memory Consolidation and Integration." *Neuron* 81, no. 1 (2014): 12–34.

Tschantz, Alexander, Manuel Baltieri, Anil Seth, and Christopher L. Buckley. "Scaling Active Inference." *2020 International Joint Conference on Neural Networks (IJCNN)*, Glasgow, UK, 2020, pp. 1-8, doi: 10.1109/IJCNN48605.2020.9207382.

Tversky, Amos, and Daniel Kahneman. "Judgment Under Uncertainty: Heuristics and Biases." *Science* 185, no. 4157 (1974): 1124–31.

Uleman, James S., S. Adil Saribay, and Celia M. Gonzalez. "Spontaneous Inferences, Implicit Impressions, and Implicit Theories." *Annual Review of Psychology* 59 (2008): 329–60.

Vance, Erik. *Suggestible You: The Curious Science of Your Brain's Ability to Deceive, Transform, and Heal.* Washington, DC: National Geographic Books, 2016.

Vander Weele, Caitlin M., Cody A. Siciliano, Gillian A. Matthews, Praneeth Namburi, Ehsan M. Izadmehr, Isabella C. Espinel, Edward H. Nieh et al. "Dopamine Enhances Signal-to-Noise Ratio in Cortical-Brainstem Encoding of Aversive Stimuli." *Nature* 563, no. 7731 (2018): 397.

Vanhamme, Joelle, and Dirk Snelders. "The Role of Surprise in Satisfaction Judgments." *Journal of Consumer Satisfaction Dissatisfaction and Complaining Behavior* 14 (2001): 27–45.

Van Prooijen, J. W., O. Klein, and J. Milošević Đorđević. "Social-Cognitive Processes Underlying Belief in Conspiracy Theories." *Handbook of Conspiracy Theories* (2020): 168–80.

Varol, Ozan. *Think Like a Rocket Scientist*. New York: PublicAffairs, 2020.

Vassena, Eliana, James Deraeve, and William H. Alexander. "Surprise, Value and Control in Anterior Cingulate Cortex During Speeded Decision-Making." *Nature Human Behaviour* (2020): 1–11.

Vincent, Peter, Thomas Parr, David Benrimoh, and Karl J. Friston. "With an Eye on Uncertainty: Modelling Pupillary Responses to Environmental Volatility." *PLoS Computational Biology* 15, no. 7 (2019): e1007126.

Visalli, Antonino, Mariagrazia Capizzi, Ettore Ambrosini, Ilaria Mazzonetto, and Antonino Vallesi. "Bayesian Modeling of Temporal Expectations in the Human Brain." *NeuroImage* (2019): 116097.

Visalli, Antonino, Mariagrazia Capizzi, Ettore Ambrosini, Bruno Kopp, and Antonino Vallesi. "Electroencephalographic Correlates of Temporal Bayesian Belief Updating and Surprise." *NeuroImage* (2020): https://doi.org/10.1016/j.neuroimage.2021.117867.

Vuilleumier, Patrik. "How Brains Beware: Neural Mechanisms of Emotional Attention." *Trends in Cognitive Sciences* 9, no. 12 (2005): 585–94.

Wang, Song, Ming Zhou, Taolin Chen, Xun Yang, Guangxiang Chen, Meiyun Wang, and Qiyong Gong. "Grit and the Brain: Spontaneous Activity of the Dorsomedial Prefrontal Cortex Mediates the Relationship Between the Trait Grit and Academic Performance." *Social Cognitive and Affective Neuroscience* 12, no. 3 (2017): 452–60.

Weems, Scott. *Ha!: The Science of When We Laugh and Why*. New York: Basic Books, 2014.

Wessel, Jan R., Ned Jenkinson, John-Stuart Brittain, Sarah H. E. M. Voets, Tipu Z. Aziz, and Adam R. Aron. "Surprise Disrupts Cognition Via a Fronto-Basal Ganglia Suppressive Mechanism." *Nature Communications* 7, no. 1 (2016): 1–10.

Wheeler, Ladd. "Social Comparison, Behavioral Contagion, and the Naturalistic Study of Social Interaction." *A Distinctive Approach to Psychological Research: The Influence of Stanley Schachter* (1987): 46–65.

Winter, David A., and Nick Reed, eds. *The Wiley Handbook of Personal Construct Psychology*. Hoboken, NJ: John Wiley & Sons, 2016.

Winograd, Eugene, and Ulric Neisser, eds. *Affect and Accuracy in Recall: Studies of 'Flashbulb' Memories*. Vol. 4. Cambridge, UK: Cambridge University Press, 2006.

Wolfe, Michael B., and Todd J. Williams. "Poor Metacognitive Awareness of Belief Change." *The Quarterly Journal of Experimental Psychology* (2017): 1–45.

Wu, Yang, and Hyowon Gweon. "Surprisingly Unsurprising! Infants' Looking Time at Probable vs. Improbable Events Is Modulated by Others' Expressions of Surprise." *PsyArXiv*. (2019).

Wu, Yang, and Hyowon Gweon. "Preschoolers Jointly Consider Others' Expressions of Surprise and Common Ground to Decide When to Explore." *PsyArXiv*. (2019).

Xu, Haitao, Brendan McCane, and Lech Szymanski. "VASE: Variational Assorted Surprise Exploration for Reinforcement Learning." *arXiv preprint arXiv:1910.14351* (2019).

Index

About the Author

Dr. Michael A. Rousell is a teacher, psychologist, and professor emeritus at Southern Oregon University. Rousell studied life-changing events for more than three decades and established his expertise by writing the internationally successful book *Sudden Influence: How Spontaneous Events Shape Our Lives* (2007). His pioneering work draws on research from a wide variety of brain sciences that show when, how, and why we instantly form new beliefs. He lives with his spouse in Edmonton, Alberta, Canada.